COLLABORATIVE THEATRE

Over the past thirty years the Théâtre du Soleil has become one of the most celebrated theatre companies in Europe, and Ariane Mnouchkine one of Europe's best-known directors. *Collaborative Theatre* is the first in-depth sourcebook on this' unique theatrical troupe, providing English readers with first-hand accounts giving rare insights into the development of its creative processes, collectivist practices and driving passions.

Collaborative Theatre presents critical and historical essays by theatre scholars from around the world as well as the writings of and interviews with members of the Théâtre du Soleil, past and present. The volume is divided into chapters on five key productions: *1789, L'Age d'Or, Richard II, L'Indiade* and *Les Atrides*.

These reveal the recurrent concerns and themes of the company, such as the ethics and politics of collaboration; the theatrical re-visioning of history; the training of performers; the role of a director in collective work.

Collaborative Theatre will be of compelling interest to students of theatre and performance studies, French cultural studies, as well as academics and theatre practitioners.

David Williams is Professor of Theatre at Dartington College of Art, Devon. He is the compiler of *Peter Brook: A Theatrical Casebook* (1988) and *Peter Brook and the Mahabharata* (Routledge 1991). He is also a theatre director.

For Rachel

COLLABORATIVE THEATRE

The Théâtre du Soleil Sourcebook

Compiled and edited by David Williams
New translations by
Eric Prenowitz and David Williams

London and New York

First published 1999 by Routledge
11 New Fetter Lane, London EC4P 4EE

Simultaneously published in the USA and Canada
by Routledge
29 West 35th Street, New York, NY 10001

© 1999 Compiled and edited by David Williams; translations by
Eric Prenowitz and David Williams

Typeset in Baskerville by J&L Composition Ltd, Filey, North Yorkshire
Printed and bound in Great Britain by
Biddles Ltd, Guildford and King's Lynn

British Library Cataloguing in Publication Data
A catalogue record for this book is available from the British Library

Library of Congress Cataloging in Publication Data
A catalogue record for this book has been requested

ISBN 0–415–08605–1 (hbk)
ISBN 0–415–08606–X (pbk)

CONTENTS

3 An apprenticeship with Shakespeare: *Richard II* (1981)

4 A modern passion play: *L'Indiade* (1987)

PLATES

ACKNOWLEDGEMENTS

My sincere thanks go to the following, for permissions to reproduce material here: in particular, members of Le Théâtre du Soleil, past and present – Ariane Mnouchkine, Guy-Claude François, Françoise Tournafond, Sophie Moscoso, Roberto Moscoso, Louis Samier, Jean-Claude Penchenat, Georges Bonnaud, Philippe Caubère, Georges Bigot, Philippe Hottier, Erhard Stiefel, Jean-Jacques Lemêtre, Hélène Cixous, Simon Abkarian and Catherine Schaub; for her photographs, Martine Franck; in addition, Victoria Nes Kirby, Emile Copfermann, Irving Wardle, Christopher Kirkland, Jacquie Bablet (for the late Denis Bablet), Yvon Davis, Michèle Raoul-Davis, Bernard Sobel, Colette Godard, Jean-Michel Déprats, Judith Miller, Gilles Costaz, Josette Féral, Alfred Simon, Sarah Bryant-Bertail, Odette Aslan and Béatrice Picon-Vallin; the editors of *Fruits*, *Travail Théâtral*, *Théâtre/Public*, *The Drama Review*, *Qui parle*, *Acteurs*, *Journal of Dramatic Theory and Criticism*, *Theatre Journal*; MIT Press Journals; and M. Élie Konigson, director of the Laboratoire de Recherches sur les Arts du Spectacle at the CNRS in Ivry-sur-Seine, and of the CNRS Éditions collection 'Arts du spectacle'.

This book is dedicated with gratitude to the following: Sophie Moscoso and Pierre Salesne at the Théâtre du Soleil, for seeing the wood for the trees; Eric Prenowitz, for the precision and generosity of his collaboration on new translations; Liliana Andreone; Peter Hulton, whose model of multi-vocality and/in the 'unwritten' in the *Theatre Papers* and *Arts Archives* monographs has my greatest respect as an ethical practice; Patrice Pavis, for his generous help in locating materials in France; Maria Shevtsova, for her encouragement and generosity; Talia Rodgers and Sophie Powell at Routledge for their extraordinary patience. Thanks also to Nina Soufy; Baz Kershaw, David Bradby and the Bangster; and to Anna Deavere Smith, Bruce Myers, John Berger, Nermin Tulic and Anne Bogart, who light the fires with compassion and *corraggio*. Finally, thanks to the Australian Academy of the Humanities, Canberra, whose award of a Travelling Fellowship in 1991 facilitated a period of research with the Théâtre du Soleil.

Unless otherwise stated, all translations from the original French texts are by Eric Prenowitz and David Williams.

INTRODUCTION: A GRAIN OF SAND IN THE WORKS: CONTINUITY AND CHANGE AT THE THÉÂTRE DU SOLEIL

David Williams

'The end of history'? That amuses me. Saying this one risks the loss of language and the loss of the possibility of thinking; one risks becoming more and more passive, able to be bought and sold [. . .] Theatre is doubtless the most fragile of the arts, the theatre public is now really a very small group, but the theatre keeps reminding us of the possibility to collectively seek the histories of people and to tell them [. . .] The contradictions, the battles of power, and the split in ourselves will always exist. I think the theatre best tells us of the enemy in ourselves. Yes, theatre is a grain of sand in the works.

Ariane Mnouchkine[1]

Turn on the television, and you will be invited to swim in a particular kind of performance according to which history, like coffee, is 'instant'. The terrible ethno-nationalist conflicts that have exploded as senescent empires unravel and collapse are played out prime-time in horrifying visual 'grabs'. Pyrotechnic displays over Baghdad, 'like the 4th of July', induce amnesia about the melting and shattering of bodies ('collateral damage'). Cameras tracking 'smart' missiles, invisibly tipped with depleted uranium, bring the obscene lie of a 'sanitised' war into our lives – bright flashes, but no blistered faces, no dismembered children; coverage becomes cover-up. Celebrity murder trials are transmitted live into our homes, star careers are manufactured; books and badges are on sale in the foyer. Politicians employ 'image consultants' and learn to exploit the coercive power of representation; Margaret Thatcher played the Iron Maiden, Bob Hawke played Pagliacci, Bill Clinton played the baby-boom sax (but never, ever inhaled). In the seductive society of the spectacle, a B-movie actor gets to occupy the Oval Office, extending the narratives of Hollywood at its most insidiously moralising into the presidency, before riding off into the sunset: the triumph of the political technologies of 'making seeming being'.[2]

'News', the great leveller, now means infotainment, a commodity driven by ratings; hyper-mediated, simulational 'realities' come to us cling-film wrapped, for instant consumption, while phenomenal embodied realities recede.[3] 'History' means a Michael Jackson CD/world tour, marketed by Sony in a campaign that draws uncritically and unashamedly on Leni Riefenstahl's Nazi films and Stalinist propaganda representations. I feel no nostalgia for the old empires or geographies of the selfsame, no yearning for a stable, monologic 'truth'. However, so many of our dominant cultural forms want us tranquil-ised, want us no longer to re-cognise ourselves; they colonise our imaginaries. We suffer from the vertiginous dis-locations generated by what McKenzie Wark has called *telesthesia*: mediated perception at a distance, constructing an illusion of proximity.[4] Our critical faculties and our memories are failing, our compassion is fatigued, and yet we have rarely been more haunted by myths and ghosts.

This is a book about theatre making, a local sub-set of global 'performance', and for many now a rather quaint anachronism. Yet certain kinds of theatre offer a site in which maybe we can rediscover 'an art of memory'[5] – in which we can re-cognise who or what haunts us, apprehend what it is we are swimming in and turn against the current. Ariane Mnouchkine's Théâtre du Soleil is one company that has tried to make oppositional interventions into popular culture by contesting the ways in which we are invited to live and represent ourselves in the self-generating hegemony of capitalism. Through the reflections of members of this group, and others familiar with their work, the present volume attempts to explore the social praxes of collaboration, creativity, resistance, pedagogy and the processes of theatre making as the elaboration of a dynamic local culture.

Over the past thirty years, since its inception by a group of ten idealistic young students in Paris in 1964, the Théâtre du Soleil has become one of the most celebrated, indeed mythologised, theatre companies in Europe.[6] In the course of its ongoing determination to privilege formal innovation, theatricality and a notion of theatre as social practice, it has explored and reassessed the legacies of some of the seminal practitioners and theorists of European Modernism – Artaud, Meyerhold, Brecht and in particular Copeau, Jouvet, Dullin and Vilar.[7] In addition, it has recuperated and reinvented 'other' techniques and traditions, from the popular (*commedia dell'arte*, clowning) to the hieratic (projected, 'imaginary' Asian theatres).

Almost all of the material included in this anthology comes from writings by or interviews with members of the Théâtre du Soleil, past and present. The plurality of voices is intended to reflect a plurality of tasks and of perspectives in a company that has endeavoured to make theatre in ways that are radically interactive and dialogic. Director, actors, designers, composer-musician, writer – all articulate the problems and pleasures that emerge from their active engagement with a network of interrelated questions about theatre making as social practice. What are the functions of theatre in a society in which, to paraphrase a memorable image of Peter Hulton's, theatre has become like an orchid on a golf course? How does one collaborate with ethical and political integrity? What processes disperse and multiply creativity and power within a collective? What are the forms of a 'popular theatre' today, and what are its narratives? How can theatre dismantle and re-vision monolithic representations of History? Which performative traditions and forms from the past can create possible futures here now? Perhaps above all, how does one *act*, and how does one make theatre 'appear'?

This volume does not seek to be an exhaustive study or history of the Théâtre du Soleil.[8] Neither is it a book of criticism *per se*, although it aims to offer an array of critical perspectives. Instead, it chooses to focus on five core projects undertaken by the company during its thirty year existence: from the 1970s, *1789*, the celebratory wake for the events of May 1968, and the *commedia*-inspired 'contemporary comedy' *L'Age d'Or* from the 1980s, *Richard II*, Artaudian affective athleticism in an auratic and imaginary medieval 'Japan', and *L'Indiade*, Hélène Cixous's epic chronicle of the partition of India; and from the 1990s, *Les Atrides*, a tetralogy of Greek tragedies tracing the fragmentation of a family at the mythical dawn of (a compromised) democracy.

Each of the five chapters comprises a description of the relevant production in performance, followed by a series of texts by some of the practitioners directly involved. These include interviews, public discussions, programme notes, extracts from rehearsal logs, open letters and essays – most of them available in English for the first time here. The detailed notes at the end of each section are intended to amplify contextual and conceptual frames for these texts, and encourage readers towards other pertinent material. At the back of the book, readers will find a complete production chronology and an extensive bibliography of published materials relating to the company.

In many ways, each of the five projects discussed in this volume constitutes a praxiological paradigm which reflects a specific set of concerns. Each of them should be taken in its own terms, in its particular political and historical context; the Soleil has always sought to engage with its sense of its historical moment. The Théâtre du Soleil's production, Molière's *Le Tartuffe* (1995–6), for example, was an explicit critique of fundamentalism, in Algeria, Israel and elsewhere; it included music by Cheb Hasni, one of Algeria's best known Raï singers, who was murdered by extremists in Oran in September 1994. The newspaper-style programme for *Le Tartuffe* provided a multi-textual collage of historical documents relating to religious intolerance and racial extremism: from the Edict of Nantes and Jansenist condemnations of theatre, to recent press reportage of the *fatwa* against Pakistani feminist writer Taslima Nasreen, and of white supremacist groups in the USA. In addition, it contained information about a number of activist human rights organisations in France, pockets of organised resistance to fundamentalisms.[9] Many of the programmes accompanying Soleil productions over the years have adopted a multi-vocal, critically activist, historicising approach of this kind.

As will become apparent, however, each of the projects discussed in this volume is closely interrelated. Collectively, they represent the development and refinement of a body of work underpinned and informed by recurrent concerns and ideals. Both differences and continuities are informative here. So, for example, a number of developmental trajectories are embedded in the material contained in this volume: a movement from collectively devised material (*la création collective*) to work that emerges from existing play texts;[10] the development from a carnival-esque historiography to epic passion play and tragedy – an evolution which Mnouchkine once compared to the relationship between Kyogen and Noh; a refashioning of the ideological and party political (a retreat, some would say) in favour of a collectivism of situational ethics that nevertheless remains wholly politicised;[11] an increasingly multi-cultural mix in personnel as the company has ballooned to over sixty members; and so on.

At the same time, continuities underlying these shifts include a negotiation of the implications and paradoxes of the idea of collectivity and civic responsibility;[12] a prioritisation of the actor and of the discipline of mask work as corporeal and imaginal preparation – the legacies of Copeau and Lecoq; the development and refinement of a shared technical discourse, a shorthand vocabulary of acting processes and 'laws';[13] a repeated rhythm of exploring forms from other times and places as a pedagogic *reculer pour mieux sauter*, a way forward into representing contemporary histories with critical distance (Cambodia, India, the recent scandal of contaminated blood transfusions in France, the French Resistance); a recurrent thematic constellation in terms of content – the impact of civil war, separation and displacement, in the widest sense of these terms ('the enemies/splits in ourselves'), and the avoidability of fratricidal conflict (what *might* have been);[14] and the generative centrality of the company's base since 1970 at the Cartoucherie de Vincennes, a former munitions factory on the eastern margins of Paris – as theatre, workplace, school, Fourier-style phalanstery, community.

The presence of company director Ariane Mnouchkine throughout this body of work represents one of the most resilient and dynamic continuities of all. As this book attests, she is forthright, articulate, passionate, demanding and dissident; and the Théâtre du Soleil is inconceivable without her. In tandem with her work as a director, she has been an active campaigner for human rights – for workers, immigrants, prisoners of conscience, HIV/AIDS communities, and most recently the people of Bosnia-Herzegovina. In 1995, for example, in Avignon and subsequently at the Cartoucherie in Paris, Mnouchkine led a group of artists in a hunger strike, in protest against the inaction of Europe and the United States with regard to Bosnia.[15]

As director of the Théâtre du Soleil, Mnouchkine has been implicated in the collisions, rifts and ruptures that are part and parcel of a utopian project of such scale, intensity and heterogeneity. The Soleil's continually reinvented brand of collectivism has rarely entailed the erasure of difference and the coercive imposition of some fictional consensus. On a number of levels, difference seems to have been privileged as a source of creative friction. As a result, it is perhaps inevitable that in reality there have been several companies called 'Soleil' over the years, a seismic upheaval every five years or so engendering departures and new arrivals. Mnouchkine seems fully aware of the paradoxical status of change in this context – as both an imperative in the avoidance of institutional ossification, and a traumatic dismembering (a 'civil war'). In a 1985 interview, she suggested:

> The Théâtre du Soleil is one of the rare troupes where change and transformation are part of the very essence of the undertaking. To create theatre is also to work relentlessly at changing oneself. This doesn't happen without pain, nor without difficulties so terrible that they tear apart the very fabric of the troupe.[16]

This pulsional rhythm of fragmentation/dispersal and renewal/consolidation continues to the present, one of the most recent departures being that of an exhausted Georges Bigot, the most lauded of the Soleil actors in the decade following the production of *Richard II* in 1981.[17] Endlessly rehearsing the fate of the good ship *Medusa*, Mnouchkine is now the only survivor from the early 1960s – the matriarch of a very young group of performers, and a seasoned hand in crisis management. Mnouchkine appears to recognise that, to borrow a phrase of John Berger's, 'utopias only exist in carpets';[18] but her energy for 'weaving' remains undiminished. Necessarily and inevitably, her articulations of her evolving role as a director of actors in a collective form a central component in this volume.

Over the last decade, the Théâtre du Soleil has collaborated extensively with the writer Hélène Cixous, who has become central to the company's work in the wake of the Shakespeare cycle. According to Mnouchkine, this cycle had been undertaken in order to learn how to produce a theatre that could articulate the complexity and polyvocality of contemporary realities. And since the mid-1980s, the company has directly confronted aspects of the late twentieth-century world with three plays by Cixous. Broadly, these plays have dealt with colonialism and its disruptive legacies in the contemporary world: the dismemberment of the Khmer people in *Sihanouk* (1985); the traumatic partitioning of India in *L'Indiade* (1987); and, most recently, government and medical scandals in France in *La Ville Parjure* (1994).[19]

The company's evolving relationship with Cixous as playwright is another of my interests here, for Cixous's writings-about-writing as an ethical practice, and their embodied exploration in the *écriture corporelle* of the Soleil's performers, continue to mark my own thinking, theatre making and teaching in substantive ways. Cixous's earlier plays have been dismissed by some critics as exercises in nostalgic or revisionist hagiography.[20] However, for Cixous, to write (and by implication, to read, or to perform) is to try to do 'the work of un-forgetting, of un-silencing, of un-earthing, of un-blinding oneself, and of un-deafening oneself';[21] to speak history is to 'sing the abyss'.[22] I would prefer to locate these plays as critical meditations on compassion and re-membering, as attempted reparation of the oblivion and loss that characterise what Genet called 'the misery plain'.[23] They deal with histories of atrocity and trauma on an enormous scale, interrogating the ideological alibis employed to conceal complicities in erasures of alterity at a personal level; in a *theatrum mundi* within which micro and macro are intertwined, they remind us that it is above all the inter-personal that is political.

Finally, this is a book about the implications of and for theatre in critical reinventions of democracy, a dynamic set of practices by definition always *in statu nascendi*, always 'to come', as Chantal Mouffe has described.[24] It speaks of a desire for compassionate and ethical change, and of the possibility of renewal through a processual fashioning of *self-in-relation*. Each of the Soleil's projects has emerged from the interrelatedness of individuals within an always temporary and volatile micro-world; in each of them, the performers have rehearsed corporeal dreams of an elsewhere that could be otherwise, a re-membering of dis-membering. These dreams, which insistently inhabit the subversive spaces between here/there, near/

far, self/other, are grains of sand in the works of a corporatised, multinational commodity culture: tiny local provocations that invite us to apprehend other (hi)stories, other possibilities – other ways of being in the present in the presence of others, face to face.

NOTES

1 Mnouchkine interviewed by Eberhard Spreng, *Theater Heute*, June 1991, p. 9; quoted in Sarah Bryant-Bertail, 'Gender, empire and body politics as mise en scène: *Les Atrides*', *Theatre Journal* 46: 1, March 1994, p. 1.

2 For an astute analysis of Reaganism as a 'regime of the visibility of seeming being', see Brian Massumi, 'The Bleed: Where Body Meets Image', in John C. Welchman (ed.), *Rethinking Borders*, Minneapolis: University of Minnesota Press, 1996, pp. 18–40.

3 Paul Virilio and others have discussed the critical erosion and collapse of temporal duration engendered by the instantaneous transmission of information in real-time technologies: 'They kill "present" time by isolating its presence here and now for the sake of another commutative space that is no longer composed of our "concrete presence" in the world, but of a "discrete telepresence" whose enigma remains intact forever'; Paul Virilio, 'The Third Interval: A Critical Transition', in Verena Andermatt Conley (ed.), *Rethinking Technologies*, Minneapolis: University of Minnesota Press, 1993, p. 4.

4 'From the telescope to the telegraph and telephone, from television to telecommunications, the development of *telesthesia* means the creation of, literally, dislocated perception and action. Dislocating the action from the site via the vector allows the use of power over the other without implicating power in the scene of the other'; McKenzie Wark, *Virtual Geography: Living with Global Media Events*, Bloomington: Indiana University Press, 1994, p. 43.

5 Michel de Certeau, *The Practice of Everyday Life*, Berkeley: University of California Press, 1988, p. 87.

6 The theatre company was christened Soleil as 'a tribute to certain film makers associated with light, generosity and pleasure, such as Max Ophüls, Jean Renoir, George Cukor'; Ariane Mnouchkine and Jean-Claude Penchenat, 'L'aventure du Théâtre du Soleil', *Preuves* 7: 3, 1971, p. 120. Interestingly, 'lightness', 'generosity' and 'pleasure' continue to be articulated as goals by/for Soleil performers.

7 When the Théâtre du Soleil was established, Jean Vilar had just stepped down as the director of the Théâtre National Populaire (TNP). The Soleil's early conception of a theatre that was both popular and political had much in common with Vilar's, although Mnouchkine's company developed it further, both in its political analysis and in its use of popular theatre forms. Two years before his death, Vilar invited the Soleil's productions of *Les Clowns* to the Festival d'Avignon in 1969. For further details on Vilar and the Soleil, see Thomas J. Donahue, 'Mnouchkine, Vilar and Copeau: popular theatre and paradox', *Modern Language Studies* 21: 4, Fall 1991, pp. 31–42.

8 For accounts of all of the Théâtre du Soleil's projects, from its prehistory in L'Association Théâtrale des Etudiants de Paris (ATEP) to *L'Indiade*, see Adrian Kiernander, *Ariane Mnouchkine*, Cambridge: Cambridge University Press, 1993; and David Bradby and David Williams, *Directors' Theatre*, Basingstoke: Macmillan, 1988, pp. 84–111.

9 These organisations included Mouvement contre le Racisme et pour l'Amitié entre les Peuples (MRAP), Groupe d'Information et de Soutien des Travailleurs Immigrés (GISTI), Ligue Internationale contre le Racisme et l'Antisémitisme (LICRA), Association Internationale de Défense des Artistes (AIDA), Ligue des Droits de l'Homme and Amnesty International.

10 In the wake of the collectively devised *L'Age d'Or*, Mnouchkine appears to have concluded that the vision of a single playwright was necessary after all; and the productions of the 1980s and 1990s that deal with contemporary political realities have all emerged from written texts. Retrospectively, Mnouchkine admits: 'The whole period of creating work collectively was, in fact, a preparation for our work on and *with* an author. I realise that now.' Mnouchkine in Maria Shevtsova, 'Sur *La Ville Parjure*: un théâtre qui parle aux citoyens', *Alternatives Théâtrales* 48, May 1995, p. 72.

11 Cf. Susan Melrose's account of the Théâtre du Soleil's gradual 'dispersal' of 'any *clear, univocal and strongly directed political action*', a process which 'rankles with those in theatre who still warm to the crusading politics of, for example, the "Brechtian" or the 1968 leftist tradition' (italics in original). I fully accept her suggestion that 'this does not indicate a lessening of the political. It indicates, instead, the ways in which myths can change, changing with them certain sorts of polarised roles, certain notions of the enemy and possible modes of intervention.' *A Semiotics of the Dramatic Text*, New York: St Martin's Press, 1994, p. 41.

12 The legal status the company adopted at its genesis, '*société coopérative ouvrière de production*', underlined the group's commitment to co-operative structures; as did its decision a few years later that every member of the company would draw the same wage, a practice that continues to the present day.

13 For example, *le psychologisme* (psychological–naturalistic acting, to be avoided at all costs in theatre), *le jeu* (game, play, acting, energy shared by complicit performers), *la création* (the generative, preparatory process as a whole, rather than simply the end product), *les évidences* (things that 'work' in a self-evident way), *l'état* (the primary state of a character), *la passion* (emotional state, drive – a term Lecoq uses for both *commedia* and melodrama), *la disponibilité* (a disposition of availability, openness, readiness), 'convex and concave' (action and receptivity, maximal exteriority and interiority), *l'écoute* (a quality of listening, a related-ness), *le paysage intérieur* ('inner lanscape'), *la transposition* (metaphoric transposition of an inner state in external space), 'autopsy' (the spatialising of interiority), *l'écriture corporelle* ('bodily writing'), and so on. Many of these stem from Copeau's and then Lecoq's endeavours to dismantle the legacies of Cartesian dualism. Many of them recur in the texts below.

14 A recent Unicef report, *State of the World's Children 1996*, records: 'Between 1945 and 1992, the world has seen 149 major conflicts in which some 23 million people have lost their lives. At the end of 1995, conflicts have been running in Angola for over 30 years, in Afghanistan for 17 years, in Sri Lanka for 11 years and in Somalia for 7 years'. Two million children have been killed in wars in the past decade. Quoted in *The Age*, Melbourne, 12 December 1995.

15 Their collective action was the end point of a process that had begun in 1993 when the Sarajevo Association was formed at the Avignon Festival; meetings and petitions were followed up with material help to artists and intellectuals with their usual petitioning by putting themselves personally at risk. On 30 August 1995, Mnouchkine received Bosnian president Alija Izetbegovic at the Cartoucherie; her words of greeting stressed the guarantee of human rights and liberties sought by the President's peace plan. She also referred emphatically to the 'multi-cultural, multi-ethnic, tolerant and politically secular' Bosnia–Herzegovina which Izetbegovic and 200,000 Sarajevo citizens, who had signed a declaration for a free and unified Sarajevo, continued to defend. (The full text of Mnouchkine's speech was published as '"Cette Bosnie-là": le message d'Ariane Mnouchkine', in *Le Nouvel Observateur*, 7–13 September, 1995, p. 41). Mnouchkine and her colleagues ended their strike after Izetbegovic's visit, with a pledge for further action for 'the principles of democracy'. [Note by Maria Shevtsova]

16 Mnouchkine in Armelle Héliot, 'Rêve oriental', *Autrement* 70, May 1985, p. 142.

17 One of the great ironies of the Soleil as 'non-hierarchical' enterprise, and a factor that has generated recurrent problems within the collective, relates to media construction of 'stars' in the company; and it has to be admitted that it has spawned a number of

extraordinarily virtuosic performers, including Philippe Caubère, Philippe Hottier and Bigot himself.

18 John Berger, *And our Faces, my Heart, Brief as Photos*, London: Readers and Writers, 1984, p. 18.

19 For a useful discussion of *La Ville Parjure*, and of theatre as 'civic' intervention, see Maria Shevtsova, 'Sur *La Ville Parjure*: un théâtre qui parle aux citoyens', op. cit., pp. 69–73.

20 See, for example, Jennifer Birkett, 'The limits of language: the theatre of Hélène Cixous', in *Voices in the Air: French Dramatists and the Resources of Language*, University of Glasgow: French and German Publications, 1992, pp. 171–86. My own reading of Cixous's concerns in *Sihanouk* relates to the precarious predicaments of individual subjects within collective structures – in other words, the status of *difference* in relation to various hegemonic regimes of power and truth, regimes that represent economies of morbidity. For a fuller discussion, see my review of the English translation of *Sihanouk* in *The Drama Review* 40: 3 (T151), Fall 1996, pp. 198–200.

21 Cixous in Susan Sellers (ed.), *The Hélène Cixous Reader*, London: Routledge, 1994, p. 83.

22 Ibid., p. 59.

23 Jean Genet, *Prisoner of Love* (trans. B. Bray), Middletown, CT, and London: Wesleyan University Press, 1992, p. 12. Genet was describing his experiences of Palestinian refugee camps.

24 'The experience of modern democracy is based on the realisation that [. . .] there is no point of equilibrium where final harmony could be attained. It is only in this precarious "in-between" that we can experience pluralism, that is to say, that this democracy will always be "to come", to use Derrida's expression, which emphasises not only the unrealised possibilities but also the radical impossibility of final completion.' Chantal Mouffe, 'For a politics of nomadic identity', in George Robertson *et al.* (eds), *Travellers' Tales: Narratives of Home and Displacement*, London: Routledge, 1994, p. 112.

CHAPTER 1
TOWARDS A POPULAR THEATRE

*1789: la révolution doit s'arrêter
à la perfection du bonheur
(1789: the revolution must end
only with the perfection of happiness)
(1970)*

Remember that the [theatre] director has already achieved the greatest degree of power he has ever had in history. And our aim is to move beyond that situation by creating a form of theatre where it will be possible for everyone to collaborate without there being directors, technicians, and so on, in the old sense.

Ariane Mnouchkine[1]

On the positive side, carnival suggests the joyful affirmation of becoming. It is ecstatic collectivity, the superseding of the individuating principle in what Nietzsche called 'the glowing life of Dionysian revellers' [. . .] On the negative, critical side, the carnivalesque suggests a demystificatory instrument for everything in the social formation which renders such collectivity difficult of access [. . .] Carnival in this sense implies an attitude of creative disrespect, a radical opposition to the illegitimately powerful, to the morose and monological.

R. Stamm[2]

1.1 *1789* AT THE CARTOUCHERIE

Victoria Nes Kirby

This detailed account of the staging of 1789, *originally published in* The Drama Review, *describes the production and its scenography from the mobile perspective of a spectator in the central 'pit' area, surrounded by the action. The production contained a number of authentic historical documents; all such texts in this section are signalled by the use of italic type.*

Inside the large rectangular building the theatre company has divided the huge space into two parts, cleaned it up and minimally painted it. One section has become a 'lobby', where tickets are picked up, some costume racks are stored and a photo display of former productions is mounted on panels. The other section, in which the play is performed, is much larger than the first. The walls and floor are stone and brick, and all the cast-iron reinforcements are visible. The rectangular space is divided down the centre by about twelve iron pillars; a wide skylight along the middle of the high ceiling is covered over during performances. The company has constructed a wooden grandstand for spectators that takes up part of the room nearest the lobby area. Behind and above it is a raised platform for the lighting boards and technical crew.

The grandstand faces five plain wooden platforms, each about five feet high, grouped around a large, empty, rectangular space. Each of the platforms can be reached from at least three sides – either along walkways or by stairs from the main floor. Inside the rectangular space, near the far platforms, are a tape deck and several kettle and snare drums. Outside the platforms and walkways there are four towers, for follow-spots at each of the corners. Above the entire playing area are rows of other spotlights, normal incandescent bulbs and several large loudspeakers.

Before the performance, the space is brightly lit, and the hall gives an impression of enormous spaciousness and simplicity. Nothing is hidden from the audience. We can see performers (of whom there are about forty) applying make-up in front of a long table and bench under the 'control tower'. More costume racks, tables and benches, trunks and lockers are located at the two far ends of the hall. The audience is free to roam about, talk to members of the company, or find a place to watch the performance. The majority of the spectators seat themselves in the raked grandstand until this area is filled. Those remaining, and those who perhaps know that the space inside the stages is available to the audience, begin drifting, searching for a stair or a cross-bar to perch on. By the time the performance begins, the grandstand is full and about two hundred people are standing in the central area. In a sense, there are two different audiences. One of them, sitting in the stands, can see all the platforms at once and has an overall, simultaneous view of the performance; it is static and distanced from the action. The other, those people within the area defined by the platforms and walkways, becomes a participating audience.[3]

The costumes and acting styles contribute to the atmosphere of a carnival or travelling show: a festival-circus. The costumes are often flamboyant, symbolic and exaggerated in scale and detail. The actors are strolling players and *bouffons* from the late 18th century. They use *commedia dell'arte, guignol* and operatic styles of acting. Gestures are often amplified, larger than life. There is virtually no 'realistic' acting.[4] [. . .]

• • •

The lights dim, and two figures appear on one of the stages. They are dressed as Louis XVI and Marie Antoinette. To the grave, slow music of a Mahler symphony, they enact the flight of the royal couple to Varennes [in June 1791], where they hope to receive help from a loyal army. An actor dressed as a strolling player during the French Revolution appears; he describes the clothes of the couple in great detail and lists the towns they pass through during their journey. The scene is melodramatic and romantic, and invokes sympathy for the miserable and bewildered 'innocents' fleeing from the revolution and the Parisian mob. The couple disappears. Then the narrator bounds up on to another stage and addresses the audience in a loud, booming voice; the Théâtre du Soleil has another story to tell about 1789.

There follows a short symbolic scene in which the King is unhorsed by the common people, who also strike out against France's two other tyrants – the Church and the Nobility. A figure appears on one of the end stages, and addresses the entire audience: 'Once upon a time, in a country that you have forgotten, there was a sick King overcome with pain. Look at him!' Leaning on a crutch, an actor dressed in the rich and flamboyant clothes of the King climbs up the stairs to the stage. The corner follow-spots brightly illuminate him, as music by Handel is played through the loudspeakers. Stepping down from the stage, the narrator grabs a microphone and tells the audience that the King, feeling death approaching, is calling his subjects to him; he introduces another actor, as a 'gander' (the Nobility), followed by another, as a 'raven' (the Clergy). These two are dressed in period costumes that are made unrealistic by the addition of extravagant feathers and plumes. The actor playing the Nobility moves slowly with courtly steps and gestures; he sniffs the King and turns away. The Clergyman has jerky, angular gestures and a harsh voice. The narrator puts a bonnet of ass-ears on his own head. As the raven and gander bang heavy wooden poles on the reverberating wooden stage, the 'ass-narrator' kneels down and the King sits on his back. Groaning, the ass begins to struggle and finally succeeds in throwing off the King. Seizing a baton, the ass threatens all three of the others. The scene ends as all of them, except for the narrator, remove their hats, making sweeping bows to the audience, and descend from the stage.

The next section is composed of simple scenes depicting the life of the common people in pre-revolutionary France. The narrator asks the audience to gather around him to hear the story of 'Marie the Miserable'. Immediately, to the accompaniment of Bach, two actors and an actress appear on another stage. Behind them, a cloth curtain is hurriedly hung from a suspended cross-bar; it is reminiscent of those hastily raised backdrops seen in travelling shows and carnival booths. The performer playing Marie squats down on the floor of the platform and begins, in mime, to eat from a pot. Her gestures are slow, simple and repetitious. One of the other actors is again the Clergy; he wears a high, clerical tiara, unrealistically decorated with fake jewels and tassels. The third actor, playing the Nobility, is also richly and colourfully dressed – a wide white ruff encircling his neck, a silk sash across his chest, long lace cuffs hanging out of his sleeves; in addition, he wears a plumed hat and carries a studded cane in one hand. Both of them ask Marie for money, for God blesses her house and armies protect it. She has nothing to give, so they snatch her pot from her. She cries in despair, her hands outstretched to the spectators standing near the stage. The spotlight on her dims as her cry and the music fade away. Opposite, another vignette takes place on a different, brightly lit stage; it involves an actor playing the King's salt-seller and an actress playing a hungry peasant. The woman drowns the salt-seller in an imaginary sea, and there is salted soup for everyone.

Momentary rejoicing is cut short as the narrator introduces another scene on another platform. 'Stagehands' quickly erect the familiar backdrop. One actress plays a pregnant peasant woman, another her friend; they are awaiting the birth of the child. The only props on the bare stage are a bucket of water and a clean white linen cloth. From an adjoining stage, an actor, dressed in the hunting clothes of the nobility, approaches the two women along the walkway. In mime, he knocks on the cottage door and enters. He demands hot water in which to wash his feet and a clean towel with which to dry them. The pregnant woman's friend begs him to return tomorrow, but the nobleman sticks his foot in the pail, splashing water over the stage, and grabs the linen cloth laid out for the imminent birth. He leaves and returns to the neighbouring stage, as the woman in labour screams and her companion weeps helplessly.

Four couples then appear on four stages, all dressed as peasants. Each woman rocks a white bundle, as if it were a baby, while the men speak to them: 'My wife, I haven't found any fire. My wife, I haven't found any bread. My wife, I haven't found any milk. I haven't brought back anything. We are lost, we are cursed. Forever. Our child too. Give him to me, my wife; so I can kiss him, my wife; so I can caress him, my wife; so I can put him to sleep.' Each father takes the bundle in his arms and strangles it.

Scenes of events leading up to the flight of the royal couple are now presented. Our eyes are drawn to another stage where an actor appears as King Louis XVI; he is a different actor from the one who impersonated the King at the opening of the performance. Imposing and lavishly dressed, he addresses the audience in an oratorical voice. He reads a paragraph from his decree for the convocation of the Estates-General (5 May 1789):

> *We, Louis, King of France by the grace of God, desire that from the extremities of our realm and from the most unknown settlements, each person should bring his wishes and complaints – in a manner that, by a mutual confidence and by a reciprocal love, will procure the quickest possible and efficient remedy to the ills of the State; and that we can restore, particularly to ourselves, the calm and tranquillity of which we have been deprived for so long.*[5]

The narrator then describes the hopes that this announcement aroused in the people of France. He points to the platform opposite where a woman stands in a spotlight; she wears a simple dress, her hair piled up on her head. Behind her hangs one of the cloth curtains as used in other scenes. After singing a song that was popular in 1789, she tells the audience that they may write to the King, informing him of who is good and who is bad, who should remain and who should disappear.

An actor dressed as a curate emerges from the darkness, beating a drum. 'Brothers!', he shouts, like a town-crier, 'the time of justice has come! Write to him quickly!' The curate says he will return in an hour to collect the people's grievances. On another stage opposite, directly in front of the grandstand, is a group of peasants, excited and happy about the news. The platforms and the pit are brightly lit; there is no music. The peasant-actors speak with a heavy regional accent, their movements are ponderous and awkward. The scene as a whole is played in a burlesque style. The peasants want to write to their 'good King', but they have no paper; so they produce the flag of France. Then they need a pen; there is a chase after an imaginary chicken, which they catch and pull out a quill. But there is no ink; so one of the women cuts her lover's arm to draw blood, and the feather is dipped into it. Finally they realise that none of them can write, and the audience laughs at their antics. The curate returns: 'If you've written nothing, we can change nothing!' The audience's laughter dies away.

A written grievance is passed through many hands on its way to the King. There are only two actors moving on bare stages, but they use popular theatre techniques and rapid costume changes to play a peasant, a man from a small market town, a man from a larger city, then a deputy. The costumes become finer, the actors' stomachs larger and their voices more solemn as the characters they portray become more elevated socially. Their means of transportation is also mimed by the actors: walking, riding a horse, riding in a carriage. Money is exchanged; the sum rises.

All of the lights go out, except for two spotlights on one of the end platforms, where two trestles are hastily lifted on stage. A board is placed on top of them to form a miniature stage, and a plain curtain is raised on poles behind. Four actors appear, dressed as strolling players of the early 19th century with huge red spots on their cheeks. They carry small marionettes, representing Louis XVI, Marie Antoinette, Monsieur Necker (the Swiss-born Director General of Finances who, in 1789, was very popular because of his economic theories), the Nobility, the Clergy and a 'brave' member of the Third Estate. Everyone can see both the marionettes and the live actors who manipulate them. They present a sketch called 'The Meeting of the Estates-General', a comic Punch and Judy show with some of the stock situations: the Queen hits the King, there are vulgar jokes, the 'villains' (Nobility and Clergy) are defeated.

As soon as the puppet-play has finished, the puppeteers again become actors. In the next scene three of them play Louis XVI, the Marquis Dreux-Brézé (a courtier and Louis's Master of Ceremonies) and Mirabeau (a noted orator and one of the great leaders in the early months of the revolution). The scene symbolises the struggle between the King and the Third Estate. Louis wished to keep a tight rein on the Estates-General by means of his royal veto; furthermore, he only gave one vote to each of the Estates, thus ensuring that the Third Estate would be out-voted by the combined votes of the clergy and the nobility. At the same time, the Third Estate naturally wanted to protect and strengthen what power it had been given by insisting that each man receive a vote, thereby outnumbering the other Estates. The scene ends as Mirabeau roars: '*For we are here by the will of the people, and we will not leave unless we are driven out at bayonet-point.*' Unable to listen to more, the King's servant Dreux-Brézé leaves to the accompaniment of a drumbeat.

An actor introduces the next scene, 'The Two-Faced King', then moves to the top of some stairs as three women gather at the foot. The women's hair is tangled and wildly dishevelled. They wear untidy but courtly clothes, and heavy, vulgar make-up; looking like witches or whores, they represent Marie Antoinette and two of her favourites. As each is introduced by the actor, she dances towards the public unrestrainedly. The announcer describes the first as 'this lewd bitch, this whore, Lamballe!', the second, Polignac, as 'an enraged she-camel'; the third woman, the Queen, he calls 'the worst of them all'. Then suddenly the announcer transforms himself into a 'terrible magician' [Cagliostro],[6] now dressed in a short velvet cloak and black shorts, over which are draped what look to be bits of an old lace curtain; pieces of netting hang out from under his hat. The scene is expressionistic, the costumes grotesque. The women come up on stage and perform a bacchic dance around him as he responds to their voices and caresses. Then the four part and form a procession as they walk towards the King, who is waiting on the platform where the puppet-show took place. Cagliostro gives a magic potion to the Queen and leaves the stage. The King, giving himself up to the women, drinks the offered beverage, then, transformed into a raging maniac, throws the only remaining puppet – Necker – off the stage. This represents the second historical dismissal of the Director of General Finances (11 July 1789). The King then orders 20,000 of his Austrian troops to surround the city of Paris.

Our attention shifts to another stage where someone is hanging up a cloth that represents the map of Paris in 1789. The actor who played the 'magician' begins speaking to the audience, pointing at the cloth behind him; he informs them of where the King's troops have been stationed and how many there are at each point. He tells us they are holding back shipments of food, and have in their clutches the people's deputies – its representatives in the newly formed National Assembly, which has developed out of the Estates-General. The actor calls on his audience to revolt.

The next section is an enactment of the events leading up to the storming of the Bastille by the people of Paris. A group of performers play de Breuil (a powerful landowner) and his servant, a banker and his wife, two brothers who own a shop and an officer who served under Lafayette in America. On hearing the news that the King has dismissed Necker, de Breuil closes the stock exchange and convinces the banker to close his bank; in turn they persuade the shopkeepers to close. The dialogue is repeated and phrases are added in each successive scene, as in the chorus of a folk song. All of the characters finally go to the soldier's house and ask him to form a citizens' militia. After being paid handsomely, the soldier instructs the banker and de Breuil how to shoot; he teaches the shopkeepers, however, how to obey the commands of their superiors. Now trained in the 'art of war', they all proceed to another stage accompanied by a military march played on a drum. They reach the home of Monsieur du Faubourg, an artisan of the working quarter. They repeat their story of closing the exchange, bank and shop, and tell him that he must free the people. There is a long silence. The members of the bourgeoisie look at each other with uneasiness as the artisan remains silent. Finally the banker speaks: 'I said, "let the people go" – I didn't say, "arm the people".' As the other characters talk amongst themselves, the artisan stands alone behind them; they begin to repeat, 'let the people go!' The sound becomes louder and louder until they are shouting, then they run off, brandishing their guns. So, having stirred up the workers, the bourgeoisie of Paris retreat to the security of their homes. The lights dim.

There is complete silence in the hall. Gradually one becomes aware of someone murmuring close by. Turning, you can see an actor sitting and beckoning spectators to gather closer around him. He is whispering about taking the Bastille. He stops, trying to recollect the events exactly, searching for the proper words; then he remembers and continues, surer of himself. The words come faster. He becomes more excited, louder. You realise that there are other actors telling other groups of spectators, including those in the raked seating, their stories of the Bastille. Their acting is very realistic, as the murmur becomes a steady stream of words. Slowly the actors rise to their feet, talking louder and louder until they are shouting out their tales. Drumbeats come faster and faster as the performers tell of entering the first, then the second courtyard of the prison, the smoke that impeded their passage, the dead bodies, the surrender. 'They have taken the Bastille!' The rolling kettle drums become deafening, the lights very bright. Suddenly a man bounds on to a central stage and announces the news; the Bastille will be demolished – the people have won.

The entire playing area is now bathed in light. Backdrops appear behind several of the stages, and every stage is occupied. It looks like a fair (Plate 1.1). Simultaneously, scenes depicting the great events of the people's victory are enacted by colourfully dressed puppeteers, wrestlers and acrobats. Three actors twirl huge flags over their heads at one end of the space. On another stage, a man symbolising Nobility is enchained. The audience is invited to step up to another stage and throw small bags stuffed with soft material at shields held by three members of the company; on the shield are painted the heads of Marie Antoinette

Plate 1.1 *1789.* The *fête populaire* after the fall of the Bastille. Photo: Martine Franck/Magnum

and Louis XVI. A large colourful wheel with words like 'Reason', 'Fraternity' and 'Happiness' painted around its rim, spins around on one of the end stages. Audience members are encouraged to bet on the winning word. Suddenly, a long chain of people holding hands comes racing across a stage. Comprising members of the audience and performers, the line sweeps across all of the stages, winding in and out among the actors on the platforms and the spectators on the ground. Acrobats take over another stage and make a pyramid, one climbing and standing on the shoulders of the others. On still another stage, an actor representing Bailly, the Mayor of Paris, pins the *tricolor* cockade on Louis XVI; another actor beats a snare drum while the King, in an effort to appease his people, receives this symbol of unity. (Red and blue were the colours of Paris, and white the colour of royalty.)

Then at one point during the fair, three of the stages are cleared to enact the flight of the Comte and Comtesse d'Artois, two of the first nobles to flee France.[7] Performers appear and announce that they are members of the Théâtre Français. They are wearing caricatural versions of the costumes that actors of the Comédie Française would wear. They waddle and strut about the stage, and speak in exaggerated parodies of the accents of the nobility. Here the Comte wears violent red lipstick in the form of a heart and large rouge dots on his cheeks; the Comtesse wears a bizarre looking hat of plumes and feathers, her face covered with heavy make-up. However, their conversation seems realistic. They enact their flight as they hurry from one stage to another, riding on the backs of their hunched-over servants.[8] The servants rebel when they reach the third platform and desert their masters. The nobles continue moving down the stairs and into the standing audience, which parts to give them passage.

The festival following the storming of the Bastille finally comes to an end with the nomination of Lafayette as commander of the National Guard (15 July 1789). Appearing on an end stage, he addresses the audience with sweeping gestures. In a booming pompous voice that carries over the music and the noise of the excited crowd, he thanks the people for giving him the command, then immediately orders them to disperse and return to their homes. The music intensifies until no one can hear his voice. Furious, he throws his hat into the crowd, then, forbidding all festivals and any signs of happiness that might trouble the property owners, yells out: 'THE REVOLUTION IS FINISHED!' An officer appears and orders the carnival people to close their booths and decamp. As the lights go down, only one booth remains dimly lit. A woman addresses the audience, trying to hold its attention: 'Don't leave, there's still something to see'. She introduces a doctor who can cure everyone; it is Jean-Paul Marat, dressed in a white robe with a white band around his head. A man emerges from the crowd, carrying in his arms a young woman who has fainted, and asks Marat if he can cure her. Taking the 'sick nation' in his arms,[9] he replies:

> *She is sick because she lacks love. I abhor licence, violence, disorder. But when I think there are actually 15 million men in the realm who languish in misery, who are nearly perishing from hunger, when I think that after having been reduced to this shocking destiny, the government*

abandons them without pity, treats as criminal those who assemble, and follows them as if they were ferocious beasts, my heart is oppressed by sorrow, and revolts with indignation. I swear to give myself wholeheartedly to instructing the people in their rights.

Marat's impassioned speech is followed by scenes of the general unrest and fear that swept France: the peasant revolts in rural areas, reprisals by the nobility and clergy and the great famine.[10]

Then the audience is reminded of the memorable night session of the reassembled National Assembly on 4 August, at which the privileged classes – the Nobility and Clergy – divested themselves of most of their prerogatives. They relinquished and abolished serfdom, titles, special hunting rights, tithes, internal customs barriers, and introduced equality for all men in regard to taxes, before the courts of law, and equal opportunity to secure governmental positions irrespective of class or wealth. On one stage, two men undress a richly ornamented woman, making flamboyant and exaggerated gestures with pieces of her clothing. Meanwhile a large group of actors, dressed in the finery of nobles, assembles on another stage. On a neighbouring stage, women in fine robes begin a slow dance movement to very 'noble', solemn music that blares from the loudspeakers overhead; they represent the higher clergy. All of the performers use grandiose pretentious gestures and statuesque poses as they take off their plumes, doublets, skirts, robes, cloaks, ruffles and other finery, then fling them high in the air and out to the waiting public. After stripping off their top garments, the women wear plain, long white robes and black veils over their heads. When the nobles and prelates are disrobed and stand in their underwear and white robes, an actor dressed as a deputy of the National Assembly appears and reads the law of Le Chapelier (the decree that abolished many of the privileges of the Nobility and Clergy).[11] While it is being read, the nobles and prelates awaken to the consequences of their act of charity, and a look of horrified consternation distorts their faces. Uttering piercing cries, they scramble for their cast-off clothing, then, clutching what they can grab back from the audience, they flee.[12]

After his speech, the deputy descends from the stage and walks among the spectators, announcing in a comic manner that they are going to witness an authentic parliamentary debate. Actors in the roles of deputies make their way through the audience and position themselves throughout the playing area. When one speaks, the others do not listen to him, and when the next speaker begins, he doesn't refer to his colleague's statement. In this disconnected, haphazard way, they discuss whether the Declaration of Human Rights should be placed at the beginning of the constitution. Their speeches – which are pompous, abstract and oratorical – are all taken from historical archives. They demonstrate the weaknesses, selfishness and treachery of those deputies who were concerned above all with preserving their own property. Finally, one deputy reads the articles of the Declaration to the audience. The first four concern man's rights to the pursuit of happiness, liberty, justice and guarantees of property rights. However, the fifth article states: '*But each man has not received from nature the same ability to use his rights. This results in an inequality between men. Inequality is, therefore, in nature itself.*' The debate ends, and the deputies congratulate each other. One of them, a bishop, remains alone. Taking off his costume, he becomes a narrator. A girl steps forward, and she is introduced by him as the 'General Will' in the clutches of the Executive and the Legislature on the question of the royal veto. 'To the gallows with the veto!', he shouts.

There is a commotion from the other end of the hall, and the audience turns to see a woman wearing the costume and make-up of a stereotyped 'black mammy' lumber onto the stage. She explains the application of the Declaration of Human Rights to a 'plantation owner' in colonialist Santa Domingo, who is sitting in a chair beneath a canopy held by an actress-slave in black face. There is momentary elation among the slaves, until one of the owners interrupts the black woman to point out that the Declaration also states that the possession of property is an inviolable and sacred right: 'They spoke of men, my dodos, not of negroes.' The male owners win the argument, and the slaves bow down in front of their masters. There then follow scenes in which the National Assembly concerns itself with etiquette rather than the raging famine, bakers are paid to withhold bread from the people, and the King and Queen stuff themselves with food while he yells out his veto to everything passed by the Assembly. In the final scene, the *tricolor* cockade is trampled underfoot during a banquet of the King's Guard Corps.

Bright lights and triumphant music announce the arrival of all the women in the company. Holding hands to form a chain, they dance diagonally across the pit area; the standing spectators separate to make a path for them. Carrying branches in their hands, they all wear white skirts and blouses, white shawls and white puffy *charlotte* bonnets with a *tricolor* pinned to them. Breaking the chain, they turn around and begin to retrace their steps, dancing and weaving their branches. They have gone to Versailles to bring the King and Queen to Paris, where they will be confined to the Tuileries (5 October 1789). The French had still not considered a republican form of government.

Then two enormous puppets come out of the darkness beyond the playing area; high above the heads of the standing spectators, each is held up by three men in white shirts. The puppets appear to float in the air as they are brought to meet the dancing women. A woman shouts through a hand-held microphone that the royal cortège is coming. The other women dance even more merrily in front of the approaching puppets and cry out: 'Long live the King! Long live the Nation! Long live the People!' The music is deafening, and the excitement contagious, especially for those spectators close to the moving procession. Spotlights follow the bobbing balloon-like figures as they make their way through the crowds. As the women reach the farthest stage, the whole cortège comes to a halt.

Three actors, representing deputies from the Assembly, dressed in sober black and the sashes of their office, hail the women from the stage. Using a microphone, one of them yells: '*Silence! A free people must be reasonable! If you do not renounce these illegal and rash acts, you will dig your own graves!*' Public assemblies disturb the increasingly powerful bourgeoisie. The women fall silent, the music stops, the lights fade on the audience, leaving only the stage and the women lit. Another deputy grabs the microphone: '*Frightened, all the honest citizens will flee your capital, which will soon be deserted!'* The first deputy shouts: 'THE REVOLUTION IS FINISHED!' The third deputy uses a microphone to read the four articles of martial law decreed by the Assembly on 21 October, which stipulate that there will be no large gatherings of people. The bewildered women slowly retreat, still watching the deputies; then, as the puppets disappear, the women leave one by one, dropping their branches in defeat. As the women disperse, the deputies unfurl a large black cloth, inscribed in big letters with the word 'ORDER'. Marat materialises out of the crowd of spectators, still wearing his white robe and headband (Plate 1.2). Pointing an accusing finger at the cowardly deputies hiding behind their black cloth, he shouts into a microphone that the French owe everything to the popular uprisings of the common people. Addressing the citizens, he yells: '*This law only serves to destroy you! Awaken, citizens, awaken!'* The spotlight on him goes out, and he disappears.

The third deputy then announces the auction of the domain and goods of the Benedictine Order of St Giles. A stage to the left is immediately lit, and performers in bourgeois clothes of the 19th century (representing the eventual rule of the *nouveaux riches* in France one hundred years later) parade in through the milling spectators. They wear an excessive amount of clothing, all of it in bad taste. Everyone greets each other as they climb up to the stage to the sound of a pompous military march. When the sale begins, however, they become increasingly unrestrained, finally insulting and hitting each other. Marat reappears and interrupts them, addressing them and the audience as a whole through his microphone:

> *Citizens, what have we gained in destroying the aristocracy of the nobles, if it is replaced by the aristocracy of the wealthy? See how many of us, by being greedy and covetous, have divided the citizens; and now the Court and the Ministers want a pretext to slaughter the good citizens. The pretext is this: the King has escaped.*

A member of the bourgeoisie, Barnave, steps out from among the group of characters on-stage. Quoting the 'real' Barnave, he states that all change is now disastrous. The revolution must be stopped immediately: 'THE REVOLUTION IS FINISHED!'

In the scene that follows, the company summarises its concept of the immediate outcome of the French Revolution: the rise in power and wealth of the bourgeoisie, as characterised by the National Guard and martial law, rather than the workers and the peasants.[13] Three loud blows are struck with a wooden staff on the stage opposite the bourgeoisie. Someone announces the beginning of a theatrical presentation. Acting like children, the bourgeoisie install themselves comfortably on the edge of their stage to become spectators at a *guignol* performance. Actors dressed as puppets act out a fable. The People of France, released from a trunk by the Bourgeoisie, kill the Nobility and the Clergy, then return to the trunk in a docile fashion. There is applause, laughter and approval from the bourgeois spectators on-stage. But the figure of the People suddenly reappears from the trunk and strangles the figure of the Bourgeoisie, who calls out in terror: 'Help me, National Guard!' Represented by another *guignol* actor, the National Guard arrives and announces martial law. 'Fire!', he commands. At first the bourgeois

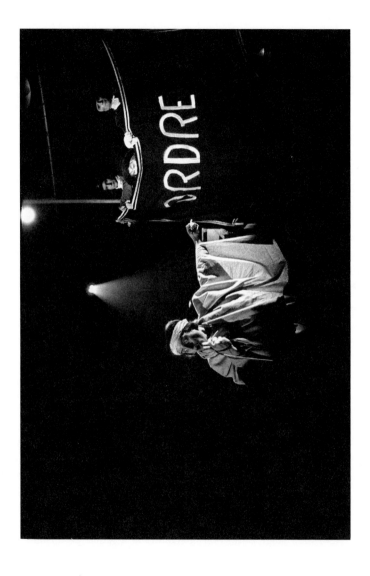

Plate 1.2 1789. Marat (René Patrignani, with microphone): behind him, the deputies with the banner marked 'ORDER'. Photo: Martine Franck/ Magnum

spectators are horrified by the turn of events in the fable, but they sigh with relief when the Guard appears and leave the 'theatre', satisfied by its outcome. As they file out, Marat reappears in a beam of light and speaks sadly of the revolutionary ardour lacking in the souls of his fellow citizens: '*I say with all sincerity from my heart that our only hope is in civil war. I hope that it erupts as soon as possible.*'

On another stage, an actor appears and from a piece of paper reads words written by François Noël Babeuf, who signed himself 'Gracchus Babeuf'. (He was a visionary revolutionary who founded the *Journal de la Liberté de la Presse* and the *Tribune du Peuple*; he also organised egalitarian groups and was an enthusiastic supporter of economic equality and communal property. Imprisoned many times, he was eventually executed in 1797.)[14] In this passage, Babeuf calls for a total upheaval of laws, institutions and social structures: '*Let's see the end of society as it is! Let's see the happiness of the common people! After a thousand years, let's at last change these rank and stupid laws!*'

Immediately after his speech, loud triumphant music fills the air, every light is turned on, and the members of the Théâtre du Soleil come running in from all directions, bound up on the stages and joyfully bow to the audience. They quickly disappear and reappear, this time holding each other's hands. Forming a long chain, they dance across the wooden structures; the audience, wildly enthusiastic, claps and cheers. The performers never stop moving, bowing, smiling, dancing, blowing kisses to the spectators. Finally, audience and performers start clapping together until a loud, boisterous rhythmic beat nearly drowns out the music. The general joy and celebration last for several minutes. Finally the tumult dies down, the members of the company disappear into the shadows and the spectators disperse. In twenty minutes, the building is cleared and quiet.

First published in *The Drama Review* 15: 4, Fall 1971.

1.2 THE SEARCH FOR A LANGUAGE
From an interview with Ariane Mnouchkine by Emile Copfermann

In an interview recorded in September 1970, two months before the opening of 1789, *Ariane Mnouchkine describes the genesis of the project, the company's critical and dialogical approach to history, and the interactive processes and ideals of collective creation.*

COPFERMANN: After having mounted *Le Songe d'une Nuit d'Eté* (*A Midsummer Night's Dream*) in 1967, you envisaged producing a work on the Paris Commune, which you intended to adapt in part from Vallès' *L'Insurgé* (*The Rebel*). This project has been abandoned and you have also dropped the idea of a production of Brecht's *Baal*. Now you're working on *1789*. What made you change your plans?

MNOUCHKINE: There were a number of reasons. In relation to Vallès and the Paris Commune project, there was a paralysis of the company. We didn't have – we still don't have – the necessary material means to realise something on such a scale. On top of that, there were difficulties of an ideological kind. Although it was tempting to commemorate the centenary of the Commune [March–May 1871], we realised that the political education of the actors, of myself, of all of us, was insufficient. And this is what gave rise to our current choice. We were in danger of producing a right-thinking chronicle and nothing else. It seemed impossible to us to launch thirty actors into work on the Commune without first acquiring some elementary notions of history. We had to go through a political apprenticeship. Having said that, we would not have managed to do anything else either, for lack of money and other reasons which almost led the company to fold, and which made me no longer want to produce *Baal*.

C: Wouldn't it have been just as productive to tackle those political problems in the production you would have done? In the course of your professional practice?

M: That's what is happening with the French Revolution. Coming to grips with the Paris Commune was extremely complex. The French Revolution is a primary event, a primary stage for a political analysis. With the Commune, we felt we were in danger of ending up with a dishonest performance, we would have tacked our opinions onto an analysis, onto an important phenomenon without having grasped its essential components.

Through working on the French Revolution, the company is learning, training itself, developing a way of thinking which will turn into performance. We have already divided it into two parts, the revolution of 1789 and that of 1793. If one considers that there were in fact three revolutions (in 1789, 1792 and 1793),[15] we realised that we needed an absolutely radical shift in tone between the first and third. It would be both stupid and naive to show the Commune without having dealt with Thermidor first,[16] it would simply be succumbing to a spirit of commemoration. In two years, three years, we will talk of the Paris Commune. The French Revolution marked the appearance of capitalism (perhaps it is naive to formulate it in this way);[17] the workers' movement subsequently defined itself in relation to it, right up until the Paris Commune . . .

C: Did you elaborate a spine for the production in advance? Did you have a preconceived form?

M: One reason for abandoning the Commune project stemmed precisely from our inability to find a form for it. This time we've outlined not one, not two, but perhaps ten productions with History as their theme; it's still too soon to know what will come from this. In our original idea, the production went from 1789 to Thermidor. We have already had to divide it in two: there will be one production on the first revolution, another on the second . . .

Through work on *Les Clowns*, we searched for a clear, direct and luminous form. Once we had this accomplished, we wanted to find a content common to both spectators and actors, and from there we would look for a form. At first we thought of a production based on folk tales, which proved to be illusory. Today, these stories are received as cultural products, almost as aesthetic products. In any case, they don't mean very much today, their meaning has been displaced.

Moving on from there, we realised that the only heritage common to all French people, even if it is distorted, is the History of France. We wanted to create a work on a subject that everyone would feel they knew. The 'spine' emerged from this desire. Next we had to decide between two possible alternatives. We could have undertaken a production on the French Revolution through its central protagonists; we would have obtained that kind of mystificatory spectacle in which History becomes a succession of psychological conflicts between 'great men'. Or else we could have taken something more anecdotal as a starting point – the story of a worker, of an ordinary family in the face of the events. When we looked closely at this option, it proved to be every bit as fraudulent as the first one, and drew us towards edifying imagery. We have opted for a third way. We try to show the Revolution played throughout on the level of the people, but with a critical distance. Mountebanks, acrobats, fairground players, town criers or agitators show what they feel, what they know, what reaches them of the 'historical' events, of the major figures. We never show Louis XVI. The spectator sees Louis XVI as seen by a fairground player, then by someone else a few months later, in a different style.

C: Don't you run the risk of dissipation in this way: there are no longer characters that are in some sense individuals, but rather one collective character: History, and from then on, a mythical history?

M: A collective vision, rather than a collective character, which is normal in a production realised by a collective. It's difficult to appraise the risks entailed. For us, it's a production that arises from the work of the actors; its form, and not only the form, is elaborated during the working process.

C: Doesn't this take us back to what happened with *Les Clowns*, where the real subject of the representation was displaced? The subject of *Les Clowns* was not so much the clowns as the actors themselves, their own creativity in fact.

M: At the beginning of work on *Les Clowns*, nothing existed: nothing, that is, except for the creativity of the actors. Here the starting point already exists. It's the interpretation of major events by actors, who try to analyse these events from the perspective of those who lived them and experienced the consequences . . .

C: The obstacle we alluded to earlier on, in relation to the Paris Commune, is just as present here. What do the actors rely on to motivate their interpretation? Their social practice? The knowledge acquired through reading? The research that they have conducted themselves? [. . .]

M: We started with what we knew about the French Revolution, from what we'd learnt about it at school and elsewhere. We started from this vast, optimistic story, with its incredibly bloodthirsty characters, with all of its clichés: the people in poverty, their revolt, the providential heroes . . .

C: The mechanism of History, a mechanism without an engine . . .

M: . . . and an extraordinary degree of mystification about the role and function of the central characters. We forced ourselves to break this mystification; we weren't trying to write a dramatic work, a play. Starting from what they knew, a group of the actors imagined the revolution as a popular conquest. They weren't aware of the theft and appropriation of this revolution by the bourgeoisie, of the ways in which the people were muzzled each time. This discovery clearly came through reading. Ultimately, the point of view of the whole production stems from a reciprocal critique. Certain scenes are played two, three times differently. Once according to a history textbook for elementary schools – a fabulous and fabulistic story. Confronting that one, a second interpretation is offered, which proposes a different perspective.

C: From the opposition of different ways of playing, a point of view is created.

M: The ways of playing oppose or complement each other. We don't often make use of the diversity of perspectives [in the final production]. The production is created by a number of people sharing an identical point of view but in several interpretations. Someone speaks of an event. Other actors immediately re-envisage the event, responding with an interpretation which is informed by what has just been shown to them. At which point the question of the production arises: this last improvisation will perhaps be retained, and be the only one retained for the production. Not all of the improvisations will form part of the production, but all of them will have contributed to its formation.

C: So to summarise: *1789, la Révolution est finie (1789, the Revolution is over)*[18] is a collective discussion of the French Revolution, led by the actors who perform it?

M: With this nuance: the 'discussion' is not the whole performance.

C: Would you call it a collective creation? This tendency was already being sketched out in *Les Clowns*.

M: I didn't want us to use this term for *Les Clowns*, which seemed to me to be the quintessence of each person's individual creation. There was no collective creation, and that was perhaps the production's major flaw.

C: An individual creation . . . but in succession?

M: We were all confronted with our own individual problems with creativity. Something different has been going on here for two months now – I'm talking about the work, not the results. We run the risk of scattering our efforts, of making mistakes, we are groping about, we risk stammering, and not only in our expression, but also in our thinking, in our political impact. But I believe that our present approach, which is that of a group, is the best one, and in any case, it's the one that interests me. It seems to me that it is right, that it's the only way of proceeding today.[19]

I'm exasperated by 'left-thinking' productions that are produced in conditions of total imbrication with the system. They are alibi-productions. As for us, we would rather see the production escape us for a certain time, but with the group's approach being in tune with it. We prefer the production created by the group to be what the group wants it to be, not what the system of production wants.

C: After this production, will you reject written works?

M: We don't pre-judge written works to be necessarily outdated. No doubt I will again direct a written play. At the present time, it is an instinctive rejection, not a judgement. Written plays are not suited to what we're searching for – still in a rather confused way, I admit.

C: They do not allow themselves to be destroyed in order to be recomposed in a collective work of the type undertaken for *1789* . . .

M: I refuse to carry out that destruction. When I produce a play, I do not wish to destroy it. This is why I wanted to say that our attitude does not include a judgement. When I wanted to direct *Midsummer Night's Dream*, it was not at all to destroy Shakespeare's play, on the contrary, it was to read it very, very deeply.

C: The example is badly chosen; old plays offer more latitude [. . .]

M: Yes and no. There is a way of reading a play, and another which consists in twisting it. I do not want to twist a text.

C: What remains for the director in this kind of collective production?

M: A great deal. In any case it's quite enough for me. I suggested the form of this production, without really imposing it. Because I have rarely seen actors launch themselves on a trail so impetuously, with such understanding, right away. I'm responsible for a part of the construction of the whole, just like the actors. I don't think one ever carries a production within oneself.

At the present moment, we're guided more by what we don't want than by what we want. What we want still remains unclear. Directing is always like that, twenty-nine times out of thirty, I don't tell an actor: do this, but rather: don't do that. As a director, I reject certain things. I think a lot of directors write what they want *before* the actual directing. In my case, I write afterwards. We recorded the text of *Les Clowns*, then transcribed it. We distributed the good improvisations among the actors, who went back over them and reworked them. They often went over what they had already done, modifying it. This time we are recording, we are reworking[20] – not in the sense of prettying, of finishing, but so as to remove the parasites, to focus the meaning, and always after the event.

When I suggest an idea for an improvisation, I also want to provide its text. I say: it would be good if you would try to do this or that, but in general the actors produce something very different from what I've suggested. Most of the time they are the ones who bring the final touch. My role consists of searching for a synthesis: articulating one improvisation with another. The actors provide more than raw materials. Some improvisations are almost fully realised straight away. On the other hand, there are others that begin to sketch something out, which one must help to develop.

C: In the absence of a pre-established text or scenario, how do you decide that the production is finished? [. . .] When you move in undefined areas, as you are doing here, what guides you? One could ask: why three hours for the performance, and not five or six, since you've rejected the duration implicit within the form of the written play?

M: It's three hours because that is what the present conditions of the performance impose on us. It is true that we've come up against this question of the conditions in which a production can be presented. We have already taken measure of this limit and divided the production in two. Other constraints weigh on us: having to perform every evening. We would prefer continuity, play for one day, two days, stop for a month, reflect, work, perform again, learn. In the production as we currently conceive of it, I don't feel any constraints. Moreover, our aim in doing it is not at all to move beyond the notion of the production . . . I am not trying to perform the reality of the Revolution, to show the 'true' Revolution . . .

C: The form of performance isn't as 'free' as you seem to think. An example: someone writes something they want to be read. It must be 'published'. The publisher imposes the norms of what is publishable [. . .] The vague, written thing is now a book; it will only be read by those who buy and read books. What is more, the system of production imposes its form on the production to such a point that a person who writes innocently will end up no longer thinking of a jumble, of a thing, but of a publishable book [. . .]

M: In this perspective, we cannot of course escape such pressure. One of the difficulties in this production relates to its scenic configuration. To my mind, it's as simple as can be, there's nothing surprising about it. But when we tell those wanting to promote the show what its characteristics are, they are frightened. It takes place on a fairground surrounded by five interconnected platform stages, two on one side, three on the other: the audience should be in the middle and on one of the exterior sides. We cannot use a conventional theatre. We anticipated this and we have asked for a gymnasium. This simple fact is an obstacle to our being able to perform in France. It is not an insoluble problem, on a material level. The dimensions weren't established in some abstract way, we established our dimensions according to those of the smallest conceivable gym space: a basketball court, 26 metres by 14, harmonious proportions. In this case, theatre people who are open to new forms of representation respond negatively when we simply express our requirement. Now, the only space that no French town whatsoever lacks is a basketball court! The production is not expensive, we have all our own electrical equipment. It makes no difference!

Placed in the centre of the performance, the spectators can sit down or remain standing. If I add: 'as in *Orlando Furioso*', everyone acquiesces: 'Ah yes, *Orlando Furioso*', with admiration. But Ronconi had to mount his production somewhere. Afterwards, everyone followed. The same people are refusing such a simple thing here. And these are theatre people! I am not talking about U.D.R. town clerks or something like that. I'm talking about theatre people, for god's sake! They have accepted to be the prisoners of their space. At least they get something in return. As for me, I do not accept it, but in addition to not having the advantages, I must put up with the disadvantages of *their* prison . . .

According to them, this is a production we should never have undertaken. We should not have mounted any of the productions we have done, and this one obviously less than the others, because it's the last.

C: The conditions of theatre production tend to reproduce themselves. The theatre produced by these conditions has engendered a type of playhouse that will impose the same conditions, maintained by the protectors of the theatrical institution, on future productions. Anyone cannot play anything anywhere. You must do theatre in theatres, basketball on basketball courts.

M: About a year ago, we found ourselves in an untenable financial situation, which we couldn't get out of. Since it exists, I went to the Ministry for Cultural Affairs to ask for some money. I explained our imminent disappearance, spoke of the publicity we planned to give them. They gave us 50,000 francs, thanks to which we survived. At which point someone at the Ministry added, 'There's no question of you continuing in this way. We will have to meet, to work out what we can do.' He seemed very uneasy. He went on to explain to me that he knew about our intransigence. Why do they know about my intransigence? I have never been intransigent with them, I asked them for money. 'We never intervene politically', he said, 'you can do what you want. But you must understand you and your company constitute a very awkward case.' I didn't understand at all. Then suddenly I understood. I can stage a production that seems totally opposed to them, they couldn't care less. But the way in which the company functions and produces its shows, the simple fact that we don't fit ourselves into a pre-existing framework – this throws them and worries them.[21] [. . .]

C: Why do you attach so much importance to this? Would you be afraid of occupying a fixed space, of the company having an administrator, of its being constrained to giving daily performances, afraid of a regular programme?

M: Having a fixed performance space would mean that instead of renting the Elysée-Montmartre [a Paris theatre] at 1,500 francs a night, we would give performances at lower cost; it would also mean that we could develop activities around this space, which is impossible at present. No, that's not it. We are capable of maintaining a regular programme. We do not want to fall into a regular and normalised mode of *production*, which would devalue our work.

C: Isn't that a rather romantic and utopian attitude? The nostalgia of a craft industry of the past . . .

M: All theatre work is craft . . . [. . .] Are we the ones who have a romantic attitude, we who live in the utopia, or they? In the short term, perhaps. We encounter material conditions that are impossible to bear. And in the long term? The actors are satisfied with this way of working, and so am I. When I go and watch a rehearsal somewhere else, when we see how other people work, I'm really staggered. If the Théâtre du Soleil closes up shop, I will switch to another profession. Because I would not tolerate entering the theatre world as it is now. Craftspeople? Yes, in this sense we are, we attach a great deal of importance to what we are working on, to its quality. We do not produce it for ourselves, but to show it, and we want what we show to satisfy us.

C: So what cements the company is a process of 'creation' on which you all reach agreement?

M: Not just that, other notions come into play. I could find a similar degree of satisfaction directing elsewhere. People tell us: you take refuge in a mini-society that you try to make ideal. Why not? If we succeed in developing a 'Théâtre du Soleil' enterprise, in which each of its members would be able to find nourishment; which we would all manage; whose course we would be able to influence; in which technical training would be continuous; in which there wouldn't be technicians on one side, workers on the other; where everyone would be trained in all the different disciplines involved in the enterprise – if we succeeded in this, would it be a communal enterprise, phalansterism, or, in more banal terms, a vibrant theatre company?

At the present moment, we're feeling our way. We are more aware of what we don't want than of what we want. The conversation at the ministry was revealing. 'We will have to meet for an in-depth exchange of views.' Why an in-depth exchange of views? Our productions are known, they're public, they are what defines us.

Our activities began in 1964, with the same core of people. We wanted a theatre different from the one we were being shown at that time, a theatre created by us, together. We knew nothing. Is that a disadvantage? The work of a group moves forward slowly, more slowly than the evolution of an individual alone. After two years, I felt a choice had to be made. At that time, in our attempts, I saw a mistrust amongst some of those who today go the furthest; I had the impression that they were afraid of being indoctrinated, that the opinion of one person might impose itself and become the only one for all, so that their thinking would no longer be free.

C: They had come to 'make theatre', not to provoke political agitation.

M: Yes. And gradually they are noticing, we are all noticing, that in working, as we make choices, soon there are only rare, very rare solutions, fewer and fewer solutions.

C: Few solutions for what? Creating, producing a collective creation?

M: Not so much creating as assuming a social function. What we are attempting, and it's still at an embryonic, faltering stage, is to find something common from which to establish a relationship with the audience. Clearly there is a wall standing between this attempt we are undertaking on the French Revolution, and the audience we want to reach. Out of 100, out of 125 performances of *Les Clowns*, perhaps we broke through this wall five times, two times, which is miserable – few, very few times.

C: How do you see this relationship with the audience?

M: Although I don't share his ideas, I agree with Grotowski that the audience should not modify the production. If it is modified, there is very little chance of improving it afterwards, or at least only in very restricted ways. At a deeper level, the intervention of the audience ought to manifest itself in some sense prior to the production. Reviews after the event have an effect . . . on the subsequent production. Sometimes they impact on the *manner* of saying, rather than on what is said: *on what has already been said.* In the course of the work, relations with the audience are bizarre; at certain moments, we forget about them completely.

C: Paradoxically, one doesn't sense this presence of the audience in your repertoire, which seems to lack any apparent continuity. *Le Capitaine Fracasse*, *Les Clowns*, *La Cuisine* (*The Kitchen*) – a social play, *Le Songe d'une nuit d'été* (*A Midsummer Night's Dream*) – a poetic play . . .

M: On the contrary, [the continuity is] in our search for a language. We take an oblique approach. Our continuity has been in abandoning the paths we had tried. Our current obstinacy is rooted in *Les Clowns*, the most contested of the productions we've created – with good reason, no doubt. But suddenly we are no longer forced to break with that approach in order to start anew. Thanks to the language generated in *Les Clowns* we are trying to talk about the French Revolution. The audience contributed to this choice. We spent a lot of time thinking about them before deciding to create a production on the Revolution.

It's difficult to describe our way of working. It takes different forms with each production. This time we know where we want to go, it's not a production we're discovering as we go along . . . It's more that we're discovering the *way* of doing it as we go along.

C: Let's return to *Baal*, by Brecht. Why did you abandon the project?

M: It was the first time such a thing had happened to me. The desire to stage the Brecht play coincided with a crisis. Several members of the company, including myself, experienced a kind of weariness under the influence of the enormous suicidal atmosphere that followed in the wake of May 1968. Emerging from this crisis, I no longer wanted to speak of the problems of a 'creator' in society – Baal is a poet. A great deal of time and energy spent on something of interest to few, at least in terms of the perspective in which I conceived the production at the time. *Baal* is a very beautiful play. No doubt there is a way of staging it by fighting against the character. It was too much for me. *Baal* is very ambiguous. Perhaps in two or three years.

From Emile Copfermann, 'Entretiens avec Ariane Mnouchkine', in *Travail Théâtral – Différent: Le Théâtre du Soleil*, Lausanne: La Cité, 1976.

1.3 EQUAL, BUT NOT IDENTICAL
An interview with Ariane Mnouchkine by Irving Wardle

In October 1971, Irving Wardle, theatre critic for The Times, *recorded the following interview with Mnouchkine at the Roundhouse in London, the venue for* 1789 *on tour. Mnouchkine provides a performative and historical frame for the production as collective creation and oppositional historiography.*

IRVING WARDLE: Do you believe that what comes across to an audience is a product of the relationships within the little society which created the performance?

ARIANE MNOUCHKINE: Yes. I'm sick of leftist plays produced in total collaboration with the commercial system. I also believe that if the show had been better acted, better directed, it wouldn't have touched French people so deeply. The political development of a group is a process of slow maturation; it cannot be ahead of how the group actually lives. And what we have been doing until now is forging our instrument. We wanted to treat a political theme, but you cannot do that without a good instrument. The failure of political theatre – if it exists – is that it's often so bad aesthetically, thus of no service to politics. So our development has been to search for an improved means of expression before trying to express anything important.

We are all ignorant, all amateurs; we didn't know anything at the start, not even what the commercial theatre knows. The actors have various origins; some are students, some from poor families, some bourgeois. Most of them had acted just once or twice before or not at all. It's hard to say what they have in common. But I think they are all conscious that they are strong as a group and would lose if they were forced to have individualistic careers. We never used to turn any applicants away. We would say, 'Come tomorrow at 7.30, there's this set to be moved', and that would discourage at least eight out of ten. The company is made up of the people who stayed. But now there are forty-one of us and financially we cannot support any more, so we have to say no.

W: How are collective decisions made?

M: We don't gather together to decide to put in a nail here or there; the person who decides is the person who knows where to put it. But if, say, a good actor has to be dropped – if, for example, he has started being destructive or wants to work outside the group – this decision will be made collectively. With our way of working, talent is easily shared, so there's no talent hierarchy; we're equal, but not identical.

W: Are improvisations allowed to clash?

M: Yes, that's encouraged. For example, at the beginning, everyone was improvising characters; we had lots of Marats, Lafayettes, Marie Antoinettes. And at first we saw a Lafayette who was exactly the fine hero described in schoolbooks. Then one group presented an improvisation on a meeting between Lafayette and Marat; Lafayette wanted to buy him. Through this scene we discovered the other face of Lafayette, and the previous improvisations were superseded. This happened very often.

But it would be wrong to describe this process as collective decision-making. It's a process of confronting evidence and solving the puzzle. And rehearsals were so enthusiastic that there were no decisions to be made. Everyone knew what was good and what was bad, so there was no conflict. Take the case of the King's flight to Varennes. One day we were completely blocked; not one good improvisation, nothing. So I suggested we forget about the play and amuse ourselves. I put on Mahler's First Symphony and said, 'Do whatever you like to that.' There were four groups; two of them independently improvised on the flight to Varennes, and the scene we play now is a synthesis of these two improvisations. Some people have objected to our use of Mahler, Handel and Beethoven. But if the music yields such results, why not keep it?[22]

W: If the history of the Revolution, as taught in schools, is a bourgeois slander, where did you go for the 'real' story?

M: We went to Mathiez, Lefebvre, de Tocqueville and Marat himself, and to the records of the National Assembly debates.[23] There was no division of the work; apart from a young woman from Martinique who instructed us in the colonial situation, the whole troupe studied together. The work was not broken down until rehearsal, when we divided into five groups, each following up its own ideas. And these groups were never the same. It was stipulated that no four people could work together for longer than a single morning, and that each person must be prepared to abandon a part.

W: Is the audience you have the audience you want to reach?

M: Like most people in this sector of the theatre, we would like to reach the workers. But that is an abstract ideal. And I do not feel that it's entirely useless for the bourgeoisie to see certain plays, because the internal bourgeois crisis between the old and the young is very important for the revolution. After all, 1789 itself started with a crisis in the aristocracy. We've heard 'Vive le Roi!' a few times. No one has yet shouted 'Vive la bourgeoisie!' When we've played to working-class spectators, they've been very respectful and attentive; they don't show off like students. And when they ask questions they're to do with fact: Is that true? Is that dangerous? How is this done?

W: What about the spatial use of the audience?

M: I don't like this expression, 'use of the audience'; we use ourselves for them. Our first intention was for the audience to be freer – which doesn't happen of course, because there are usually too many people. But at the first few performances in Milan, when we had only about six hundred people, it was incredible to see how they did move around, in order to get in closer. We began originally with the idea of the fairground – we didn't know what shape it would be, it changed with the size and placement of the rostra. We knew only that it would be a fairground: a form which is simple and popular, which existed at that time, and both before and after that time.

W: Would you make any comparison between *1789* and Ronconi's production of *Orlando Furioso*?

M: Our purpose and Ronconi's are entirely different. Our aim is to tell as clearly as possible a story which all French people already know. Not all Italians know the story of Orlando, and anyway Ronconi's aim is not to tell it. The pleasure and magic of *Orlando* are in spatial organisation, not content. It's a completely different process, apart from the superficial similarities in our experimentation with space. But I do accept comparisons with the Bread and Puppet Theatre; *The Cry of the People for Meat* is one of the greatest experiences I've had in a theatre, and I'm sure it influenced me.[24]

W: Would the production have taken its present form without the events of May 1968?

M: Yes, because the idea was already there. Though May '68 has been important to us, this is not a play about 1968 but about something more important. In the middle of the play, with the fall of the Bastille, there is a most important moment – the moment of success. Repression follows, but because we couldn't finish on a note of defeat, we added a speech from Babeuf at the end: 'Let us see the happiness of the common people! After a thousand years let us at last change these rank, stupid laws!'

W: In his *Memoirs*, Herzen quotes a decree Babeuf drafted for post-revolutionary government, in which he lays down rules relating to forcible direction of labour, houses of correction, confiscation of property, offences punishable with perpetual slavery. Doesn't that rather undermine him as a champion of freedom?

M: That is exactly the problem that will face us in the sequel to *1789* on the next phase of the Revolution, especially in the case of Robespierre. You cannot deal with Robespierre as you can deal with Mirabeau, by criticising only one aspect, or by saying the man was extraordinary up to that point but then became corrupted. Robespierre was never corrupted, and in a way he was the heart of the Revolution. When he died the Revolution stopped for almost a hundred years. But still he did a few things we wish he hadn't. How are we going to show that, to show the massacres of that period, both as a horrible fact and as something that can be explained? And without losing the simplicity we need to address the working class – an audience we rarely have?

I'm just a little frightened. Because we are the only theatre of this kind, we are in danger. It is difficult being so terribly isolated; I wish some other groups would start making their way through to a mass audience. Our worst periods are like now, when we have success but no real work. Periods of adversity are best for us.

From an interview with Ariane Mnouchkine by Irving Wardle,
Performance 1: 2, April 1972.

1.4 WHAT IS THE DIFFERENCE? COLLECTIVE CREATION AND *1789*
From interviews with members of the Théâtre du Soleil
by Emile Copfermann

This text comes from an interview with a range of company members recorded in October 1970, shortly before the première of 1789 *in Milan. They describe working in a collective, its formal structure, and the company's differences from experiences of other theatre contexts, particularly in terms of the ethos of multi-functionality and multi-vocality.*

EMILE COPFERMANN: Ariane Mnouchkine has talked to me of a theatre, a company that are 'different'. Where do these 'differences' lie?

LOUIS SAMIER (actor): I joined the Théâtre du Soleil a very short time ago. I felt that difference from the very beginning in terms of the way daily work is conceived. In other theatres, I was hired, paid for rehearsals and performances, but I remained a visitor, an outsider, an employee. I was accepted by the others here right away. They integrated me into the group they were forming, I felt a member of a company. *1789* has also prompted me to learn: I have read a great deal, thought about things. I discovered [the historians] Matthiez, Lefebvre, etc. The work with others is also different; I improvise, and am criticised by them. In other places you remain on your own.

Not only do I feel like an actor here, but I find myself in tune with what I'm making; and what I'm making is myself, in the same way as my thirty-five comrades, in performance and outside of it. I can't imagine a professional future anywhere else, because I can no longer imagine working in 'the profession' as it's usually understood. Here an actor is required to be a creator *in the production*. What comes through in the performance stems from what's outside the performance and is intimately connected to the group's life and work. The fact that I've only recently joined the company hasn't complicated my relationships with the 'old' members. For example, I can't distinguish between those who are members of the cooperative and those who aren't.

GUY-CLAUDE FRANÇOIS (technical director): The difference can be seen in the fact that here there isn't really any specialisation. [. . .] For us, on the technical team, everyone, or almost everyone, has worked in the carpentry workshop. Lighting and acoustics require more knowledge, but present no more difficulties. Perhaps a further difference is that our aim is to attain a quality which doesn't correspond to the norms in theatre today. [. . .]

JEAN-CLAUDE PENCHENAT (actor, administrator):[25] We have almost no contact with the theatre milieu outside. When we're working on a production, we work all day every day. [. . .] All members of the company receive the same monthly salary, twelve months a year: 1200 francs at the moment – or partial payment on account when money's too tight! The company is constituted as a workers' cooperative, directed by an elected committee. Members of the cooperative have more duties than rights. Out of thirty-five present members of the company, twenty-two are cooperative members. One can become a member upon request, after a six-month probationary period.

ARIANE MNOUCHKINE: Like any group, obviously we experience conflicts and difficulties. Certain members of the company reproached me for monopolising information, only making it available to a few privileged colleagues around me. One of us was chosen specifically to communicate information. [. . .]

Leftist theatres don't care what's going on in their actors' heads. Whether they're performing Brecht or something else, it's exactly the same. I find it appalling that after years of activity they continue to engage actors who are so-called 'names', but who don't participate at all in the collective enterprise. We haven't yet created a society of equals, but that's what we're aiming for. Inequalities subsist in the preparation of a production, in the aptitudes of each person, inequalities that are conflictual and lead at times to crises. However, in the work itself, an extremely profound harmony arises between us, which is not limited to the production.

GEORGES BONNAUD (actor, administrator): That's what generally strikes the public. We are often told: 'when we see the performance we sense that you are a group.' We're neither a contemplative community nor a group of 'different' people; our only communal life is in the work itself. We share the same aims, we pursue the same interests, and we've chosen the same kind of life, but this in no way cuts into the private lives of each of us.

From Emile Copfermann, 'Où est la différence? Premier entretien avec les membres de la troupe', in *Travail Théâtral – Différent: Le Théâtre du Soleil*, Lausanne: La Cité, 1976.

1.5 DEVISING THROUGH IMPROVISATION: THE STORMING OF THE BASTILLE

The Théâtre du Soleil

The following extract describes the elaboration through improvisation of one of the most celebrated sequences in 1789: the multi-vocal narration of the fall of the Bastille, a central symbol of the inequities of the absolutist ancien régime.

WEDNESDAY 29 JULY

First improvisations on the storming of the Bastille. It is presented in the form of a retrospective vision: acrobat-actors tell of how they took the Bastille, they look amongst themselves for the one who could be the most terrifying, and thus play Delaunay, the prison governor. Perched on a chair, he derides them with a big fairground laugh when they besiege him; the big laugh comes to an end: *Look!* . . . he says. On the stage opposite, the 'real' Delaunay – perhaps this is a competing troupe of acrobats performing the storming of the Bastille in their own way? – is surrounded, thrown to the ground and led away. The first group watches the scene, which assumes a particular dramatic colouring in its juxtaposition with the playfulness of the first sequence. Here two different modes of representation coexist within the same improvisation (the fairground laughter of the first Delaunay and the more realistic encirclement of the second) and it is this which holds our interest. The improvisation is then reworked by linking it with others: a scene from Marivaux is played on one of the stages. How will these actors from a 'conventional' theatre, and at the same time the nobles they represent, react to the storming of the Bastille? They are interrupted by messengers running in from all directions: *Necker's been dismissed, the Stock Exchange has closed, Paris is surrounded by 20,000 men!*

Then there follows an improvisation that has already been elaborated, the 'little nails' scene: having discovered some guns, a humble clock-maker goes in search of ammunition at a grocer's. She suggests chick peas to him, then little nails. He rejoins his companions who relate to the audience 'their' storming of the Bastille. This scene is then followed by the initial improvisation with the two Delaunays.

This linkage does not seem satisfactory, and the Bastille is abandoned for a while so as to be able to talk about it a little later on and verify the effectiveness or non-effectiveness of these improvisations.[26]

FRIDAY 14 AUGUST

In the meantime, some very strong improvisations have been found, such as that of the Night of August Fourth! Everyone thinks the improvisations on the storming of the Bastille need to be reassessed.

The actors read the text of an account made by a clock-maker of how he spent 14 July 1789;[27] the story is simple, precise and alive. They try to improvise, on the one hand drawing on previous improvisations, and on the other using this account: a storyteller begins to describe his day, then he is joined by others.

Halt: general dissatisfaction.

– It seems this scene should be rid of everything that is trivial and 'day-to-day'; this gathering of old friends is reminiscent of a derisory, 'war veteran' style.

– This account should be treated as a truly epic tale.

– Perhaps this story should be intercut with a number of more familiar scenes, like the 'little nails', so that we know and recognise those who are going to perform the storming of the Bastille for us: the 14th of July was the first day of the Revolution that involved the masses; those who recount it must be flesh and blood characters. What's more, that would enable us to give the story a new fairground performance dimension, since it would be intercut with played scenes.

There then follow some improvisations about the people's activities during this particular day: a disabled soldier refusing to give an officer weapons, a wig-maker handing over his work instruments, etc. But the day comes to an end, the actors go off dissatisfied, the 'storming of the Bastille' has not been found.

MONDAY 17 AUGUST

The company gathers to discuss and try to define the difficulties:

– In popular imagination, the Bastille is not even a myth any more, it's almost a fossil. The difficulty stems from the danger of only creating pleonasms with popular imagination, within which the storming of the Bastille is a 'fixed monument'.

– All that has been done up until now has been too realistic. The only elements that seem right are on the one hand, the laugh of the fairground Delaunay, and on the other, the encirclement of the 'real' Delaunay.

– We must watch out for embellishments, for anecdotes. The tone of the performance is being forgotten, we're avoiding what is essential.

– What's essential is for this event to arrive in a flash; so we have to find a very simple signifier for it, without making concessions with stage 'tricks'.

New groups are formed, and work starts again from scratch.

An initial improvisation, in the form of a fable, uses legendary characters. For centuries, Samson, Spartacus and a Knight from the Middle Ages have been trying to cross a deep chasm, 'Tyranny', but all of them have lost their lives there; then along comes the patriot, who wins victory. The idea seems very nice, but the problem is badly put: from the outset the chasm should be the Bastille. Second attempt in a totally different direction: the actors draw on an improvisation about the women's return from Versailles with the King during the *journées d'octobre* [in early October 1789 when the people brought the royal family back to Paris] (a scene which remains in the final production). All the actors enter the central pit area, to the accompaniment of Beethoven's Seventh Symphony.

The formalism of dance gives a new dimension to the vision of the event; in addition, one should feel the combativeness of the crowd and the rupture in the music and dance for the encirclement of the 'real' Delaunay. But a counter-effect of this is that the appearance of the performer playing the laughing Delaunay is no longer justified, the playfulness is no longer felt as such.

Start again, then stop: this view ends up giving the image of an illusory victory, of a rather jingoistic and nationalistic celebration, whereas the company does not feel the event to be like that at all.

WEDNESDAY 2 SEPTEMBER

New attempts at improvisations in small groups. The first deals with the creation of a national guard: two members of the bourgeoisie go to Lafayette to start military training. It's an interesting idea, and the rapid rhythm of the improvisation is in keeping with fairground theatre.

Second improvisation, on the visits of a banker and his faithful clerk to a demolition contractor at the Bastille,[28] and to Santerre, 'defender' of the people.[29] This improvisation arouses general interest: it shows the dispassionate dismantling of a political mechanism. Forgetting for a moment that the Bastille is a symbol for us, it provides a few illuminating flashes regarding some of the elements that preceded and provoke the 14th of July, with notarial precision and a total absence of lyricism.

Afternoon: this improvisation is taken up again, but there is no longer the dryness and clarity of the first sketch. Almost everyone is discouraged!

So, as an exercise, Ariane suggests that the actors, in small groups of three or four, tell the story of the storming of the Bastille as they would to children of five or six, keeping to a strict narration of events, and forgetting any political interpretation for the time being.

The same story is retold, but for adults, keeping the same economy of means: a very simple story, with concern for making it intelligible without grand declarations. After this attempt, discussion:

– What is nice is that gradually, imperceptibly, the tension mounted, we sensed the riot. What's more, fairground theatre is part of an oral tradition, this is its specificity.

Legibility is privileged: we feel the anger of the people.

– But has the *storming of the Bastille* itself been found? What is its true meaning? Why did this event happen?

– If one managed to give a genuinely mythical vision of the storming of the

Bastille, then one would have a critical vision: traditional visions contain their own denunciation within themselves, through *distancing*.

– This is the first time that the people of Paris overcame their fear, took the initiative and felt their victory.

Exercise: the riot is interrupted by a messenger who announces that the Bastille has been taken. An actor suggests continuing with short fairground scenes to signify the people's explosion of joy.

Evening: This sequence is taken up again: account by the fairground performers which starts very softly and gradually builds up; interruption with the announcement of the people's victory, and explosion into a street fair celebration. This image rekindles enthusiasm: through the very means of street fair productions, and in a way that's both entirely logical and devoid of realism, we return to the chosen scenic space: the fairground.

FRIDAY 4 SEPTEMBER

Work on the political analysis of what provoked the 14th of July. Earlier improvisations on this theme are taken up again, while structuring and linking them in a very linear fashion to signify an itinerary (a banker, a bourgeois family, two shopkeepers and a soldier) which ends with the leader, Monsieur du Faubourg. Everything culminates with the decision to 'unleash the people'. The itinerary is then linked with the fairground performers' story and the street fair, into which several improvisations are inserted: the one about the Comte d'Artois, which existed already, was adapted to the fairground atmosphere; those of the King being received by Bailly and Lafayette were found later on.

Every stage in this lengthy and sometimes difficult progression was necessary to enable the constitutive elements of this event to emerge, and to discover a meaningful theatrical situation:

– the portrayal of the functioning of a political mechanism;

– the account by the people of their own victory;

– and the fairground celebration, which places all of these elements back into the context of theatrical performance and efficacy which constitute the life of the production.

From 'Les improvisations: Un exemple du travail: la prise de la Bastille', in Le Théâtre du Soleil, *1789* 'texte-programme', Paris, 1971.

1.6 DEVISING A NEW SCENOGRAPHY FOR EACH PRODUCTION

Guy-Claude François

Like Peter Brook, I work on the concept of the empty space. [. . .] I like purity,
but I hate austerity. I think an actor needs a magnificent empty space.

Ariane Mnouchkine[30]

*In the following extract, the Théâtre du Soleil's technical director describes the elaboration of the
scenographic configuration for 1789 – an empty space with multiple stages and mobile audience
perspectives – and the collective's 'artisanal' approach to the acquisition of skills.*

Every production possesses its own characteristics, and it's precisely for that
reason that we have no fixed criteria in terms of scenography. Only three years
ago, we had certain ideas, we wanted a multi-purpose hall. Now our thinking is
rather that each production requires a different form of scenography, even
(almost) a form of architecture.[31] [. . .]

On the scenographic level, *1789* is a production we intended to be performed
in a gymnasium – an option chosen by us not for aesthetic reasons, but because we
were never able to fit it into existing theatres. For reasons that were both practical
and technical, we said to ourselves that a gymnasium is a sufficiently big and free
space. Eventually, by studying documentation on the architecture of sports
centres, on everything to do with sports and recreational areas, we realised that
certain norms, certain dimensions of the basketball court, which is built as soon as
one builds a gymnasium – that is, the smallest facility in the smallest French town
– corresponded to what we were looking for. [. . .]

Thinking back on the production, Ariane inevitably had a scenographic view, a
view of the relations between actors and spectators, and naturally she expressed
her ideas. Roberto Moscoso [who designed the décor for the production]
proposed a model, although we didn't really make a model – and fortunately. If
I remember correctly, Ariane talked of a kind of 'itinerary'. Out of that came the
idea for the platform stages and interconnecting runways, of a number of spaces
responding to, commenting upon and opposing each other.

Starting in the first few days of the rehearsal period, we constructed makeshift
'Italian-style' demountable stages; in other words, we used planks and nails to
make runways for provisional configurations which could be transformed very
quickly, always using a very fast method of joinery. It's called 'Italian-style' because

Italian stage technicians are in the habit of making stripped demountables, without wooden jointing.

After about a week, the actors already had a configuration quite like this one, but we experimented with a number of different possibilities. It soon became evident that the layout worked best like this, the actors performed around the spectators, enveloping them; some of the spectators had the possibility of watching the whole space from above, from the side, etc. And that was in fact our 'model'. When I say I don't really like models, it's because I prefer this type of model. In the end it's not much more expensive. When I describe this system to other theatre people, technicians or directors, they tell me: 'That's madness, it costs a fortune'. In actual fact, it's not at all expensive because it's made out of recuperable wood. It's an investment sanctioned by the performance style.

The system of constructing the demountables was discovered not in documents (we didn't manage to find any), but in carpentry books. We saw how carpenters assembled their frames, and that gave us the idea of pegging everything instead of nailing; that's how things were made at the time. The lads worked during the night, with wood squared with an adze rather than in the current way; and we used tools that were employed at that time.

The characteristics of each space were then found, bit by bit. [. . .] I worked on fitting the scenic configuration into different spaces – hence the idea of the gym, the basketball court. We travelled to Milan to see the performance space there.[32] We realised – and this was a real discovery for us – that a basketball court is well conceived architecturally: basketball is a sport that needs to be seen from sufficiently close up, because individual players' actions are interesting to follow, but it also needs a certain distance, to enable the spectator to see the strategy of the game. In this way we discovered that the dimensions of handball or football pitches are large because these sports are particularly interesting on a tactical and strategic level. The 'scenography' of sports fields was also interesting and it turned out to be a good thing!

Ultimately, this prompted us to ask further questions: the details of what's performed will not be seen in one space, and the opposite will be true in another. We can no longer try to establish the relations existing in a closed theatre, where everything is performed frontally.

In *1789*, there are two areas reserved for the spectators: the tiered seating on the outside, and a space inside, between the stages and runways. People will have the choice of one or the other of these spaces, they will walk around. If I am inside, I can have much closer, tighter relations with the production. If I am on the outside, I see its development more. The spectator will have the choice between these two relationships, each one more interesting, in my opinion, than what's possible in a fixed and frontal theatre – forget the proscenium stage.

There is no mystery between technical and performance aspects because there is a wonderful understanding between us. Human relations eliminate the mystery and sectarianism much more than technology. Actors took part in the construction, even in the assembly, particularly for *Les Clowns*. One actress was involved in the construction from beginning to end because she wasn't cast in the show. Later, two other actors were added to the crew, one of whom is part of the technical team for assembly. I hope this kind of thing recurs often, and I think we'll manage it, even though it is difficult. For example, when we began rehearsals on 20 July, all the actors were cast. If this had not been the case, actors would have done the work very well, rather than taking on non-members of the company – I do not want to say *people from outside* because in the end the person I took is henceforth a part of the team and has become extraordinarily well integrated. [. . .]

The difference between us and other theatres is that they have a notion of consumption that presupposes specialist knowledge, a certificate, and in some sense you sell your knowledge. With us, it's not the same, a collective evolution occurs, and it takes a particular direction. Elsewhere, you are obliged to produce. Here, you have the impression you are acquiring something, or at least the impression that you are alive. For me, the notion of creation is a bit outdated. At the Théâtre du Soleil, we 'create' more than elsewhere, in my opinion, even if we only make one 'creation' a year, and elsewhere they make two or three.

From 'Guy-Claude François: A chaque spectacle sa scénographie' and 'Roberto Moscoso: Un théâtre pour chaque spectacle', in *Travail Théâtral – Différent: Le Théâtre du Soleil*, Lausanne: La Cité, 1976.

NOTES

1 Ariane Mnouchkine, '*L'Age d'Or:* the long journey from 1793 to 1975', in *Theatre Quarterly* 5: 18, 1975, p. 12.
2 R. Stamm, 'On the carnivalesque', *Wedge* 1, 1982; quoted in Peter Stallybrass and Allon White, *The Politics and Poetics of Transgression,* London: Methuen, 1986, pp. 18–9.
3 Cf. Pierre Bourdieu: 'Nothing more radically distinguishes popular spectacles – the football match, Punch and Judy, the circus, wrestling, even in some cases the cinema – from bourgeois spectacles, than the form of the participation of the public'; *La Distinction,* Paris: Editions de Minuit, 1979, p. 569.
4 The Soleil's theatrical aesthetic at this time owed much to melodrama, and to what Peter Brooks has called 'the "bodiliness" of revolutionary language and representation' (*Body Work,* Cambridge, Mass.: Harvard University Press, 1993, p. 55). Brooks locates an origin of an 'aesthetics of embodiment' in the Revolution, and analyses the performative quality of revolutionary oratory, iconography and events. He describes the revolutionary body as a 'melodramatic body seized by meaning'; contemporary melodramas, he suggests, simply enacted in 'a heightened excessive, Manichaean, hyperbolic form the national drama being played out in the Convention, in the sections, in the tribunals and on the scaffold' (64–6). See also Peter Brooks' foundational text, *The Melodramatic Imagination,* New Haven: Yale University Press, 1976.
5 As Danièle de Ruyter-Tognotti has suggested, the use of authentic documents in *1789* often exploits the interrogative and contradictory slippages between written History (e.g. records of parliamentary rhetoric) and enacted/spoken histories in performance, in a way that is contestatory and critical. See 'Théâtre et histoire: position critique dans *1789* du Théâtre du Soleil', in *Néophilologus* 75: 3, July 1991, pp. 373–6.
6 This figure represents the infamous Cagliostro, a charlatan 'count' and Rasputin-like occultist who at one time appears to have had enormous influence over the Queen. For further details, see John Hearsey, *Marie Antoinette,* London: Constable, 1972, pp. 82–93. The ill-fated Princesse de Lamballe and the Comtesse de Polignac, intimates of Marie Antoinette who drained her financially, were both instrumental in court intrigue and factional cliques in Versailles.
7 Le Comte d'Artois was Louis XVI's youngest brother, later Charles X; he 'emigrated' on 16 July 1789, and became an aggressive counter-revolutionary advocating a war of restoration for an absolutist monarchy.
8 Such polemical literalisation of the inequities of the *ancien régime* was very common in contemporary political cartoons. See, for example, Lynne Hockman (ed.), *French Caricature and the French Revolution,* Los Angeles: Grunwald Center for the Graphic Arts, 1988, pp. 161–2. See also pp. 204–5, re. an anonymous cartoon called 'The Great French Puppeteers', in which *émigrés* (including d'Artois) are represented as clowns and marionettes in a circus sideshow farce. Clearly these critical, performative and comic representations, as well as some of Honoré Daumier's later drawings, proved to be a rich iconic and improvisatory source for the members of the company.
9 Such representations, employing women as allegorical figures, were very common at the time. For a fascinating critical analysis, see Madelyn Gutwirth, *The Twilight of the Goddesses: Women and Representation in the French Revolutionary Era,* New Jersey: Rutgers University

Press, 1992. The Soleil's rather idealised representation of Marat – the 'friend of the people', the Cassandra of the Revolution – meant that Marat was the only recurrent figure in the production to be performed by a single actor throughout.

10 This sequence represents the so-called 'Grande Peur' of late July and early August 1789.

11 The Le Chapelier law also outlawed workers' associations. Like the Allarde law which abolished guilds, it was part of a series of reforms implicitly designed to promote bourgeois interests. See T.C.W. Blanning, *The French Revolution: Aristocrats versus Bourgeois?*, Basingstoke: Macmillan, 1987, p. 43 ff.

12 During the devising period, the group had studied early films, including Jean Renoir's *La Marseillaise*, D.W. Griffiths' *Orphans of the Storm* and Abel Gance's epic *Napoléon*. Although silent film language and rhythmic textures were perhaps most directly cited in this scene (as were the rhetorical attitudes of melodrama and grand opera), traces of these films recurred throughout the production. This scene also seemed to contain critical allusions to Géricault's painting *The Raft of the Medusa* (1819). (For a discussion of silent film's recuperation from revolutionary melodrama of a semiotics of the body, see Peter Brooks, 'Melodrama, body, revolution', in Jacky Bratton, Jim Cook and Christine Gledhill (eds), *Melodrama: Stage, Picture, Screen*, London: British Film Institute, 1994, pp. 11–24.)

13 This scene, with its sudden jump to a Daumier-esque 19th century, marks the second dislocation of an otherwise linear structure in *1789*. This 'play-within-the-play' epilogue mirrors the first dislocation, the melodramatic prologue to the production representing the flight to Varennes of the King and Queen. In both cases, representation is critical and gestic, received narratives of History are destabilised.

14 'Babouvism' is often located as the precursor of both Communism and Marxism. For an interesting critical overview of Babeuf, which compares and contrasts him with Marat, see Eric Walter's essay 'Babeuf's candour: the rhetorical invention of a prophet' in John Renwick (ed.), *Language and Rhetoric of the Revolution*, Edinburgh: Edinburgh University Press, 1990, pp. 75–99.

15 The 'second revolution' was that of August–September 1792: the overthrowing of the monarchy, the establishment of the Republic and of the revolutionary Commune of Paris, and so on. (For full production details of the Théâtre du Soleil's *1793*, please refer to the Chronology in the appendices.) The 'third revolution' comprised the *sans-culottes* coup of September 1793, the institution of the Jacobin Republic and adoption of the revolutionary calendar in October (Year II), the commencement of the Terror, and so on.

16 Thermidor (July–August 1794) was the time of the so-called 'Great Terror', the purging of 'enemies of the Republic'. It climaxed on 27 July ('9 Thermidor Year II' in the Revolutionary calendar), when Robespierre, Saint-Just, Couthon and eighty-seven other members of the revolutionary Commune were summarily arrested and guillotined without trial in the largest mass execution of the Revolution.

17 Mnouchkine's formulation of the Revolution in these loosely Marxist terms is in the prevailing ('orthodox') historiographical tradition in France, perhaps best represented in the works of the French revolutionary historians since Jean Jaurès, including Albert Mathiez, Georges Lefebvre, Jean Massin, Albert Soboul and Jacques Godechot. Inevitably this reading has been vigorously contested by conservative revisionists, such as the English historian Alfred Cobban.

18 This was the intended subtitle at the time of the interview. The subtitle eventually chosen was a quotation from the revolutionary orator Antoine Saint-Just.

19 Evidently *création collective* in *1789* represented a 'new' way of constructing a history play, entirely by means of improvisations based on the pooling of historiographic and political research. In the production that emerged from this process, not only the salient historical facts, but also the very problematic of establishing 'historical fact', became central concerns. As will be clear from Victoria Nes Kirby's account above, each of the

scenes depicted an event that was well-known to its audiences from their study of the French Revolution in school, but each of them was presented from different points of view, frequently in contradiction with one another. In this way, *création collective* allowed the company to generate a densely layered, decentred and *critical* re-presentation of history, which demonstrated that there are a great many ways of articulating history, and that our constructions of events cannot avoid being marked by our own socio-political perspectives and assumptions.

20 According to Denis and Marie-Louise Bablet, during the *1789* rehearsals, more than a thousand improvisations were recorded on tape. See *Le Théâtre du Soleil, ou la quête de la bonheur (Diapolivre 1)*, Ivry, Paris: CNRS, 1979, p. 46.

21 For a detailed discussion of the Soleil's troubled relations with funding bodies in the early 1970s, see Renée Saurel, 'Deniers publics ou cassette royale?', *Les Temps Modernes* no. 321, April 1973, pp. 1907–18. In May 1973, the Soleil and other groups staged a large demonstration and procession from the Place de la Nation, in response to remarks by the then Minister of Culture, Maurice Druon, to the effect that, 'People who come to the door of the Ministry with a beggar's bowl in one hand and a Molotov cocktail in the other will have to choose'; quoted in Lenora Champagne, *French Theatre Experiment since 1968*, Ann Arbor: UMI Research Press, 1984, p. 30.

22 Cf.: 'Music is a vehicle of understanding, and rhythm facilitates dialogue and a relationship with an audience enormously'; Ariane Mnouchkine and Jean-Claude Penchenat in 'L'aventure du Théâtre du Soleil', *Preuves* 7: 3, 1971, p. 124.

23 Socialist historian Albert Mathiez published three very small but influential volumes on the subject, *La Révolution Français* (1922). Georges Lefebvre's work is perhaps best summarised in his two-volume *The French Revolution* (1962, 1964). Alexis de Tocqueville's *L'ancien régime et la Révolution* was first published in 1856. Records of the National Assembly debates are held in the Bibliothèque Nationale in Paris. The company also read Patrick Kessel's *La nuit du 4 août*. For the *1789* project, the company included a historical adviser, Elisabeth Brisson, a teacher at the Lycée Michelet and former pupil of Jean Massin; she conducted regular evening classes with the group.

24 Cf: 'We have used theatre references in the same way as recollections from school, pictures and images etched into our memories forever, although we have shifted their meaning through the ways in which they are composed'; Mnouchkine in *Preuves*, op. cit., p. 124. *Orlando Furioso* was first performed in Milan in the summer of 1969; see Franco Quadri's account in *The Drama Review* 14: 3, 1970, pp. 116–24. Peter Schumann's Bread and Puppet Theatre had performed their epic Vietnam passion play *The Cry of the People for Meat* in France in 1969; the production involved extensive use of masks and giant puppets, including the celebrated 'Grey Lady'. See Stefan Brecht's accounts in *The Drama Review*, op. cit., pp. 44–90.

25 In 1976, the year of his departure from the Théâtre du Soleil, Jean-Claude Penchenat established his own company, le Théâtre du Campagnol. There he has remained close to the spirit of *la création collective*, continuing some of the Soleil's experimental work on the recovery of French popular performance styles, most notably in its productions of *David Copperfield* (1977) and *Le Bal* (1981); the latter was subsequently filmed by Ettore Scola. For further details, see Jean-Claude Penchenat and Evelyne Loew, 'Le Théâtre du Campagnol', *Theatre Papers: Fifth Series*, no. 8, Dartington: Dartington College of Arts, 1985.

26 Mnouchkine's devising process is indebted to Jacques Lecoq's teaching practice of the *autocours*, in which students are asked to prepare scenes to be presented to others in class. The *autocours* reflect a developmental pedagogy of auto-didacticism, according to which what is learnt by performers emerges most forcibly from their experiences of performing in front of others.

27 Cf. 'Le journal de J.B. Humbert, horloger, qui le premier a monté sur les tours de la Bastille', in Albert Soboul, *1789: l'an un de la liberté*, Paris: Editions Sociales, pp. 147–52.

28 After the fall of the Bastille, a certain 'citizen Palloy' made a vast fortune out of

demolishing the prison and selling the stones and other fragments as souvenirs. This kind of commodification of the revolution by the bourgeoisie seems to be the target of the company's critique here. See Simon Schama, *Citizens: a Chronicle of the French Revolution*, New York: Random House, 1989, p. 406 ff.

29 Antoine Joseph Santerre (1752–1809), a wealthy brewer and commander of the National Guard. He took part in the storming of the Bastille.

30 Quoted in Anne Tremblay, 'A French director gives Shakespeare a new look', *New York Times*, 10 June 1984.

31 The practice of changing the performance environment for each new production has become a permanent feature of the Théâtre du Soleil's productions. In *Méphisto* (1979), for example, the coexistence of multiple, contradictory spaces within the Cartoucherie unsettled the possibility of fixed spectatorial perspectives. A double-ended performance space was devised. At one end of the space was the stage of the State Theatre of Hamburg; at the other, the cabaret stage of 'The Peppermill'. Spectators sat on fixed benches running laterally across the space; the back-rests of these benches could be rotated, allowing audience members to switch viewing directions – from the official State culture of Nazism to its dissident, subversive 'other'. The sides of the hall were also activated: on one wall, a grand heroic fresco evoked Prussian military might; on the other, wire mesh screened off a vast empty space – a permanent reminder of the death camps into which the victims of Nazism disappeared. For *Sihanouk* (1985), the space resembled a Cambodian temple; for *L'Indiade* (1987), the actors animated a bare white-walled space constructed around a raised central area of reflective marble and terracotta-brick; for *Les Atrides* (1990–2) audiences accessed the performance space via an 'archaeological excavation', while the playing space itself carried suggestions of a weathered bullring. Since the Shakespeare cycle in the early 1980s, however, the arrangement of seating has remained essentially unaltered. The large open stage has been set in opposition to a bank of tiered benches and, once installed, audiences have remained static throughout. The experiments in audience mobility that made for some of the dynamic excitement of the productions in the 1970s have been largely abandoned, as Mnouchkine's focus has shifted towards the 'bodily writing' of texts.

32 The Palazzo Lido, a sports centre with seating for 2,000 spectators; the venue was proposed by Paolo Grassi, co-founder (with Giorgio Strehler) and producer of the Piccolo Teatro di Milano, which had already played host to the Soleil's productions of *La Cuisine* and *Les Clowns*.

CHAPTER 2
THE COMEDY OF OUR TIME
L'Age d'Or: première ébauche
(The Golden Age: first draft)
(1975)

There is no question of making historical reconstructions
[. . .] We shall study the *commedia dell'arte* and the
fairground theatre. We shall learn the history and
development of improvisation, the manners, the methods and
the peculiarities of the actors who practised it. But our goal is
to create a new improvised comedy using contemporary
types and subjects.
Jacques Copeau[1]

Commedia has nothing to do with those little Italian troupes
who export precious entertainments. It's about misery, a
world where life's a luxury.
Jacques Lecoq[2]

2.1 *L'AGE D'OR* IN PERFORMANCE

Christopher D. Kirkland

Writing in The Drama Review, *Christopher Kirkland offers a description of the spatial configuration at the Cartoucherie, a detailed account of the production and its performance styles, as well as a narrative synopsis of this 'comedy of our time'.*[3]

With *L'Age d'Or*, the Théâtre du Soleil addresses itself more directly than previously to the issues of contemporary social reality – to investigating the everyday struggles, the events hardly familiar before they come to seem banal, which fill newspapers and newscasts, that unite and divide all manner of political groups, and which compel the erratic push and pull of government in France. Topics for the play's episodes originate in a published chronology of events,[4] dating from the 1973 cholera epidemic in Naples to the December 1974 deaths of forty-two coal miners in northern France. It includes specific instances of strikes, workers' solidarity, factory occupation, injury and fatality in industry and commerce, prison brutality, military indignity, individual rights, over-crowded low-income housing, price fixing, government repression, bribery, favouritism and racism. The actors approach socio-political events and issues with the techniques of improvisation and the character-types of the three theatrical styles in which they have been working intensively over the last eighteen months: *commedia dell'arte*, ancient Chinese theatre and circus.

Some episodes were developed from talks with workers in factories, mines, hospitals and schools [. . .] So for example the current production's final episode comes directly from discussions and improvisations with a committee of workers from the nearby Kodak factory, its setting now changed to a construction site. A group of high school students helped the troupe develop through improvisation an opium den scene from traditional Chinese theatre into an episode about family television and drugs. A group of young immigrants participated in the develop-ment of an episode relating to a recent rent-strike scandal, involving 240 workers housed in twenty-six rooms of a low-income apartment building.

For the current production, technical director Guy-Claude François conceived 'a *free space*, with no defined architecture, something modern but not modernist; a place in which people tell a story to others, a place which makes people want to tell stories and to listen, a sort of agora – *a meeting place*, where one likes to be because it's a pleasant environment. And the second core idea was to use the interior of the space as a whole, without the separations that existed in *1789* and *1793*'.[5] So he removed a wall that separated the two warehouses to open up a space of about 120 by 150 feet, bisected by a row of eight pillars which proved too expensive to remove. He then brought in earth and concrete by the truck-load to build up a cruciform ridge about 10 feet above the floor, which fell gracefully away in a 30° rake towards the corners. In this way the room was quartered into almost identical amphitheatres. Next he covered the entire contoured floor with rough, light-brown hessian matting. Seventy-two loudspeakers, which worked off a sixteen-track tape deck, were set into the walls. He lined the two peaked ceilings in bright copper, and placed thousands of small light bulbs at eight- to ten-inch intervals along every beam and rafter.

Before the performance begins, the resplendent, warmly hued space prompts youthful spirits to run up one of the hills and to run, roll or slide down the other side. Performers change into extravagantly padded costumes and chat in one of the flat corners. A dancer-gymnast limbers up while another actor plays bongo drum rhythms; another props his mirror up against one of the pillars to paint his lower face in white, and to line it heavily with a black pencil. Savvy spectators, aware of Mnouchkine's tendency to move her audiences around, try to outguess her by perching along the ridge, from where they can sit to see all of one amphitheatre and stand to see into the others. In the adjoining warehouse, about 60 by 150 feet, narrow balconies and symmetrical staircases built of dark-stained wood line two of the walls. Colourful banners hang from the rafters. Costumed actors, most with *commedia* half-masks pushed up onto their foreheads, sell fruit, sandwiches, wine and coffee from a stand.

In grand design and in small detail, the performance as a whole seeks to keep its audience mentally and physically alert. Even the ambiguity of the title compels speculation. Is the 'Golden Age' past, present or future? Does it offer the point of view of an ironic pessimist or of a sincere optimist? Is 1975 an age of ultimate submission to the lure of gold, or the dawn of the long-awaited awakening to the golden rule? Might 'first draft' apply to each of these senses of the title as well as to an 'unfinished' production?[6] Similarly, the eight scenes of the production, which vary in length from twenty to thirty-five minutes, cause the audience to shift positions constantly. Even during the first scene in 1720 Naples, performed in the smaller space, the action draws the standing audience from one playing area to another. Some 450 people climb and slide between valley spaces so similar that one begins to look hard for the differences. What's changed? The audience. Spectators re-settle in an almost identical theatre space, with new neighbours and a changed perspective [. . .]

• • •

Circus music gives way to Renaissance fanfare, and it is the year 1720; the Prince of Naples glowers over his noisy, standing audience from one of the wooden balconies. Actors move people from their chosen spots in the larger room to the smaller room, where Arlequin[7] appears in a yellow spotlight on a high stage. In animate mime, he begs the audience not to smoke so that they can see what they have paid to see, and not to carry bottles into the other room 'because it's we who have to sweep and sweep, and we don't like that'. The Prince descends to ask Arlequin about life in the city; sickened by Arlequin's lively account of shopping among the corpses, the Prince sends Arlequin to summon Mayor Antoine Raspi and his businessman friend Pantalon, the two responsible for allowing infectious ships into the harbour of the plague-ridden city. The Prince orders them to produce a culprit in three days, and just before the stage manager yells them off stage, they pass on this task to Arlequin. Anachronistically, he happens upon an amiable, 20th-century Algerian immigrant labourer named Abdallah, who is sailing towards Marseilles on the *Mea Culpa*. Arlequin, Raspi and Pantalon will conspire to blame the plague on Abdallah, ignoring the 250-year discrepancy of his presence. So the first scene sets the *commedia dell'arte* style of the performance, and introduces the play's major theme: the struggle of those workers at the very bottom of hierarchies of strength, profit and power.

The performers funnel the spectators through double doors into the nearest amphitheatre. Two actors, carrying 250 watt portable follow-spots, settle among the audience. This valley becomes the space of the sub-proletariat, the setting for the story of Abdallah's arrival, life and death in France, a story interrupted by trips to the other valleys for indirectly related scenes. Abdallah arrives in Marseilles where he admires a dock-worker called M. La Ficelle ('String', a character borrowed directly from Chinese theatre) as he moors the ship with a lively dance of busy arms. A group of actors on the ridge provides the rhythms with bongos, sticks, rattles, gourds and jangles. Then Max, the customs officer, impersonates a new-horizons, see-the-world American tourist, who has lost her baggage, before he turns to harassing Abdallah.

The narrator Salouha, who has an Algerian accent, suggests that the audience move to a different setting for another story. 'This is the best part of the show', she says, 'because the matting is very slippery. Help one another!' The audience struggles up to the ridge and skids down into another space where a Spanish maid (Bernarda) refuses to serve anything but ham sandwiches to an elegant dinner party, during which a real estate promoter and a dreamy young architect conspire to blame their collapsed building and its one hundred fatalities on striking, careless workers. Actors sit at the edge of the playing area to watch their colleagues work; they hiss and comment, jump up to enter the scene through a mimed door, and drop out of character among the other actors in the audience. They raise and lower their masks, just as tournament knights raise and lower their visors between engaging and disengaging.

The spectators then move back over to the first space, where imaginary droppings of mimed seagulls and a ring-studded, immigrant con-man contribute to the miseries of the naive Abdallah ('he who falls into every trap'), who only survives by ruse as his first and his last resort. He finally manages to get to sleep, balanced on a shoulder and an ear, in an over-crowded workers' dormitory. Next the spectators move diagonally over the centre to watch a housewife called Irene as she mimes her dinner-time routines. She never takes her eyes from an imaginary TV set, which puts her through the whole repertoire of soap-opera sentiments. Her husband, shoe salesman Aimé L'heureux, returns from work. Even as he scorns it,

Plate 2.1 *L'Age d'Or.* After Abdallah's death, the site workers pursue Pantalon and his accomplices 'up the scaffolding'. Photo: Martine Franck/Magnum

he gets caught up in the TV show. 'These two are really good together', he tells the audience, 'too bad you can't see them.' A daughter named Mimi ('la minette') arrives from high school to boast of the latest factory strike before she too gets caught up in the TV trance, which continues as a mimed spaghetti dinner is spilled onto the table and eaten while no one notices. The parents go off to bed; Mimi's boyfriends arrive with some pot, which induces a bar-room brawl performed in the style of a silent film in slow-motion.

Then the spectators move back over the ridge's centre to Abdallah's space, where a grotesquely bulbous woman called 'Lou la Grosse' ('Fat Lou'), with an orange beach-ball of an Afro, delivers a deliberately gratuitous English lesson and ends it with a feminist twist. Two semi-literate workers dodge searchlights to smear walls with graffiti ('Who wastes? Not us!'), and a husband avoids hearing his wife break the news of yet another pregnancy ('One more word and I'm leaving!' – 'I'm pregnant' – 'That's it, I'm leaving'). Then we move back to the fourth of the valleys where pushy actors – sometimes polite, sometimes brusque – herd the spectators into a new configuration, in which we look up from the flat corner towards the ridge with the rafter bulbs glowing against the copper ceiling. Here, by night on the virgin shore, mouthing the surge and hiss of midnight surf, two young lovers meet, play adolescent games and undress. The Mayor Dussouille, the real-estate promoter Pantalon and the hopelessly romantic architect Olivier arrive to chase the lovers away before they can 'pollute the beach with fornication'; they have other developments in mind for this sea-shore.

Finally, we go back to Abdallah, who is bribed by the promotion-seeking director of a construction project and his slavish site foreman Max into working on a high scaffold in a fierce wind. Abdallah dances his fall to the thundering chorus of Verdi's *Requiem*. Even during the mutely screamed laments of Abdallah's wife, Pantalon interrupts to declare the show over: 'You didn't come to hear a story like this.' But the others persist, and like messengers in Greek tragedy, they run on-stage to call Pantalon's attention to vivid examples of social injustice in every direction: 'If you want to see people swimming in their own excrement . . .' Pantalon leads his establishment accomplices up rungs in the wall (Plate 2.1) where they fasten themselves as the lights dim and the theatre fills with primitive noises.

Then neon lights, in exterior boxes built around the warehouse windows, gradually come up to shine through frosted glass, filling the room with a clear, bluish dawn. It is a second and wholly different triumph of atmospheric lighting in a production continuously dependent on original lighting effects and devices. The audience has already risen for sustained and rhythmic applause, but Salouha finally quietens them to eternalise Abdallah in the epilogue. She tells us that Abdallah always falls, that Pantalon always covers up the scandal, that the powerful haven't yet been driven to climb the wall: 'but perhaps you will begin . . .'

From '*The Golden Age: first draft*', first published in *The Drama Review* 19: 2, 1975.

2.2 'A SERENE AND VIOLENT CELEBRATION': A STATEMENT OF INTENT
The Théâtre du Soleil

The following is an extract from the company's programme notes for L'Age d'Or, *describing its genesis and goals, and the production's intervention as critical social praxis.*

The social reality of 1975 seems to us like a mosaic of worlds that are unequal and impermeable between themselves, and whose workings are concealed from us. To describe it, to try to make its motivating forces understood, we chose to recreate it with the means of theatre. We want to show the farce of our world, to create a serene and violent celebration by reinventing the principles of traditional popular theatres.

The actors have created characters using those of the *commedia dell'arte* for inspiration. Defined in human and social terms, Arlequin, Matamore, Pantalon, Polichinelle, Zerbine, Isabelle or Brighella only exist through and for theatre. We are not resuscitating past theatrical forms, whether from *commedia* or traditional Chinese theatre. We want to reinvent rules of acting [*des règles du jeu*] which uncover everyday reality, showing it to be not familiar and immutable, but surprising and transformable. We are trying to create a theatre of representation in which each gesture, each word, each intonation has its own importance, and is a sign that is immediately perceptible by the spectator.

It's not a question of dealing in abstractions, in 'opinions', but of imagining concrete and theatrical situations in which these characters assume functions. The roles of police officer, valet or foreman can be adopted by a single character, each of them having his or her way of perceiving reality and of showing it to us.

Our goal is a theatre that is directly engaged with social reality, not a simple report, but an encouragement to change the conditions in which we live. We want to recount our History to make it move forward – if this can be the role of theatre.

From 'Pourquoi *L'Age d'Or*?', in Le Théâtre du Soleil, *L'Age d'Or, Première Ebauche* (*'Texte–Programme'*), Paris: Stock, 1975.

2.3 TOWARDS A NEW FORM
From an interview with Ariane Mnouchkine by Denis Bablet

In an interview recorded in the autumn of 1974, about six months before the opening of L'Age d'Or, *Mnouchkine describes the company's difficulties and aspirations in this project. She discusses the group's generative processes (including improvisation), its re-vision of a* commedia dell'arte *character typology, the role of the director in collective creation, and the nature of contemporary popular theatre.*

DENIS BABLET: On 15 April 1972, during an interview with Françoise Kourilsky for *Travail Théâtral*, she said to you that: 'After *1793*, the transition to the contemporary period seems inevitable.' You replied: 'Yes, that's true. [. . .] I want to see if we can make something about contemporary history, to talk about today in the theatre. But I'm not sure that we're ready' [. . .] And indeed *L'Age d'Or* will talk about contemporary reality. How have you approached it?

ARIANE MNOUCHKINE: I think that the amount of time we have spent in order to dare taking on contemporary reality confirms what I said to Françoise. 'I don't think we're ready.' We have been working now for more than a year on this subject. Of course when I say 'a year', you have to take into account the fact that we were unemployed in 1973–4, we only worked every second day.[8] Nevertheless a long period of time has passed before approaching this possibility of speaking about today – and we are still not there, far from it. Françoise put it very well; after *1793* we had to get to the point where we would have the courage to talk about our times, but as it was we were not ready.

B: On what levels?

M: On every level.

B: On that of knowledge concerning today's reality?

M: Certainly. I don't think anyone is ready in that domain. But primarily on the level of improvisational technique, of theatrical forms which would enable us to treat contemporary reality as we wanted – without it becoming derisory, caricatural, psychological of course, parodic, or a sort of tract and placard, etc.

B: 'Contemporary reality' is extremely broad as a term. What exactly do you mean by it?

M: If you like, we could replace the terms 'contemporary reality' with the struggles of today – struggles or non-struggles for some. Then, and above all else, the contradictions within people. But the problem is different from what it was for *1789*, where it was possible to quickly make a decision and take a stand. As far as immediately contemporary events are concerned, we still don't think that we have at our disposal an analysis which would enable us to say: Here, this event has this signification . . . ' We know full well that it fluctuates; something that's self-evident one day is contradicted the next. For us, today's reality is much more complex, much more fleeting.

B: In *1793*, reality was seen through the eyes of the *sectionnaires*, that is, through the people. Is it also seen through the people's eyes today?

M: No, I think it is seen quite simply through the eyes of the actors. Perhaps this fact will not remain: it is seen in about fifty years' time by actors who will tell how it was today. In fifty years, what will one tell about today's reality? The people who will do the '89 of our times, what will they talk about? The scheming of politicians, showing Giscard d'Estaing[9] and the rest of them? Or the contradictions within the people, the divisions in the working class, their every-day struggles, etc.? We chose the second of these solutions.

B: So these future actors make use of the daily life of today?

M: Absolutely.

B: And not of a history reduced to its great events?

M: Certainly not. And if we wanted to, we would not be able. With *1789*, we could address the problem at a certain point, but today it cannot be imagined without running the risk of condemning ourselves to the most insubstantial, in my opinion insignificant kind of theatre. And anyway, what is a great event today? The Lip strike?[10] The Six Day War?[11] Or the women's movement? Things are not equal, but they all interpenetrate; all struggles are useful.

B: You mentioned the Lip strike. Do you still think you will have recourse to events of this kind in the production, or will you concentrate more on people's situations?

M: It's primarily to do with the situations. Naturally there will be some references, I think. If you see a workshop, those who knew the Lip strike will recognise part of their situation. But we won't show all of the Lip strike, in the first version at least.

B: So you already envisage several versions?

M: That is certain. It's a production which will change.

B: Will it evolve from day to day? Or will you present a first version, then a second six months later?

M: I think things will happen rather more quickly, and that both aspects will occur at once. I think this production will evolve just like any production, all the more so given that it will come before the audience really as an experimental product: so it will automatically change. On the other hand, bits will be replaced progressively –

B: – as a result of the improvisational work –

M: – which will be ongoing. In a way we already know we will not be able to include all the material that's available to us in the initial production. On the other hand, there are really no criteria to say that one situation is more important than another. In what way is the situation of a woman in a council flat expecting a child she doesn't want of greater importance than that of a despised boss in an office? Given that we already have an amount of material that is unstructured – this is the problem – not finished, entirely raw, but enormous, we already know that we will have material for two or three productions.

B: In terms of construction, for both *1789* and *1793*, history at least provided a base –

M: – a linear construction. That's one of the problems. For now we're confronting the difficulties of the acting: never lapsing into realism, never being psychological, working with masks is extremely difficult. There is also political analysis: we must not show a false situation, because, even if the relationships between the characters seem right, the situation can be falsified by a wrong fact attributed to a character. [. . .]

B: When you talk of political analysis, do you say to yourself, 'I will do a Marxist analysis of this situation'?

M: Let me tell you: I do not say to myself – we didn't say to ourselves with *1789* and *1793*, 'Let's do a Marxist analysis.' It's true that we were more inclined to do so. It is necessary to know on which side you position yourself. If for *1793*, you choose to take the side of the *sectionnaires*, if you defend them to the end, at a certain point you are forced into an analysis which is that one and not another. It is the same thing when working on today's world.

We have chosen to talk about people rather than great events. And in order to do so, we have tried to get groups of workers from particular factories, groups of nurses or soldiers to come tell us not what we already know about them – in other words, what one reads in any of the left-wing newspapers – but what we don't know. And that's what's most difficult to get them to express. For the first hour, at the beginning, the people we meet give general opinion. We meet workers' councils, so there are militants among them, and they are always the ones to speak first; listening to them is a bit like reading passages from *Libération*, *Politique-Hebdo*, *L'Huma*. So after a while we say: Yes, we know that, we read the papers. But what we want to know is the other side of all of this. Repression with a capital R doesn't exist; what does exist is one person repressing another. How does that happen? how is it manifested? and also how is it betrayed, how can you fight against it?

If we manage to have in the production even a half hour at the beginning dictated by workers, or nurses or others . . ., I would be very happy. I would say to myself that perhaps we have at last found the dramatic author. [. . .]

B: For *'89*, there was an enormous amount of documentation.

M: Here too. It takes on a bookish form for some, a form which others, while not rejecting it, don't need. And then there is this new form we are now trying to elaborate, the direct contact with certain social classes, certain companies.

B: Did you envisage these contacts with workers from the beginning?

M: No, it happened when you came to see us, a month ago, a month and a half ago. It was a very bad moment. We felt we needed a rupture. I thought that the actors needed to act. I say the actors, but I was also scared. We needed our work to be confirmed. [. . .] We needed at once holidays and work. We went to the Cévennes, because we had a place to stay there, and we said to ourselves: 'No one knows who we are. No one expects us to put on "great productions".' We played every day, sometimes even two times a day, in villages that had only been informed the previous day, by a little parade, that actors would come and improvise. One beautiful day we performed in a little square, and otherwise in church or municipal halls. [. . .] Since that experience of the Ardèche, we have decided to have a great deal of contact with various social categories.[12] Yesterday, for example, a group of workers from Kodak came here [. . .]

B: Will these contacts, these situations given by people who come at your request, oblige you to modify considerably the situations in the material you already have?

M: No, they will provide us with more, and help us to complete, to finish the situations we have already elaborated. It's thrilling work, although sometimes it also drives us to despair. At times we think that we'll never get there. We're all so conditioned by the idea of a finished work, of a completed production! [. . .]

B: To make theatre dealing with contemporary reality, why remain faithful to improvisation?

M: Give me a way to do it otherwise. [. . .]

B: Why not ask an author to collaborate in the production?

M: We have authors, we are all authors. It is more and more true. I do not see why one only has the right to be called an author if one has a pen. *An improvising actor is an author*, an author in the broadest sense of the term. So we have authors. But the problem is that we are very much novices in this practice. With each production we are very much novices. We do not want authors now because authors never consider themselves to be novices.

Why be faithful to improvisation? Because I think the actors are authors more with their sensibilities and their bodies than they would be with a blank sheet of paper. Remember the postulate of the production: actors who recount in fifty years . . . They are actors who have found character-types for today, like Balzac in his own time when he recounted the 'human comedy'. The term 'character-type' sounds a bit stupid, but that's what it's about: characters who are not limited, crass or incomplete, who tell the story of a particular society. Naturally one can say that the character-type is the wicked capitalist with his fat cigar and top hat. This kind of cliché is clearly what we have wanted to avoid. Our capitalist is the result of a long period of work on Pantalon. In *commedia dell'arte*, Pantalon is a fantastic emanation of the bourgeoisie.[13] We took him, worked him to death, transposed him, and we find ourselves with a capitalist endowed with all of Pantalon's guile, his intelligence, his violence, etc. and who is not at all the general *opinion* of a capitalist. That's what we're looking for; I'm not saying we always succeed.

B: Why choose to talk about contemporary reality by means of characters borrowed from *commedia dell'arte*?

M: These are not borrowed characters. I think it's a bit like if you said: 'You are building a house: why are you using bricks when today all houses are made with concrete?' To which one could respond: 'Because we think brick is the most economical, least polluting, most essential method.' That's exactly it. It happens that we have a certain way of treating theatre. We did not go steal a character. In the case of *commedia dell'arte*, we went back to take up a kind of work which seemed to us to have been interrupted, and we have attempted to take it to the limit. [. . .]

When we started work, I proposed: let's stage the Thévenin affair.[14] It was an exercise. Immediately a problem crops up: either you deal with it in the manner of 'I have faith in my country's justice system', which does not satisfy me; or you decide to tell the story in such a way that the motives of the people present – the courage of some, the cowardice of others – are exposed, so that one understands the mechanisms, which are human mechanisms. Then you realise that, at the present time, there's no form that can serve as a support. Brecht is not a form, it's a vision of theatre, and if you tell yourself: we're going to deal with it like Brecht, that's where all sorts of heresies appear.

The Thévenin affair was a contemporary event for the actors, and it involved people of about the same age as them. So they found it impossible to set about performing it directly as if it were distant from them. So I proposed a number of ways of performing it, and my suggestions were not entirely instinctive: play it in China a thousand years ago, play it in Italy three hundred years ago, and I added: play it in France in the middle ages. That was when I recognised just how ignorant I was when I said to myself: temporal distance will suffice. We did this experiment in a single day. With the first two modes, we instantly realised we had everything we needed. The third produced a dreadful TV programme. For actors, time is nothing. We had lots of suggestions for costumes, etc. for the middle ages, but not a form of theatre.

After a while we found ourselves with a number of work platforms: the *commedia dell'arte*; the Chinese, who were very important too. We also worked on the tragic narratives (as we found characters, even very comical ones, we had them do the messenger in *Antigone*), and, more recently, on Molière. Personally, I think this makes a whole. [. . .]

B: The first time I came to see you working, you were all sitting around a table in the foyer, and you were reading extracts from Jacques Copeau's *Appels*,[15] which had just come out. They were about improvisation and Copeau's desire to create an improvised comedy for today which would take up the principles of *commedia dell'arte*. You seemed to find your own preoccupations in his. You were very enthusiastic.

M: Yes, I was discovering . . . You know, I have no culture in theatrical theory. I know Brecht a little, and Meyerhold. But I think there are some extraordinary things in Copeau. The only thing that worries me is that he didn't succeed in realising the 'New Improvised Comedy' that he wished for. I feel that like a sword of Damocles hanging over my head. [. . .]

B: You remember the conference you attended on collective creation at the Théâtre Récamier with Peter Brook, Armand Gatti, etc. When you were asked if the Théâtre du Soleil had achieved collective creation, you responded by saying something like: 'Listen, I do not know . . . But what I can tell you – and it's all I can tell you – is that collective work is a sort of ideal toward which we direct all our efforts.' What can you say about this today? Have you advanced on this path? Do you feel you are closer to a true collective creation, in so far as it can exist?

M: I think it is spreading out. In *Les Clowns* already, there was a big part of collective creation, in *1789* there was still more, and in *1793* still more. At the present time, we are making great progress in terms of everyone taking on more and more responsibilities in the production. Of course, there are still actors in this production who have not contributed much, but there are others who have taken on an incalculable number of things, who have invented continually. In particular, there are two who had not been able to do '93 and who are among the *leaders* this time. [. . .]

B: As you know, people have often talked of the problem of the relations between the actors and you, between the group and you. I have just returned from abroad, where I was asked this question as it is asked about a traditional theatre where the actors are *interpreters* directed by a director. Some people will go so far as to deny more or less explicitly the group, and to consider the Théâtre du Soleil to be Mnouchkine. [. . .]

M: You ask the question badly. Within the Théâtre du Soleil, I don't think my role is diminishing; I think that the roles of the others are increasing. This is a somewhat different analysis. I don't think that we will achieve collective work only when I'm no longer anything, because this is also an incorrect attitude. I believe it's a mistake to say that collective work implies the suppression of the specific place of each individual. I'm not talking about hierarchy, but about function. I think that the role of the actors will always remain fundamentally different from mine. The only thing – and it's fundamental – is that dialogue should become increasingly rich, increasingly equal, but it remains a dialogue between two people who fulfil two different functions. Perhaps we still need to find a certain democratic centralism. The real problem is not for me to diminish, but for each individual to increase, which is in the process of happening.

I am in no way the originator of everything. There are many things that occur without me, that take place beyond me. [. . .]

B: Certain far-leftists talk of a sort of absolute collective creation (let's all create together!). I don't think it is really possible.

M: But creation can be collective, and absolutely collective, precisely if everyone is in his or her place, ensures maximum creativity in each function, and if there's someone who centralises. This does not imply any hierarchical vision. One does not create all together, it is not true. Everyone creates, one after the other, and if everyone creates at once, there's a short circuit, like when everyone speaks at the same time. Each person must at least be able to have the floor; otherwise it's a brouhaha, and the brouhaha exists in improvisation! [. . .]

B: In a very beautiful text [published in 1968], very simple and very lucid, you expressed your aspiration towards a theatre of the people as well as your doubts about its possibility in today's world. [. . .] Do you have the impression that you are progressing on the path to a theatre of the people, and if so, of what kind?

M: I think we are preparing ourselves for the possibility of a transformation which will mean that a theatre of the people could exist. We're getting ready so as not to be too outflanked, and in order to be able to offer the necessary tools. In the wake of meetings like last night's, with the Kodak workers, I would say that if we really get to the point where part of a production is provoked, and written by the workers themselves, then we will have come closer to a popular theatre. It's difficult to see any other definition.

Naturally, it would also have to be workers who watch the production. But we're also aware of the fact that that depends on events, I would even say on episodic crises. It's well known that, in May 1968, performances which would normally have had no opportunity to reach audiences of this kind did just that. But we also know that, at times like the present, that's utopian. With *1789*, which was seen by 350,000 to 400,000 spectators, we reached more than just the people who normally go to the theatre. But you cannot achieve this every time. There are meetings, strikes on occasion, militant performances (organised by militants) where you touch a working audience, but a popular audience does not only comprise workers. I am quite conscious of the fact that we reach a very small percentage of the popular audience, six or seven per cent as opposed to two or three elsewhere [i.e. reached by other companies in other venues]. But in any case I don't think it's possible to create a *popular* theatre by performing certain productions produced in conditions of wage hierarchy, or hierarchy at all, of aestheticism, even if these are so-called Marxist 'readings' of certain plays, and by some miracle they manage to be performed before 3,000 workers.

For our own part, we are preparing ourselves so that the functioning of the Théâtre du Soleil can be as democratic as possible, something which doesn't preclude centralism, so that the actors and technicians can be in the fullest possession of their art, so that they can be as available and ready as possible to put it at the service of what people will want. Not by asking them what they wish to see, but by performing what they live. That's what popular theatre is. Now . . . it does not exist.

But one shouldn't say that it cannot exist.

From Denis Bablet, 'Rencontres: un entretien avec Ariane Mnouchkine', in *Travail Théâtral – Différent: le Théâtre du Soleil*, Lausanne: La Cité, 1976.

2.4 THE INDIVIDUAL AND THE COLLECTIVE
From an interview with Ariane Mnouchkine
by the editors of *Théâtre/Public*

In this interview recorded shortly after the opening of L'Age d'Or, *Ariane Mnouchkine tussles with the editors of* Théâtre/Public *over collective creation as social praxis, the relationship between politics and ethics in the production, and the problems of presenting a 'work-in-progress'.*

THÉÂTRE/PUBLIC: Examining the situation of theatre today, one might well ask oneself whether it's still capable of representing the world. With *L'Age d'Or*, you seem to have made the opposite gamble.

MNOUCHKINE: I must posit as an assumption that it is still capable, otherwise I would immediately stop doing theatre. In order to find out, you have to try.

T: Do you think that the number of spectators and their satisfaction constitute sufficient criteria?

M: You can certainly fool people, but not many of them and not for very long. Contrary to what you might believe, we don't have an audience that is always unanimous in its responses. *1793* generated much harsher reactions than *1789*, and yet we are more satisfied with it. Having said that, the pleasure that one can procure is a significant factor, although it doesn't blind us. We are conscious that with *L'Age d'Or*, we have only moved towards what we wanted to do, from every point of view: that of the form, of the thinking, of political independence. That's why we called the production a 'first draft'. We have not waited longer before presenting it because we absolutely needed to meet the audience.

T: In 'traditional' theatre practice, the text exists independently from the production, and constitutes the principal instrument of theatricality. What is primary with you is the actor, who generates texts by using major forms stemming from popular traditions. What led you to set the terms in this order? Why this suspicion with regard to the text?

M: There is no suspicion with regard to the text. Before *Les Clowns*, we read hundreds of them. If we didn't want to stage any of them it was because they no longer corresponded – not to our tastes, but to the functioning of our group. We want to eliminate all hierarchy, to make sure that each person can develop and contribute his or her best. When great plays are performed, the same people always take the major roles, and one must acknowledge that they allow more progress than the little ones. After a certain amount of time you become a company like any other. Of course, all of this was not entirely conscious at the time. In this production, if an actor does not do much in front of the audience, he has nonetheless worked a great deal beforehand, his creative share is large. In fact, it is the texts that rejected us. They were written for companies different from our own.

T: Certain eras give rise to collective artistic expression, the works are anonymous. In others, it is a man, an individual who crystallises and amplifies the questions of his time, sometimes answers them. Do you think a collective can perform this crystallising role?

M: A collective is not the negation of the individuals of which it's composed. It would be dangerous to think that a collective can exist without eyes, without mouths, without hands. A collective is the grouping of several creators. If Shakespeare crystallised the questions of the society of his time, it's no doubt also because he reworked those of his company, of his actors.

T: The major problem is to ask the right questions. With *L'Age d'Or*, one gets the impression of a theatre of reflection, which remains on the surface of things, rather than of an interrogative practice, which would make contemporary reality unfamiliar.

M: That's why the production is called a 'first draft'. But its inadequacies don't only stem from the fact that we are a collective. All writers in the last thirty years, apart from Brecht, have merely brushed the surface of things. This comes from the fact that contemporary reality is very difficult to analyse.

T: You call it a 'first draft', and yet as it unfolds the production never signals to the audience that this is a first attempt. It feels like a closed object.

M: Pointing out that *L'Age d'Or* was a first draft was a painful confession. We didn't do it with a light heart. We have not quite managed to accomplish what we wanted to, but we had to meet the audience. Now it is a broad audience, and I don't think that they are prepared to accept something unfinished. Especially since a show that is less finished, closer to improvisation, if it is performed regularly, can easily degenerate into a false happening, a false celebration, a false participation.

T: It's true that the rules of our society prohibit us from confessing to an attempt.

M: When we were in the Cévennes, we performed for free, improvising on themes suggested by the audience. We experienced such pleasure with this that we arrived at the point of thinking that only this was valid, that we should no longer do anything else. We were mistaken. There is a dialectic between experiences of this kind and the realisation of a full production. The laws of production don't allow us to offer just any experience. And yet, to my mind, the exploratory character of *L'Age d'Or* is clearly palpable in the very form of the production itself.

T: It seems to me that one of the production's difficulties relates to the articulation of the form and the story, which is sometimes problematic. Take for example the changing-room sequence at the construction site. The situation seems to have been invented only to allow for the gag.

M: In fact, we didn't invent any of that. The story was told to us by the workers at Kodak. If it made you feel uncomfortable, it stems from the fact that, on the night you saw the production, the actor may have allowed himself to become carried away by the pleasure of performing and have forgotten the story. For the actors, that's one of the dangers of our work. But if they remain conscious of what they have to perform, there's no disjunction. I believe that those people who consider the main value of *L'Age d'Or* to be in the actors' performances and the work with forms, but that the underlying base is weak, are completely mistaken. The best moments of the form are also the best moments of the story and meaning, and vice versa. For example the sequence in the immigrants' hostel is a moment at which the form is pushed to its limits starting from a very rich base.

T: Doesn't the use of old forms to talk about the contemporary world impose constraints?

M: It necessarily imposes some. But I don't agree with talking of old forms; they are simply pure theatrical forms. Amongst other things, they enable us to avoid what I would call the constraints of aesthetic realism, which is widespread today. For me, this aesthetic realism is a true perversion of Brechtian realism. One must shun this realism, one must shun the object. More often than not in theatre, everything is meaningful except for the actors and what they say. This aesthetic realism is real terrorism. The spectator is assailed with signs which for the most part aren't signs at all; they are simple presentations, a jumble.[17] The imagination is sterilised, the audience can no longer play. True realism is a transposition, a dialogue; it permits the development of the art of the spectator. Brecht, who stressed the importance of this, nonetheless gave rise to a school which has taken all talent away from the spectator.

T: But a form is never empty. Isn't it also ideology?

M: We worked on *commedia dell'arte* and Chinese theatre to deepen the relationship between actor, story and spectator. The improvisations stemming from *commedia* produced different results from those that stemmed from Chinese theatre. More than anything else, *commedia* allows us to fabricate characters. Asian theatre allows us to structure a story. We have also noticed that, depending on the form being used, we would invent very different characters who would nevertheless function very well together. Apart from Arlequin, the *commedia* primarily produces characters representing the powerful, whereas Asian theatre produces gods (whom we don't need) and ordinary people. Having said that, the work on the mask and the *commedia* was in fact privileged over the rest, precisely because it gave us so much difficulty. But this is a first stage. We did not take these forms as old forms; we gave ourselves forms of a level below which we did not want to descend.

T: One wonders whether the use of the *commedia* character typology doesn't have repercussions for the production. By choosing Pantalon to represent the capitalist, for example, one runs the risk of transforming the capitalist into an entity, the 'Bad Guy'. One no longer sees a man within a system, and who can't act differently than he does.

M: Pantalon is not an entity. He is a complex being driven by self-interest and passion. One must not lose sight of this last element. We never wanted spectators to think, 'Pantalon is a bastard.' If that's what occurs, it's quite involuntary on our part, it has to do with the exploratory character of the production. I think in fact there's only one scene which could support that criticism with any evidence, and that's the dinner party. But neither the character-type nor the actor are at fault; they are victims of the inadequacy of the story at that particular moment. I might add that, during the rehearsals, we took great delight in this character because he was so sympathetic.

T: What's important is to make a production manageable. When Brecht showed the suicide of a worker in *Kuhle Wampe*,[18] he represented it in a non-tragic way, as a banal and everyday act. Which the censor at the time decided was more dangerous than a dramatised – and therefore more exceptional – death. Isn't this precisely the case with the death of Abdallah?

M: You're forgetting the degree to which we can be victims of the press. We are used to reading every day in a dispassionate way that French or Portuguese or Algerian workers have died from industrial accidents.[19] As a reaction to this, we wanted to show that, however common it is, the death of a worker is an exceptional event, a tragedy, every time it happens. That's why Abdallah's death is recounted as if it were that of a great king from Shakespeare. Furthermore, this character does not commit suicide; in fact he protests violently against his own death.

T: Couldn't there have been more cruelty in the production? Take Arlequin as an example; the character is driven by physiological needs – hunger, sex, etc. . . . .

That is why his behaviour eludes any moral judgement.[20] But Abdallah's motivations seem a bit vague. For example, it's a shame that we never see him queuing up outside the door of a brothel.

M: That scene does exist, although we didn't include it in the final performance; it would have been too long. However I agree with you about Abdallah's character. I have the feeling that we have not been entirely free with regard to him. We have undoubtedly been victims of a taboo.

T: Wouldn't the problems have been diminished with a more marginal character, like those that Chaplin can play? His marginality and his aspirations turn him into a tool which allows the behaviour of others to be read.

M: It's relatively easy to construct a strongly individualised character on the borderline between classes. It is difficult, however, to make one who is representative of a class, someone who can speak for that class. I would take the absence of unionists in our production as proof of this. The danger is universality, anonymity. I think that a mass event, such as a demonstration, can only be shown through individuals. The question we ask ourselves is how to perform the masses. You won't succeed by embodying them in an exemplary character. Maybe we should draw inspiration from the past, returning to the techniques of narration. But the messenger must not have been only a witness to an event, he must have participated in it, lived it.

T: Doesn't this problem connect back to that of the mask?

M: Indeed, in a mask there is both the individual who is unlike anyone else, and all of those that resemble him. The mask enables us to present collective experience by means of individual experience [. . .]

T: One could wonder whether ethics don't take precedence over politics in the production? It seems that what is put into question is a way of life and modes of behaviour much more than processes.

M: Processes are only visible through behaviour. And besides, an actor can't work from the process. If he does, he loses the imagination of behaviour. The reverse seems to me to be more productive. Nevertheless, as I have already said, the production is dangerous for the actors insofar as, in their relationship with the audience, it is possible for them to lose sight of the process. Having said that, the processes are much more difficult to grasp today than they were in the past. But in the struggle, facts and personalities are what's important, not abstractions.

T: In abandoning the playwright, do you ever get the feeling that you have lost something?

M: Of course. So we're not Shakespeare! In the passage to socialism, perhaps we'll also lose certain things, but what's important is what is gained in the change. Perhaps what will have been lost will be found again later.

From Yvon Davis, Michèle Raoul-Davis and Bernard Sobel, 'Première Ebauche: entretien avec Ariane Mnouchkine', in *Théâtre/Public* 4–6, June–August, 1975.

2.5 DEVISING THROUGH IMPROVISATION: THE CONSTRUCTION SITE

Sophie Lemasson (Moscoso)

> The art of the actor is transposition. He is an actor set-designer.
> He plays with emptiness. He begins the image; the spectator follows.
> Ariane Mnouchkine[21]

Sophie Moscoso has been integral to the Théâtre du Soleil's working processes since the early 1970s, when, as a young postgraduate student, she attended rehearsals for 1789. As assistant to Mnouchkine, she records every working session in detail, and her status as 'living archive' of the company has earnt her the title of aide-mémoire. *In the following extracts from the rehearsal log for* L'Age d'Or, *Moscoso offers a detailed description of the evolution through improvisation of a core sequence in the production. Her account contains a range of perceptive observations in relation to mask work: in particular, the importance of transposition and rhythm in the development of character and situation.*

The origins of the construction site scene are simple: *on 3 December 1973*, Ariane suggested that the actors work from tapes (recordings of the 'sounds' of a construction site, of a printing press, of the Stock Exchange). Without us ever formulating it in precisely this way at the time, at this stage in our work these sounds enabled us to avoid the clichéd ideas that the words 'construction site' evoke in our imaginations. At the beginning, these tapes allowed us to transpose the *realistic data of workplaces.*

A remark that seems important to me: *historical distance* offers more images to the actors' consciousness, to their imagination than the present time, which has not yet produced an imaginary landscape in the unconscious of each one of us. [. . .]

The suggestion to use these tapes opened two areas of work:

– *On rhythm*: The tape of the construction site is composed, as a musical score can be, on one hand of 'background noise', whose essential characteristic is to muffle, and on the other, of a thematic 'leitmotiv': the noise of a machine which *crushes*. As the sound envelops and directs, the actors are obliged to improvise without speaking, or at least without wanting their words to be heard and understood: to dominate the recording *gesturally.*

– Second necessity emerging from the first: the *creation of a space*. How can this rhythm of the tape help the actors to create, with their own means, *the space of their work site*, a space in which each of their characters will move, act, encounter others, provoke conflicts, and thus tell a story?

Note: this analysis is possible with hindsight, but was not at the moment of the original suggestion. The work that this led to brought forth a very important notion: rhythm, the *internal music*, that every masked character must possess in a specific way. [. . .]

By 3 December, the only attempt at a contemporary transposition had been the 'dinner party' scene – which can be seen in the first draft of the production. [. . .]

So on 3 December 1973, the actors improvise the construction site scene in the style of the old *commedia*, which is to say in the old costumes. The anachronisms are of no importance; what is crucial is that the actors' imaginations be free of clichés! This is the first time that the Arlequins and Brighella[22] must throw themselves into exploring functions other than those traditionally ascribed to them as valets accomplishing particular tasks for Pantalon, their master.

Two working stipulations:

– find a *directly* sensorial relationship between the space created by the sound and that created by the internal music of each character;

– show the work at a temperature of minus 15°C: midwinter is already a suggestion for a first conflict.

In addition, the permanent stipulations of any 'masked' improvisation: each character must make their *own* entrance, *showing*, with the general *lines* of their body, a specific *state*. This state creates a *parallel situation* which will encounter the general situation in the work site, either by clashing or by harmonising with it. In this way, through their entrance each character presents and *shows* him- or herself to the audience in the place where the action will unfold.

When a character creates the place, it is not so much the objective givens of this place that are of interest, but what these details – certain details chosen by the actor for his or her character – provoke in Arlequin or Brighella. (In reference to his films, Jean Renoir talks of 'internal realism'.)

First difficulties during first improvisations:

– The characters automatically saturate themselves with the rhythm of the machine: there's no conflict, so no story can emerge.

– The difficulty of playing work. We're not dealing here with 'workers', but with characters who live and show us a certain number of situations and conflicts: it's from these that the function arises.

– We are working primarily on Arlequins and Brighella, and we try in vain to find the 'spitefulness' necessary for a foreman Arlequin. However, driven by an urgent need for such a character, we witness the *birth of the character Aimé Lheureux*. The actor only found this name later; we always called him 'the Foreman'. At this point he could be a rag trader, a shopkeeper . . . and in the future he will find many other functions.

An important remark: the creation of a new character usually happens in an obvious and comical way from the moment of his or her first entrance. All of Aimé

Lheureux's characteristics were present during his first appearance on the construction site.

From this work on characters at the construction site emerged two skeletal outlines of conflicts which seemed interesting enough for us to keep for future work. On one hand, the appearance of an immigrant Arlequin from Senegal: M'boro. Only recently arrived, he doesn't as yet possess within him the alienating rhythm of the machine. On the other, given that his sole aim is to work, there still remains in him a certain lack of consciousness, a degree of submissive zeal. So he is easily manipulable, either by the foreman or by the French Arlequins.

First sketch of an improvised framework:

– The entrances of the two French Arlequins; very early morning, cold, frost; their arrival at the work site; coffee made on a portable stove in the corner; two aims: to warm themselves up, to delay starting the machine for as long as possible.

– The entrance of the foreman, who sets the machine going; the sound-tape starts playing. At this point a difficult moment arises: finding a way of showing the work. The actors don't succeed in this.

– The entrance of M'boro, with his own rhythm, which is antinomic to the rhythm of the machine; he asks for work; distrust of the Arlequins; the foreman takes advantage of the enthusiasm and obedience of this new arrival; through a piece of theatrical artifice, M'boro is able to stop and start the machine at will; caught between the very different orders of the Arlequins and of the foreman, M'boro no longer understands anything and seems rather to give way to the foreman's offers.

– He gets beaten up by the two Arlequins behind a wall; and in a vital revolt fuelled by his lack of understanding of what is happening to him, he grabs a shovel and threatens the other characters very violently; he is driven by both anger and fear at the same time. The improvisation ends there.

Even though it's not entirely successful, the improvisation seems interesting because it allows us to see, through the relationships between the characters, the range of divisions that prevent solidarity from arising. Furthermore, it leaves its own conclusion open: what will be the impact of M'boro's revolt on each of the other characters? [. . .]

Then on 18 December 1973: a day of improvisations on topics freely chosen by the actors from newspaper cuttings. One group chooses the theme of an *accident at a construction site in Fos-sur-Mer*. The location: a girder thirty metres above the ground. So the actors must play the height and the wind (the *mistral* of southern France); above all they must avoid starting from a moral idea, but rather from a basis in the unconscious and in play.

With these suggestions, the improvisation really begins with a *lazzi*[23] – which we will refer to for ourselves as 'the balls *lazzi*', provoked essentially by the physical situation of the characters on the girder: their 'acrobatics' to stop themselves from falling and in their struggle with the wind.

Abdallah–Arlequin: 'Vertigo gets me right there!', pointing to his balls. Out of this emerges an outrageous joke about his penis swelling and being used by him as a stabiliser for his balance. It's a piece of theatrical play, but it's also emblematic of a kind of derivative behaviour that Abdallah–Arlequin finds to forget where he is: the height, the fear can thus be played in a true and 'masked' way.

On this particular day, the 'dramatic' objective was not achieved, but it seems indispensable, in order to obtain it, to start the improvisations in this way: the most tragic of situations, to begin with, can provoke a great deal of laughter.

Abdallah's death was found much later, on 6 October 1974, during an exercise around a passage from Verdi's *Requiem* [the 'Dies Irae']. The exercise consisted of the individual entrances of characters who had to show us a simple situation, an adventure, and to use Verdi's music at a moment of their choosing. This music provides an explosive dramatic quality which forced the actors to perform on the same scale.

Abdallah died on that day, almost exactly the way he dies in the first draft of *L'Age d'Or*.

A last element that will nourish in a very important way the theme of work, hence of the work site: on 3 December 1974, a meeting with workers from the Kodak factory in Vincennes. At first the discussions occur in an abstract theoretical language – that of Exploitation with a capital E. Gradually, however, the mutual understanding becomes more precise, and 'anecdotes' are formulated in such a way that the actors can more easily imagine a theatrical transposition. On that particular evening, the Kodak workers are the *authors* of what will be improvised.

One anecdote caught our attention because it contained pretty much all of the remarks expressed: the organisation of work so as to accentuate division; the existence of 'small bosses'; the functioning of promotion procedures, etc.: a department head, who is poorly thought of and unpopular in the firm, is transferred to Marseilles; 'someone', we do not know who, suggests the idea of giving him a present; a collection is organised and the secretary delegated with this task must make a list of the generous donors . . . This is the anecdote! The actors request further information about the hierarchy of functions: a department head – this will be M. Dussouille; a lab head – Max; and two workers – Ramon Granada (a bearded Polichinelle)[24] and La Ficelle. This casting establishes the typical relationships of hierarchical organisation as it was described to us, and obeys a fundamental law discovered during the work: masked acting forbids improvisations with too many characters; each character is a hero who tells his own story, and cannot be a secondary character [. . .]

Last step, 6 February 1974: it seems to us that the theme of the work site should be included in the first draft of the production of *L'Age d'Or*. Today's task is to re-improvise the work site, taking into account everything that has been accumulated thus far, in terms of the characters, the creation of the space and locations, of the rhythm. Since Abdallah's story now seems sufficiently structured for the first draft, it seems justified to make the construction site scene its final episode. Knowing that Abdallah will die here, Ariane offers two suggestions: firstly, a return to the situation of the wind and the worker high up; secondly, after Abdallah's death, in order for his adventure not to become a simple negative statement, imagine that the other characters present in the site oblige Pantalon himself to climb the crane.

Although the sound-tape had permitted a shift away from realism a year beforehand, we realise that now it only evokes a realistic universe. This is a measure of the trail of discoveries we have travelled over the past year!

We find ourselves confronted with the same problem, the work itself: right from the various entrances of the characters, playing the wind and the cold, in settling down to the work that is to be accomplished there is a slackening of pace and rhythm. Time and space become realistic. So Ariane suggests combining the elements of the construction site (the wind, the death of Abdallah) with those discovered with the Kodak workers (the relationships between the characters). [. . .]

So, the itinerary leading to the scene of the construction site is still unfinished. Even so, the creation of this *typical place* in our contemporary world leaves all the possibilities open for encounters of characters, for conflicts, for *lazzis*, for farce . . . for what will come after the first draft of *L'Age d'Or*.

From 'Raconter *L'Age d'Or*: le chantier' (Sophie Lemasson's rehearsal log, 20 February 1975), in Le Théâtre du Soleil, *L'Age d'Or ('Texte–Programme')*, Paris: Stock, 1975.

2.6 IMPROVISATION AND THE MASK: FROM ARLEQUIN TO ABDALLAH

Philippe Caubère

> Force yourself to draw pleasure from the accomplishment of
> your scenic task. It's the number one axiom.
> Vsevolod Meyerhold[25]

Philippe Caubère first joined the Théâtre du Soleil for the revival of 1789 *in* 1972. *In this extract, he recounts his experiences in rehearsal for* L'Age d'Or *of some of the trials, joys and 'laws' of mask work: the 'still-point', temporal manipulation, the 'state', and so on. He describes the transposition from the* commedia Arlequin *to Abdallah, the interactive relationship between actors and director, and the role of pleasure in performance.*

RECOGNISING THE CHARACTER

When Ariane talked about making a production about the present time using masked performance, I have to admit that the latter part of her proposition did not really grab me. I thought that this bit of cardboard or leather that we were going to place in front of our faces would hinder me rather than anything else. In fact, the more the work progressed, the more I recognised the freedom and strength that the mask could provide me with, once I could manage to find the rules implied by wearing it.

Initially it was by watching others that I began to understand the extent to which mask work was an essential means of expression for an actor. To begin with, the mask was the first transposition from the 'natural' to the 'theatrical'. If a masked actor performed 'naturally', all I saw was someone wearing a bothersome and dead object on his face. However, once the same actor began to make the mask live, to give it a meaning, a rhythm, a balance, to 'inhabit' it, then an image was born, another face was suggested and mysteriously a character appeared. This character was called Arlequin, Pantalon, Matamore or Bisognoso, depending on which mask the actor had chosen. I didn't know who they were, but I recognised this character; I had already encountered him in my life, or perhaps in the cinema, or even in my childhood. And I realised that the same thing was happening all around me, everyone had recognised him instantly; and everything that this actor had evoked in our memories was already there in the theatre, translated into theatrical signs. So confronted with this incredible human marionette with his clown-like clothes, his false stomach and his disproportionately large nose, all this fabricated gear that nonetheless evoked the most intimate reality, we roared with laughter.[26] I laughed all the more because the actor did not disappear during this phenomenon. On the contrary, he was there, present; under the mask, his eyes never left us. He had sensed that we had seen and recognised his character, our laughter had alerted him. And he took an ever greater pleasure in showing us, before we had even thought of them, the most hidden contradictions, the most secret passions of the character, using all of the means at his disposal: his body, his voice, his gaze, his mask. Caught between the unreal, the mystery of his art and that raw reality he was continuously suggesting, arousing, revealing, he was making fun of this character, like a cruel and clever juggler. This miracle could last for hours; when we were on the same wavelength, complicitous in terms of look and pleasure, we played the 'magical' game of theatre with him. Undoubtedly it was Mario's 'Pantalon' who gave me my first experience of this immense pleasure; there were many others later on.

THE TRANSPOSITION OF *COMMEDIA* CHARACTERS: ARLEQUIN

When we refer to Matamore, Pantalon or Arlequin, it should be pointed out that we have never tried to 'reconstruct' any of these characters. We simply decided to use certain basic elements of a genre of theatre, that was represented by the *commedia dell'arte*, amongst others: i.e. masks, character types, improvisation, the body. I think that rather than the *commedia* characters themselves (only known to us through a few theoretical definitions), we used the image that they suggested to us, the conscious or unconscious memories that they triggered in us, through the intermediary of their representative masks. Between an actor and a mask something happens, or else nothing happens. But if something does happen, it is because the sight of this particular mask has awakened in the actor a memory, of greater or lesser distinctness, which he will use to propel his imagination on the trail of a character. However, many of the masks that we use are not directly descended from the traditional characters of the *commedia dell'arte*; and yet the characters which they have generated are just as universal as Pantalon or Matamore. One could say, reversing the terms, that Lheureux or Dussouille, both characters found in the 'modern' world, are in fact characters from the *commedia*, although there is no proof of this.

For myself, what image could I have of Arlequin? Definitions of the character were rather simplistic: poor, intelligent, ignorant, violent, sensual. The rest had to be invented. Furthermore, the psychological characteristics could only be of use to me if I transposed them into theatrical signs. On the level of reality, they no longer meant anything. For me, Arlequin no longer exists – if he ever has. And yet some actors putting this traditional mask on their faces, giving their bodies to a celebration of the imagination, created in front of us an incredibly concrete, real and contemporary character. So, drawing inspiration from what I was seeing, I too set off in search of this internal image and this character.

I had this mask on my face, and I was being asked to *show*. Knowing that I could only use words accessorily, knowing that I could hide nothing, that everything that I could imagine for Arlequin had to be seen, felt and immediately understood by the spectators, knowing also (whatever one says) that their laughter would guide me, I soon understood that whatever I chose to show through my body – feelings, objects, places – would be infinitely quicker and more effective, if I succeeded, than if I settled for saying it in words. Which is to say that the more raw and precise I could make the outline traced in my mind and projected into space by means of my body and my mask, the more people would laugh. It was infinitely preferable to see Arlequin squirming with pleasure before a female servant, jumping up and down, having an erection like a donkey, than simply to hear him say: 'I want to sleep with her.'

So I did the squirming and jumping. But unfortunately all that those watching could see was the frenetic gesticulations of a sweating and puffing wretch, struggling to convey something that they had understood from the very beginning, and they were wondering 'But why doesn't he simply say that he wants to sleep with her?' Then it was explained to me that if I wanted to be understood, I would have to 'stop' myself, in other words, whenever possible, I should freeze the outline of body and mask in space for a fraction of a second; in this way, I would give the audience the time to receive the images, to understand them and to laugh at them.[27] Delighted with this discovery, I set about 'stopping'! Unfortunately, the same audience now saw little more than a studious demonstration of limp buffoonery, a succession of conventional postures which were exhausting for the actor: hands on the hips, hopping from one foot to the other, joy-arms-in-the-air-smile-from-ear-to-ear, etc. Still they were wondering: 'Why doesn't he just spit it out?' In both cases, the ideal would have been to say nothing at all, not to move at all and for the scene not to exist at all.

So what could I do? First of all, 'gather' my body into a position which was both a position of rest and a starting point. Be as relaxed and as taut as possible in my body and my mind. Allow both blood and ideas to flow freely. Then, at the first idea, enter and allow things to come.

It's in this entrance that everything happened, that's when they would think: 'Ah yes! that's Arlequin, what fun we'll have!' That's when they would recognise me. But in order for that, something had to take place – an incident, a particular location – something through which the audience would react. We called these *lazzi*. Anything can serve as a starting point for a *lazzi*: a fall, rain, wind, snow, a theft, a fair, a cabaret. And that's where, through the work of the actor and his character, the spectator discovers him and prepares to follow him in his adventures.

'THE STATE'

Subsequently I discovered that, in order for this to occur, a 'state' was also necessary, in other words that I had to choose to have Arlequin enter in a particular mood: happy, unhappy, shivery, famished, stuffed with food, etc. What was important was that this be visible, and even better, that it be made visible through contradiction. For example, I could show that Arlequin was cold by shivering. But I could also show him playing the-one-who's-never-cold-and-who's-out-for-a-walk-in-a-singlet-in-the-middle-of-December (when in fact he's absolutely freezing). Strutting like a rooster in front of another Arlequin, I could show the audience that I was freezing; or else, strutting in front of the audience, I could convey to the other Arlequin that I was just showing off; which allowed me not only to play 'Arlequin is cold', but also 'Arlequin is bragging.'

The difficulty came from learning that it was not possible to play these two states simultaneously if I wanted to be understood and to make the audience laugh. Instead, I had to play the two states successively, sequence after sequence: *one* state, in *one* given time, with *one* given sign, and then the other. From the two images played in succession an order could emerge: that of the character. And then they would laugh, and the pleasure that this would give me could incite me to find other incidents through which, bit by bit, Arlequin would exist.

In the wake of this extraordinary discovery, I was obliged to make another one: this performance required sequential cutting of this type because *time* itself became a tool for the performance. Each of these sequences could have the time and the rhythm that I wanted to give it, according to its importance. In this way, time itself would be completely transposed and would become theatrical time. The same thing applies to the voice, same thing for speech. Everything could become an instrument of creation and of theatre.

All of this can seem extremely complicated. In fact, so long as we couldn't 'find' a scene, it was extremely complicated. We thought it would drive us mad.

And then one day, without our really being fully aware of it, something would be released: the desire to make friends laugh, to make oneself laugh, and all this became extremely simple, utterly self-evident. We saw ourselves becoming in turn the famous magician puppeteer of men [*montreur d'hommes*]; I saw myself tracing in space décors, places, objects, towns, and in particular I saw myself animating Arlequin inside them, running around, falling in love, saving his skin. I heard the others laugh on recognising him; and I caught myself laughing at what I made him do, at the tricks I played on him, the world I invented for him. I revelled in the great pleasure of hearing people laugh at these images of the world and of people, when there was only me – running, jumping, sweating, shouting in the theatre. Then I used Arlequin's character and mask to play one of the characters in the performance: Abdallah. [. . .]

ACTOR AND DIRECTOR IN COLLECTIVE CREATION

As I describe all of these discoveries, one might well wonder who made them, how they appeared and how they were conveyed. It would be as wrong to believe that the actors could have found them out by themselves, as to think that Ariane plucked them out of a magic box for us – a box to which, miraculously, she

Plate 2.2   *L'Age d'Or.* Abdallah (Philippe Caubère) asleep in the workers' dormitory. Photo: Martine Franck/Magnum

possessed the key. 'Collective creation' is not some miracle process which erases all difficulties. On the contrary, it invariably brings them together every time that an actor enters; and on each occasion, everything has to be revised and reinvented.

When I begin to improvise, I know that everything will come from me and from those with whom I'm going to perform – or that nothing will come.

Ariane's work, apart from the general project of the production and the choice of style, begins at this moment. Either I'll offer nothing and she will be unable to invent, or I'll propose the image of a character. If the image lasts a few seconds, she will focus my attention, get me to glimpse whatever it is towards which I must be able to go, what means I should prioritise to get there and what dead-ends I should avoid. And so on in this way, from image to image. If, instead of a fleeting image, I immediately outline a recognisable character with a physical attitude, a voice, passions, and even a tradition (in *commedia dell'arte*, for example), Ariane will orient her work in two contradictory and complementary directions: backwards and forwards. Backwards, because she will be striving to relocate the essence of the character. She will incite me to abandon what she calls its 'parasites': gratuitous gestures, imprecise rhythms, folklore, psychologising. Gradually I will be able to shed all that's useless, which is to say insignificant, everything that doesn't immediately connect back to one of the character's essential passions or to a precise social relation – in short, everything that would take me further away from theatre. In this way, I will be able to concentrate my invention and my art into two or three chosen and determinant areas, so as to give this character every opportunity to open out and to find his fullest possible dimensions. But Ariane will also work forwards; she'll never stop 'talking' with me about this character, about what she has already glimpsed of him, his possible functions in society, his connections with a particular family of the *commedia*, his possible relationships with the other characters, the name he could have. After a number of stages in this exchange between my performing and her critical gaze, a relationship will be established between the image that I have of the character and the one she had glimpsed.

But it's a long road and often it doesn't lead anywhere. At the best of times, it takes us through reciprocal stimulation, amazement, the complicitous mobilisation of memory and intuition; and at the worst, through confrontation, my own inability to translate what she wants to have me perform, her impotence in releasing the spring in me that would lead me to that point. So it happens that after periods of exaltation and an unbelievably rich inventiveness, we would pass through long tunnels of emptiness, doubt and uncertainty, some of us even coming close to despair. At these moments, we tried to make use of all of the discoveries I have described above. Ariane had brought these 'laws' or 'frequent risks' to light progressively during the work; and watching the others improvise, we too had come to distinguish certain of these constants. Month after month, we had accumulated a number of them that we could no longer ignore. So we tried to let them permeate us; but alas! Ariane would say to me 'The state!', and I found myself in a 'terrible state'; she would say to me 'The body!', 'The mask', and I couldn't seem to understand what that might mean. Our difficulty was amplified by the fact that, although these givens were valid for all of the actors, their application or interpretation differed according to each temperament. This became apparent when some of us attempted to convey our own discoveries to others. Sometimes it would work well, so that an actor was able to adapt someone else's mechanisms to their own temperament; sometimes it didn't at all, and we wept with rage.

The failure was because it lacked that mysterious clarity and self-evidence[29] that nothing could replace: the inventive state, the desire to have fun, pleasure. But what was clear was that when the improvisation found its true dimensions again and the actors their freedom, then mask, body, pauses, states, sequences, all these 'laws' were there, united at the same time through a sort of diabolical chance. So contact was re-established, the journey which had been stopped for lack of ideas got underway again, and once more we trembled with the intense pleasure stemming from that acute and violent relationship between us (creating through performance), and her (creating through her gaze).[30]

From Philippe Caubère, 'A nous la liberté', in Le Théâtre du Soleil,
L'Age d'Or ('Texte–Programme'), Paris: Stock, 1975.

2.7 FROM MASK TO CHARACTER: SALOUHA
Lucia Bensasson

Lucia Bensasson played the central part of the narrator Salouha in L'Age d'Or. *Here she describes the evolution and elaboration of this character, some of her difficulties with masks and the gender implications inscribed in the* commedia *typology.*

The creation of the character of Salouha occurred in successive stages, and through the intermediary of other characters developed in the course of improvisations. [. . .] One day Stiefel brought some new masks for modern comedy, which he was producing with increasing regularity. One of them captivates me. It seems somewhat Semitic to me, I try it on, it seems to fit my face perfectly. I look at it, I desperately want to do something with it. I show it to Ariane, it seems to inspire her as much as me. It has a despondent look and all the weight of a history.

The first time I use it, I enter into an entirely psychological state: I feel the mask only from the inside, without managing to externalise it, to show it, to take it into my body. So Ariane simply reminds me not to forget that we are in a fairground. I start again, and all of a sudden something clicks: I find the signs to show what I feel on the inside, in other words, I see my character at the same time as I show it, as I sketch it. Mademoiselle Lanzberg was born; she gained confirmation as the work progressed.

I really believe in the encounter with a mask, but also in the encounter of a mask with one's own history, one's roots (mine are Judeo-Arab, and I use them in both of my characters). However, as women, the actresses involved in the production had particular problems with transposition. In the *commedia dell'arte*, the women were not masked, and their characters were not as representative, as symbolic, as Arlequin, Pantalon or Polichinelle were: they were the counterpoint to the male characters. It was necessary not only to overcome this counterpoint, or secondary-image attitude, but also to find an exemplary symbolic image, and that search immediately made us fall into the masculine schemata. In order to find a female character, I had to use a male mask; there were no equivalent masks for women. Stiefel's task was difficult on this level. Initially the female masks he brought us were pretty, but without any expression, unlike the male masks. He had in mind a traditional representation of woman as secondary image, male object; but this was a way of seeing he had to revise progressively.

So once the character of Mademoiselle Lanzberg was solid, I tried out various new masks, but without much success. In our work we returned constantly to the old comedic forms, and I hadn't abandoned the idea of trying Polichinelle. This work generated a colourful character, a Neapolitan like its model, but I quickly lapsed into a kind of facile folklore, relying on language and remaining too static corporeally. Nevertheless I had discovered the importance of contact with the audience, a prerequisite for any mask to exist.

I started to sketch out this character shortly before a trip to Tunisia. I thought a lot about the gestural qualities of the Tunisian women I knew well: one of the characteristics of Mediterranean women is their role in the fair, the market, the *souk*, their sense of performance through their gestural behaviour. Upon returning, when I picked up the Polichinelle mask again, the similarity between the everyday characters I had been able to see and their typical characteristics became very apparent to me, and also enabled me to recognise that this was a support that could bring out the contradictions of a civilised society.

The character of Salouha, in her reality, is very legible in terms of her relations with an audience, and at the same time she offers sufficient contrast with everyday reality for her contestations or resentments to appear without too much talk. So I had the right mask: complicity with the audience, an exemplary and symbolic attitude, the possibility of exposing the contradictions of everyday life. There remained the task of finding the limits of her own contradictions. This was by no means easy: she knew too many things, nothing seemed to surprise her, as a heroine she was too much the heroine, finding a way out of any situation. Today, she makes us witnesses to her contradictions and weaknesses.

From Lucia Bensasson, 'Autour de Salouha', in Le Théâtre du Soleil, *L'Age d'Or* ('*Texte–Programme*'), Paris: Stock, 1975.

2.8 SOCIETY CAN BE UNMASKED WITH A MASK
Erhard Stiefel

The Swiss mask-maker and sculptor Erhard Stiefel has become integral to the work of the Théâtre du Soleil over the last twenty years. After completing a Fine Arts degree, he studied with Jacques Lecoq (like Mnouchkine), then with Italian mask specialist Amleto Sartori. The following text was included in the 'texte–programme' *for* L'Age d'Or.

A mask begins its life from the moment it is created in its living material. It has its own life. It is no longer a new object. It simply demands to be able to continue to live, to be played.

The mask: expression-force that can dominate a theatrical space and forestall words. The birth of a mask is also a revelation of the philosophical, the political life ethics of whoever creates it. Between the mask and him, there is a trans-position of his lived life.

A mask must be mobile: this means that the mask does not have a fixed and defined expression. Only fundamental and essential traits exist, giving it every possibility of revealing the depth of the character's life. It reaches fullness at the moment of its encounter with the actor who plays it. A complicity must exist between them as soon as the mask comes to life. Its revelatory power is in not giving the audience (and the actor) the possibility of constructing a preconceived stereotypical identification, but on the contrary, in giving them the means to see a particular class through the character, with which they can identify.

All too often in the West, the mask is conceived of and realised merely as a decorative accessory, or as a caricature of some other character. This does not leave any opening for the blossoming of its life, its existence, its reasons for living and moving in the space of its social role.

In performance, a mask is both mask and counter-mask. In its movements it makes its destination, which is to say itself in the face of its authenticity, vibrate and resonate in the theatrical space. This revelation is also apparent as the performance unfolds through actions in their theatrical time, through criticism and self-criticism, the dialogic traits that distinguish the character and its life. The mask imposes a multiplication of time and its duration, which enables a better, deeper understanding of a fact or a gesture without deforming it. This time belongs to a kind of theatrical acting which excludes any interpretation of its psychology. Its duration amplifies and at the same time details an action, an event, a cry with great precision. It provides the signs that are being outlined and translated with a heightened power and resonance in the perception of meaning.

Thus, society can be unmasked with a mask, which becomes revelatory and makes life's truth, which we have never known how to see, spring forth.

In its performance, a mask creates a magical power in the theatrical space through its intensity and vividness, a power which invites the audience – at last – to participate in genuine dialogue. The beauty and precision of its gestures generate a radiance which reveals and distinguishes the inner workings of society, which denounces them, but at the same time invokes hope of a different life.

From 'Le masque et l'univers', in Le Théâtre du Soleil,
L'Age d'Or *('Texte–Programme')*, Paris: Stock, 1975.

2.9 TRANSPOSITIONS AND SILHOUETTES
From an interview with Françoise Tournafond
by Catherine Mounier

Françoise Tournafond was the Théâtre du Soleil's costume designer from Gengis Khan *in 1961 to* Dom Juan *in 1977. In an interview published in the* 'texte–programme' *for* L'Age d'Or, *she describes the nature of her collaboration with the Soleil performers in transposing* commedia *characters to a contemporary context. She highlights the importance of* 'silhouettes' *in mask work, the tracing in space of a character's volume and outline as a legible signifier, as well as a 'masking' of the body as a whole. The silhouettes have a gestic function here: they are socially contextualising, critical and self-consciously theatrical.*

The search for characters and the search for costumes are indissociable. In order to give an image of his or her character, the actor must necessarily invent a silhouette which makes it immediately recognisable. Ideally, even before it opens its mouth, simply thanks to its silhouette, a spectator should be able to locate a character socially, imagine its family life, its way of thinking . . .

So I have only been able to intervene once a character already existed, and from that point, I can only contribute a few details. Here too, the creation is the work of the actors. Rather than any personal creation on my part, one could speak of my *collaboration* with actors who have gone on a quest for characters. The 'beautiful costume' no longer exists, it's an ensemble: masks, costumes and the actor's performance should constitute the inseparable and equally powerful elements of a *sketch* or *outline*. It's not a matter of looking for details, but of looking for silhouettes: in other words, for *volumes*.

How does one achieve what is essential for the costumes? By doing exactly what the actors did in working on their performance: refining as much as is possible the silhouettes which define the characters socially. The actors found the volumes, very effectively. So for example 'Max', who's little more than a stocky bulk in overalls, was entirely invented by Jonathan [Sutton]. For those who experienced difficulties, the work consisted of ridding the costumes of parasitic elements so as to achieve a certain purity. In most cases, the actors found their own silhouettes by building up different paddings available to them. Very often my own work consisted in finding ways of arranging and constructing, erasing what was false and trying to valorise the costumes through certain details: patches of colour, for example.

As is the case for the work as a whole, problems of transposition cropped up here in a particularly acute way. So for example, the passage from old to modern was very difficult, because without a certain distance the imagination doesn't transpose as well, it tends to lock in on the anecdotal [. . .] The *commedia dell'arte* helped us rediscover a certain strength. It is important to think of the Polichinelles, the Arlequins, the Pantalons, the Doctors, in an attempt to find the theatrical correspondence in modern costumes and make it less anecdotal.

For Salouha's costume, we had to discover a quality which recalled her country of origin, for she is an immigrant, while inventing a silhouette for her which was not folksy. We discussed it with Lucia, and chose a blue like the blue of the Tuaregs, the blue people of the desert. The form of the costume (a dress which passes between the legs) was generated by thinking about the character's attitude, the 'diamond' shape she traces (in fact it seems that North African women wear this type of clothing under their dresses, something I didn't know). In relation to her very powerful mask and her attitudes, we needed to affirm her silhouette, free up her movements and enhance her attractive arms. I did not try to stick to the reality of the Tunisian costume, but to establish the relation between this immigrant woman and Polichinelle. The material chosen as a function of these elements could not be light, it needed to be a fairly heavy and rough cotton which I dyed and went over with a paintbrush to darken it slightly. The result needed to be sober and theatrical.

For M'boro, Josette [Josephine Derenne] herself found a silhouette that was just right and very beautiful. Certain details underline the fact that this is an Arlequin: the coloured woven cap, a sign of the black immigrant worker, perhaps a brightly coloured cotton pullover. Abdallah's costume is the result of the same sort of approach. For Monsieur Gueulette, Salouha's Polichinelle husband, I looked for shoes that were a bit heavy, in a yellow colour. In fact, the masculine characters' feet have generally been enlarged. Perhaps the cut of his shirt should echo Polichinelle's in the *commedia*; the actor [Philippe Hottier] has his silhouette, with his very particular false stomach.

For the modern Pantalon, Mario [Gonzales] found everything. His silhouette is perfect, his little limbs, his deformed body, the limp material of his costume which augments his senile aspect. If need be we could complete it with a detail, a rich lining for example, but it's not certain. For Dussouille, who's from the family of doctors in the *commedia dell'arte*, Alain [Salomon] found a fantastic silhouette for himself; certain details have been improved – a nylon shirt, a spotted tie, because he's both shabby and dapper, and a pair of boxer shorts, because he loses his trousers [. . .]

The colours must stand out against that of the carpet, and mustn't kill those of the masks. To achieve this, we have avoided on the one hand rusts, browns, tobacco hues, which are too close to the colour of the ground [the matting covering the floor], and on the other, half-tints that are a bit too subtle as well as refined harmonies. We have deliberately opted for pure colours: dark greys, whites, blacks for those with power, with, in contrast, the dazzlingly bright colours reserved for the workers on the building site (very blue work overalls, perhaps fluorescent oilskins, coloured helmets).

In addition to the discussions I had with the performers and some specific pointers from Ariane, during the rehearsals I did sketches based on improvisations both in the old contexts and the modern contexts. It was a way of forcing myself to get to know bodies, the attitudes, to take into account the masks, which helped me because they define the characters to such an extent. Observation was necessary, but I had to remain vigilant. In the *métro*, I've often noticed people whose clothing totally adheres to their characters; but if it were used as such in our production, it would not be credible.

From Catherine Mounier, 'Des silhouettes pour le théâtre', in Le Théâtre du Soleil, *L'Age d'Or ('Texte-Programme')*, Paris: Stock, 1975.

NOTES

1 Copeau in John Rudlin and Norman H. Paul (eds), *Copeau: Texts on Theatre*, London: Routledge, 1990, p. 153.

2 Lecoq quoted in Jim Hiley, 'Moving heaven and earth', *The Observer*, 20 March 1988.

3 At one point in rehearsal, *L'Age d'Or* was subtitled 'La comédie de ce temps' ('the comedy of our time'), but this was abandoned as being 'too pretentious'.

4 'Points de repères', in Théâtre du Soleil, *L'Age d'Or: première ébauche ('Texte–Programme')*, Paris: Stock, 1975, pp. 159–73.

5 Quoted in Denis Bablet, 'Avec Guy-Claude François', in *Travail Théâtral: Différent*, Lausanne: La Cité, 1976, p. 123.

6 Jean-Jacques Roubine argues that all of the Théâtre du Soleil's productions, from *Les Clowns* to *L'Indiade*, can be read as 'works-in-progress' – theatrically, socially and politically. With detailed reference to the productions' subtitles and contents, and the Soleil's 'collective memory' and development, he suggests 'the company wants to show us an unfinished world, a history in progress [. . .] Incompletion is the point where history and reality converge'; 'The Théâtre du Soleil: a French postmodernist itinerary', in Erika Fischer-Lichte *et al.* (eds), *The Dramatic Touch of Difference*, Tübingen: Gunter Narr Verlag Tübingen, 1990, pp. 77–8.

7 Throughout this section, the French versions of characters' names used by the Théâtre du Soleil have been retained: e.g. Arlequin, rather than Arlecchino/Harlequin, Pantalon rather than Pantalone/Pantaloon, etc.

8 For over half of the eighteen months between *1793* and the opening of *L'Age d'Or*, the Soleil members were on unemployment benefits of about 800 francs a month each; during rehearsal, many of them worked elsewhere on alternate days. For the remainder of this period, they each received a basic wage of 1,750 francs a month.

9 The right-wing patrician Valéry Giscard d'Estaing was President of France (1974–81); his government was defeated by François Mitterrand's Socialists in May 1981.

10 On 14 August 1973, police stormed the Lip factory in Besançon to break a strike and clear the factory of its occupiers; thirty-three workers were arrested and subsequently tried. The strike began again on 31 August, with enormous community support. Finally in January 1974, the Lip employees went back to work with new terms of employment. Information collated from 'Points de repères', in *L'Age d'Or ('Texte–Programme')*, op. cit.

11 The Six Day War occurred in June 1967, when Arab nationalists, led by Egyptian President Nasser's forces, mobilised to try to invade Israel. For further details, see John Pimlott (ed.), *The Middle East Conflicts, from 1945 to the Present*, London: Orbis Publishing, 1983, pp. 54–71.

12 During the preparation of *L'Age d'Or* the Soleil left Paris to travel to rural and industrial communities in the Cévennes, as part of a kind of 'fieldwork' to receive input and feedback from different kinds of audiences, in relation to the forms and characters they were elaborating. Improvisations with local people took place in parish halls, schools, community centres, working social clubs and so on, in Lussan, Les Mages (a mining community) and other villages near Alès. This contact was felt by the company to have been enormously productive, and a great success in terms of validating the work.

13 John Rudlin locates Pantalon's origins in the city-state of Venice, one of Europe's most powerful commercial trading centres during the 15th and 16th centuries. 'Pantalone *is* money: he controls all the finance available within the world of *commedia dell'arte*, and therefore his orders have, ultimately, to be obeyed [. . .] Little by little, he seems to have lost his puissance and retained power only in his purse'; *Commedia dell'arte: an Actor's Handbook*, London: Routledge, 1994, pp. 93–4.

14 Jean-Pierre Thévenin, a twenty-four year old precision welder arrested for a minor offence in Chambéry on 15 December 1968, died in suspicious circumstances in police custody later that day. 'L'affaire Thévenin', which involved a number of unresolved public inquiries into contradictory 'evidence', and produced accusations of police conspiracy, was widely discussed in the media at the time. For further details, see René Backmann, 'Le "pendu" de Chambéry', *Le Nouvel Observateur*, 5 January, 1970, pp. 24–5.

15 Jacques Copeau, *Appels: Registres 1*, Paris: Gallimard, 1974.

16 André Gide, *Journal 1889–1939*, Paris: Gallimard, 1948, p. 529. For further details of Copeau's exploration of 'la nouvelle comédie', see John Rudlin, *Jacques Copeau*, Cambridge: Cambridge University Press, 1986 – in particular 'The new *commedia*', pp. 95–110.

17 Mnouchkine's conception of the 'sign' seems to relate both to the inseparability of 'meaning' and its occasion as described in Barthes' later work (indexical, iconic and symbolic signifying functions and relations actively negotiated *with-in* specific cultural and historical moments) and to the critical slippages and legibilities of Brechtian *gestus*.

18 Brecht co-wrote the script for the 1932 film *Kuhle Wampe* with Ernst Ottwalt; the film was a quasi-documentary of working-class life in Berlin.

19 'Ministerial report on accidents in the workplace in France: in 1972, 1,125,000 industrial accidents were recorded, alongside job losses of 13,000,000. Of these accidents, 118,000 were serious and 2,406 were fatal; more than 22 per cent of industrial accidents involved immigrant workers, although they only represent 9.4 per cent of the total number of workers; in 1973, there were on average three deaths a day in the building and public works sectors.' From 'Points de repère', in *L'Age d'Or ('Texte– Programme')*, op. cit., p. 169.

20 For a description of Arlequin, see John Rudlin, *Commedia dell'arte*, op. cit., pp. 76–9. See also Dario Fo, *The Tricks of the Trade*, London: Metheun, 1991, pp. 45–50; Fo's book contains many pertinent insights into *commedia*, improvisation and mask work.

21 Mnouchkine in Colette Godard, '*L'Age d'Or*, demain', *Le Monde*, 20 February 1975. For *L'Age d'Or* each performer was conceived of as an 'acteur–décorateur', augmenting the work of the scenic designer by creating through their bodies temporary, metonymic contexts and spaces (council flat, bourgeois dining room, fairground, beach, building site, temperature, wind, etc.) within the non-specific playing space. One of the most celebrated instances of this in the production was Caubère's suggestion of the constricted nature of Abdallah's sleeping quarters in a *foyer* for immigrant workers – he 'slept' in a shoulder-stand on one cheek, with his legs up in the air. Of course, all such signifying practices require the play-ful imaginative complicity of spectators.

22 Brighella is a high status *zanni*, an astute and cunning servant, a jack-of-all-trades and a generator of intrigue. See John Rudlin, *Commedia dell'arte*, op. cit., pp. 84–7.

23 Dario Fo: 'The [*commedia*] actors had at their disposal an incredible store of stage business, called *lazzi* – situations, dialogues, gags, rhymes and rigmaroles which they could call up at a moment's notice to give the impression of on-stage improvisation'; *The Tricks of the Trade*, op. cit., pp. 8–10. Also see Mel Gordon (ed.), *Lazzi*, New York: PAJ Publications, 1983.

24 For an account of the mercurial and cynical Polichinelle (Pulcinella, forebear of the English Punch), see John Rudlin, *Commedia dell'arte*, op. cit., pp. 138–42.

25 Meyerhold's statement was included in *L'Age d'Or ('Texte–Programme')*, op. cit., p. 27, as

part of a section entitled 'Encouragements': a collection of citations from Jacques Copeau, Henri Michaux (on Chinese theatre) and Meyerhold himself.

26 For an anlaysis of the relationship between the comic physicalities/gestural vocabularies of the performers in *L'Age d'Or* and comic strips and cartoons, see Katherina Thomadaki's essay in Bernard Dort and Anne Ubersfeld (eds), *Le texte et la scène*, Paris: Université de la Sorbonne Nouvelle III, 1978, pp. 125–35.

27 Cf. Jacques Lecoq re. masks and the still-point: '[Masks] allow one to search for the pivotal point within an action, within a conflict; allow one to find the essential, the gesture that will epitomise the many gestures of daily life, the word of all words. All that is great tends towards immobility (immobility is also a gesture).' Quoted in Bari Rolfe, 'Magic century of French mime', *Mime, Mask and Marionette* 1, 1978, p. 153.

28 Demosthème, created by Jean-Claude Bourbault, was just one of a range of characters that ultimately were not included in this 'first draft' of *L'Age d'Or*.

29 '*Les évidences*', a recurrent term in the Soleil's working vocabulary, refers to things that are clear to all, legible, indisputable, 'objectively' self-evident or obvious. In rehearsal, it is used as the ultimate sanction in determining what works *for the group*, thereby (somewhat) obviating the imposition of uni-vocal, centralised decisions. In general in this volume, '*une évidence*' has been translated as 'something self-evident', or 'a self-evidence'.

30 Philippe Caubère left the Théâtre du Soleil in 1978, after his production of *Dom Juan* at the Cartoucherie. Since then, Caubère has remained in the paradoxical situation of both rejecting and clinging on to his apprenticeship in the Théâtre du Soleil; over the past fifteen years, he has developed a series of one-man performances, collectively entitled *Ariane, ou l'age d'or*, in which he recounts his memories of the way the company worked and developed during his period of involvement. For a critical reflection on his years with the Soleil, see Philippe Caubère, 'De la vie collective au one-man show', *Acteurs* 8, April 1982, pp. 48–51; and Philippe Caubère and Jean-Claude Penchenat, 'Les rescapés du Soleil', *Autrement* 70, May 1985.

CHAPTER 3
AN APPRENTICESHIP WITH SHAKESPEARE
Richard II
(1981)

Shakespeare takes me back to a culture from which I have been freed – or of which I'm deprived [. . .] The theatre must reflect the image of the other, far off in time and space.
Ariane Mnouchkine[1]

What [. . .] of our delight in comparisons, in distance, in dissimilarity – which is at the same time a delight in what is close and proper to ourselves?
Bertolt Brecht[2]

What interests me in Asian theatre is that actors are creators of metaphors. Their art consists of showing passions, recounting the interiority of human beings [. . .] the actors' aim is to open up human beings, like a pomegranate. Not to display their guts, but to depict what is internal and transform it into signs, shapes, movements, rhythms.
Ariane Mnouchkine[3]

3.1 PERFORMANCE AS AUTOPSY

The Théâtre du Soleil

The programme notes accompanying the first play in the proposed Shakespeare cycle located the pedagogic nature of this project in terms of the company's development. Mnouchkine believed that Shakespeare proposed a dramaturgical model for representing history. Paradoxically, the way forward into contemporary history seemed to be to go back to the Renaissance – a reculer pour mieux sauter. *These notes (in which the company displays its relish for metaphor) also touch on parallels perceived in classical Japanese performance forms, and on the notion of acting as 'autopsy'; what at first sounds like the positivist discourse of Zola's naturalism becomes a metaphor for both spatialising interiority and for the heightened ('meta-physical') state of being palpably 'in the present'.*

Six plays by Shakespeare: four historical tragedies (*Richard II*, the two parts of *Henry IV, Henry V*) and two comedies (*Twelfth Night, Love's Labour's Lost*).[4] We're embarking on this cycle rather in the way that one embarks on an apprenticeship with a master craftsman, hoping to learn how to perform the world in a theatre. We are consulting Shakespeare now as preparation for us to be able to tell a contemporary story in a future production, for Shakespeare is an expert who knows the tools that are most apt and fitting for narratives of the passions and destinies of human beings.

The historical tragedies tell us 'the sad stories of the death of kings, how some have been deposed, others killed in battle, others haunted by the spectres of those they had deposed' (*Richard II*), and so many other things . . . *Richard II* is the first chapter in this chronicle of a tribe of characters who struggle to construct the world, as they cling to their savage, tormented island, which is still almost deserted (at the end of the 14th century, the Britain of Richard II had about three million inhabitants).

For every one of these adventurers, 'this royal throne of kings, this sceptred isle, this earth of majesty, this seat of Mars, this other Eden, demi-paradise' (*Richard II*) is the image of the world. And when they discover and recount their internal landscapes, they become the universe for themselves.

Each of them sings of the terrible storms they see rumbling around and within them. They look closely at themselves, analyse themselves: they give breath to a flood of images – raw, sumptuous, bloody, extreme – at every moment bringing their destiny and their mortality to the surface, as in a vivisection of the soul. Confronted with this text, we have worked from word to word, as if we were at the foot of a mountain, attentive to each word pronounced by these great visionary primitives, trying to see what they see, in order for us in turn to be able to show it, to place it in space, in bright light.

The example of Asian theatre, in particular Japanese theatre, imposed itself upon us as indispensable, with its stories peopled with great warriors, nobles, princes and kings. In its discipline, this theatre sweeps away the clichés that come to us so easily when we try to represent the heroes of the medieval Western world, and reminds us that one needs 'an unshakeable, firmly drawn contour to circumscribe great upheavals' (Alain).

The reference to this great traditional form (Noh, Kabuki, Bunraku) establishes the working rules: gestural precision, clarity of line, bringing an extreme truth and an extreme artifice together in a performance style that one might call hyper-realist. With their bodies, the actors must draw the portrait and the actions of a hero, with clearly marked lines, without blurring or half-tones. With the drive and self-control of a draughtsman led on by his hand, and who still hears the pen's nib scratching the paper. Like a surgeon who is cold and impassioned at the same time, the actor's task is to present the public anatomy of a soul; it is to be and to display one of those cruel, instructive and beautiful paintings that were called *écorchés*.[5]

Dullin once exclaimed: 'It isn't the machine for bringing the Gods down onto the stage that we need, it's the Gods themselves!'[6] We believe that this arrogant and intimidating demand calls on us to attempt, for the public good, the autopsy of man, this operation which, like the art of the actor, is sacrilegious and was long cursed. The word 'autopsy' originally meant 'an inspection, a careful examination made by oneself'; but also 'a state in which ancient pagans believed they had intimate dealings with the gods, and a sort of participation in their omnipotence' (Littré).

From the Théâtre du Soleil's published programme
notes for the production of *Richard II*, 1981.

3.2 SHAKESPEARE'S SAMURAI

Colette Godard

These 'English cavaliers' wear wide, dark skirts shot through with reflective brocade, which swirl around speckled felt leggings. Embroidered head-dresses frame faces, some masked, some painted white. Beneath Tudor ruffs, doublets are criss-crossed with obis and the flapping scarves of kimonos draped over shoulders; they resemble glittering scarabs. Cousins to the samurai in *Kagemusha*, these theatrical warriors flank their young king Richard, enveloped in the white drapes of his robes like a tiny bird.

Ariane Mnouchkine takes us into a mythic land which is neither Japanese nor British, a timeless world which links Shakespeare to the Théâtre du Soleil. The surfaces of a vast Kabuki-style stage are covered in black-banded coconut matting; this central space is flanked by long runways, along which actors enter in cavalcades. The rough-cast walls of the theatre look as though they have been brushed with flaking gilding.

With their backs to a shimmering curtain of fluid silk in gold spattered with blood-red, the actors stop face to face with the audience, knees flexed, elbows turned out, hands ceremoniously spread. With their heads held erect, almost never looking at each other, hardly moving, they project their lines directly at the audience, articulating each syllable in a sustained, sonorous delivery punctuated by Jean-Jacques Lemêtre's percussive score. The words come across with incredible clarity, like music drawn in the air, and the story kicks into gear – an inexorable sequence of events, moving straight forward, dragging these men who are striving to fashion a new country. Their lives and deaths are played out in a universe devoid of compassion. But pleasure, anguish and love too have their place in this violent world, which teems with every kind of desire, acknowledged and gratified shamelessly.

This 'sad story of the death of kings' emerges as clear as a folk-tale from the morass of terrible detail. It's as if these weren't characters, but bodies traversed by a single voice whose tonality shifts according to what it recounts. The performers make a whole. The scenic writing obliges us to leave our habits to one side. There is nothing here to distract us from the text and its complex jostle of murder, treason and madness, triggered by the fiery confrontation of Richard (Georges Bigot; Plate 3.1) and Bolingbroke (Cyrille Bosc): contenders for the crown, no doubt, but first and foremost for the love of 'this blessed plot, this earth' – an arid and still savage island, a stage the colour of straw.

It doesn't help much to refer to the conventions of traditional Japanese theatre. Here the text is what is essential. Moreover, Mnouchkine hasn't attempted to reconstruct Asian forms; she doesn't want to adapt Shakespeare to the codes of

Plate 3.1 Richard II. The court, with Richard (Georges Bigot) at the centre. Photo: Martine Franck/Magnum

Noh, Kabuki or Bunraku. She borrows from them for the immediate distance they impose, which quells any temptation to naturalism. She uses them because they conflate a very Shakespearean mélange: of rough ill-formed manners, subtlety, dazzling metaphysics – a mix of crudeness and preciosity which she has foregrounded in her translation. Finally, she uses them because of their unparalleled attention to detail.

Once again, it's not a question of borrowing a vocabulary from the Japanese theatre, but of saying everything through gesture; even the naked face becomes a mask. The production is both a continuation of what the Théâtre du Soleil has done in the past and an entirely new area of work. The actors have abandoned the immediately accessible generosity of *L'Age d'Or, 1789* or *Les Clowns*; the acting is stripped and sparse, and the actors remain physically isolated from the audience, never trying to approach it.

Although much is restrained, there is no hint of coldness, thanks in part to Guy-Claude François's design materials: the warm carpeting, the blazing scarlets in the shadows and the bright white costumes, the silk drops in greys and blues with gold leaf tracing lunar horizons – silks which float down and fly away in silence. And then there is so much tenderness in the way in which death is represented in the final tableau; Bolingbroke finally dares kiss the lips of the murdered king, before laying himself out like the figure on a sarcophagus, tiny and fragile at the centre of an enormous bare carpet, as the darkness encroaches.

From Colette Godard, 'Les samouraïs de Shakespeare', in *Le Monde*, 15 December 1981. Translation by Colette Godard and David Williams.

3.3 SHAKESPEARE IS NOT OUR CONTEMPORARY
An interview with Ariane Mnouchkine
by Jean-Michel Déprats

In an interview recorded in May 1982, Ariane Mnouchkine describes the 'influence' of Asian theatre forms on Richard II. *She outlines the key technical notion of the actor's 'state' as structural principle in the metaphorising transpositions that characterise her conception of performance, before outlining her broad plans for the Shakespeare cycle as a whole. Surprisingly, for a director with a reputation for consistently prioritising the physical and the visual over the verbal, she emphasises the importance of Shakespeare's text as a site for making dynamic meaning(s).*

JEAN-MICHEL DÉPRATS: Spectators at a performance of *Richard II*, whether they are captivated or disconcerted, are confronted with a universe that is unfamiliar, ritualised and heavily theatricalised; it's a universe within which one thinks one recognises an image of medieval Japan. Many spectators attribute this reference to Japan to a desire to establish an analogy in content between the feudal Japanese world and that of Shakespeare's warriors. It seems to me that this is a misunderstanding. Isn't the core of this choice in fact the need to resort to a strong theatricality in order to deal with Shakespeare?

ARIANE MNOUCHKINE: There are several misunderstandings. First of all, there's no exclusive reference to Japan. As the basis for our work we took Asian *theatres*, Japanese theatre (Noh, Kabuki), but also Balinese theatre, Kathakali, etc. Secondly, the choice of a ritual: the play itself is a ritual. Shakespeare is not our contemporary and shouldn't be treated as such. He is far from us as our own profoundest depths are far from us.

Finally, for all theatre one needs a form. My conviction is that Shakespeare lived in an era of theatre in which it was not the theatrical form that was strong, but the architecture which encompassed the theatre and the poetic form of the text. We looked for a basis for our work in Asian theatre because that's where the very origin of theatrical form is. In the West, apart from Greek tragedy and the *commedia dell'arte*, there is no great theatrical form. Now it's true that there is also the necessity of offering images of the ritual and chivalric universe of *Richard II*, and for me, such images are much more vibrant in certain Japanese novels and films than they are in *Thierry la Fronde* or certain engravings of the *Très Riches Heures du Duc de Berry*.[7] Given that Japan left its Middle Ages much later than we did, the closest Middle Ages we have are probably Japanese.

The misunderstanding stems from those critics who have taken the Japanese reference literally. For example, some have said that the costumes are Japanese costumes. This is wrong. There is a mix of typically Elizabethan doublets, ruffs which date from a slightly earlier period, skirts of the kind one finds in certain costumes from the Middle Ages, and then over the top cloaks which, it is true, suggest kimonos.[8]

Fundamentally, it's a question of *influence*, in exactly the same way that modern painting of a particular period was invigorated by its encounter with African art. In the series of Shakespeare productions we're presenting there is an *influence* from Asian theatre. This is nothing new at the Théâtre du Soleil, where we've always conducted research with the mask. It's nothing new in the history of theatre either. With Brecht, with Meyerhold, with all theatre people who have searched for forms, there has always been an immediate voyage towards Asia, because everything is there, for music, dance, sacred art, or theatre.

D: In your production, the text is addressed to the audience throughout. Is it your personal belief that the traditional means of Western theatre, and in particular the 'fourth wall', are inadequate in representing Shakespeare?

M: Not only inadequate, deadly. In rehearsal every time the actors found themselves talking *to each other*, it didn't work. I said to them, 'Tell it *to the audience*.' It's the secret one must never lose. Having said that, it's extremely difficult for the actor. When the 'state', the passion that he must express in relation to the character, is not sufficiently clear, there's always a tendency to take refuge in a psychological relationship with one's partner on-stage. The psychological venom has been injected deep inside us – by cinema and television – and the actors have been deformed by it. But I'm convinced that Shakespeare's text was made to be spoken in this way. As soon as you begin to modulate, to refine, to make it subtle, you water it down. To their great credit, the actors understood this immediately, and found ways of tackling this difficult work during three months of rehearsal.

D: The relationship with the audience implies another corollary, in terms of how Shakespeare's text is heard. In your production, it's quite apparent that the text speaks the characters as much as the characters speak the text. It is not only the voice of the characters' interiority, but also the voice of history in its making, the voice of the world in the process of speaking itself.

M: It is above all the voice of a man in the process of understanding each one of his characters. There are both things. On one hand there is constantly the voice of this extraordinary man who seems to have absorbed everything, understood everything, transposed everything into poetry, and on the other hand there is the no less extraordinary ability Shakespeare has to speak in the voice of a character. Shakespeare is always speaking through his characters, but he is also always speaking about them. At moments Richard is only Shakespeare's Pythia,

Plate 3.2   Richard II. 'A great epic form' (Moscoso): the deposition of King Richard; to the left, Bolingbroke (Cyrille Bosc) with the crown. Photo: Martine Franck/Magnum

but he's also an incarnated character. There is this double phenomenon and in it resides a great part of the miracle of Shakespeare.

Shakespeare is nothing but compassion for his characters, and through the passions of his characters he expresses his understanding of human beings. But he nonetheless creates differentiated characters. In *Henry IV,* between Falstaff, Henry IV, Prince Hal, Poins and Peto, etc., there are the differences of races of men. But not all of these characters do have a psychology. There is not a psychology of Richard. *A fortiori,* none of the nobles have a psychology. The only characteristics of a figure such as Northumberland, for example, are the images that the actor who plays him lends him. He is devoid of psychological motivations. Above all else, these 'characters' are receptacles, for Shakespeare as for the spectators, who sometimes catch sight of themselves and sometimes discover themselves to be different. It's only because there are works of this nature that the theatre is not dead. If there had only ever been psychological-realist works, the theatre would have been swept away in ten years by cinema. Our survival consists in putting into theatre what can only exist in the theatre.

D: Certain kinds of Shakespearean productions are characterised by a simplistic determination to transform everything into gesture, scenic images. In *Richard II,* even though there is a constant and very strong theatricality, the production gives the text an autonomy. It enables images within the text to be inscribed in the spectator's imagination, and encourages a theatre of listening.

M: A theatre of listening, but which is visionary. One can't use scenery when staging Shakespeare, because a décor would be a wall for the countless individual visions of each spectator. It would block the immediate echo of the words the spectator receives, and the words provide *everything*. If you try to get a décor to perform rather than getting the actors to perform, you miss the mark. At one point I wanted to put a tree on-stage. I abandoned this idea. One can have a space, blazing lights, but nothing figurative. The words are so figurative in our souls, in what they provoke in us, that anything which encumbers the stage must be banished. The flatter the carpet is, the higher Lear's cliff will be.[9] This raises the question of the actors' training, of their commitment, of what I would call their courage in their capacity to bring the imagination into play in their work. It's a theatre of the actor-king, yes, but at what a price in terms of humility, of commitment!

D: Can we try to define the notion of the 'state' which you often use in rehearsal?

M: It's difficult. I often say to the actors: 'Let Shakespeare take care of the words, he does that very well, you're here for something else.' The actor's task is to show what situation and what *state* the character who utters the words is in. Everything comes from the words, but the words should come from what the actor has produced as *performance*. Meyerhold said: 'In our age, we should print on posters for the theatre: "The play will be read without script in hand, with scenery and costumes," but we don't have the right to print: "We will perform," because we no longer know how to perform.' I often have the feeling that people content themselves today with 'performing the words'. In our work, what we call the 'state' is the primary passion which preoccupies the actor. So when he is 'angry', he must *draw* the anger, he must *act*. Shakespeare's characters often contemplate their interior landscapes. The passion they feel must be translated by the actor. There is a chemistry. It isn't only a question of feeling, it's a question of showing. Of course one can't show what one doesn't know or what one can't imagine, but there should be a chemistry, a transformation. An actor is a person who metaphorises a feeling. On the other hand, a 'state' is never lukewarm. This doesn't mean that you can only show extreme states, but it is very difficult to show intermediary states. If one wants to show lukewarmness, that lukewarmness must be extreme. Finally, one can only show successive states, in ruptured discontinuity.

D: Nonetheless it's the images in the text that nourish the 'state'?

M: All of the images that motivate the work are to be drawn from the text. Whenever we have tried to impose images from outside, we were soon forced to abandon them and by necessity replace them with what's in the text. The images produced by Shakespeare's text aren't images all by themselves; they are a raw material for performance. What's extraordinary with Shakespeare is that this immense poet, this immense metaphysician, this immense historian transformed all his images, all his intuitions, all his thoughts into performance instruments for actors. The actor's work should be to capture these images and convey them in a decoded form. If he only conveys the word, it will not be decoded for the theatrical representation. The actor is someone who decodes signals, and communicates them through the filter of his performance. Then, and only then, do the images become emotion.

D: Does the fact that the images are raw material for performance have implications in terms of the translation?

M: I believe that one shouldn't adapt or naturalise in relation to modes of expression that are more French. One must accept and maintain the distance, as much as possible. Respect the distance not only between English and French, but also between Shakespeare's language and our modern use of language. I suppose, moreover, that English and French were much closer in Shakespeare's time than they are now.

Fundamentally, despite the difference in date, Shakespeare is no more remote from us in the use of language than . . . Chrétien de Troyes.[10]

D: In your translation, there seems to be a desire to follow the networks of images step by step, without dissecting them.

M: Because I had confidence in the actors. My task was to translate the material that Shakespeare provided for them. People who have no contact with the reality of the theatre and of actors try to make their translation sufficient in itself, forgetting that performance is the relay of the text.

D: I have a few questions on certain specific moments in the production. The caracoling entrances, the cavalcades:[11] is this a recreation of the ritual entrances in Asian theatre, or the actors' own invention?

M: The actors' own invention. In Kabuki, there are solemn formal entrances, but they are very slow and involve a single character, with stops along the raised walkway [the *hanamichi*]. For the first entrance of Richard, I wanted us to begin in the heart of the action, in the maelstrom of the conflict. The King enters, surrounded by hornets who don't touch him yet, but wait for their moment.

D: The jesters you introduced into the tournament scene [I, iii] reminded me of certain figures in Balinese *topeng*.

M: It's also a vision of the Court. I was determined to differentiate between the two long scenes at the beginning: the appearance before the King and the tournament. For the second scene, the introduction of these two characters who continually disrupt the ritual enables us to affirm it and to show it to a greater degree. We needed to establish the ritual very very quickly.

D: In the gardeners' scene [III, iv], is it out of fidelity to the Asian tradition, where popular characters are comic characters, that the form you've adopted is that of the clown?

M: No. Initially, there was an old masked man. It was quite a lovely character, but the scene lacked insolence, it remained too proper. So one day I asked Philippe Hottier to take off his mask and to play him as a clown. The scene immediately took on another dimension. It became the very voice of the theatre.

D: Will the work on the comedies also rely on a great theatrical form?

M: The rehearsals for *La Nuit des Rois* [*Twelfth Night*] are progressing very slowly, because we're not really relying on any existing form of theatre. In order to work on this play, there's no equivalent to the Japanese theatre forms which, it should be said, are regal forms. We will have to invent still more, as the sources of inspiration are more fragile, more internal. The relation to the sacred is also not at all the same. For *Richard II*, we decided that the characters were men-gods. The characters in *La Nuit des Rois* are more like polychrome gods, wooden idols or terracotta divinities. They're little carnival gods.

D: Why the choice of two comedies and history plays?

M: So as to have both worlds: the world of love, of desire, with the comedies, and the world of history, of power, which is to say, the world of men, with the histories. *Richard II* and *Henry IV* rather than *Hamlet* or *King Lear* (neither of which I feel ready for) because of the relation to History, which has always been one of the unwavering interests of the Théâtre du Soleil.

D: Do you really believe that this journey in Shakespeare has a preliminary instructive value for writing about today?

M: Perhaps not for writing, but for remembering certain laws of construction, how Shakespeare never beats about the bush, which we never have the courage to attempt. Also that way of writing from the interior of the characters, without imposing an ideology. He is wholly within each of his characters, who are all his messengers; yet each character remains a whole person.

From Jean-Michel Déprats, 'Le besoin d'une forme: entretien avec
Ariane Mnouchkine', in *Théâtre/Public* 46–7, July–October, 1982.

3.4 OF LOSS AND LIBERATION
From an interview with Ariane Mnouchkine
by Alfred Simon

In an interview conducted after the opening of Richard II, *Mnouchkine locates the production as a development of the practices of collective creation, engendered in the wake of her own difficulties as the writer of a contemporary history play, and of an enforced renewal of the company with the addition of a new generation of younger performers. Through a conception of Shakespeare as 'metaphysical alchemist', that is related to Peter Brook's notion of 'holy theatre', she articulates the mysterious psycho-physical connections and reverberations the production seemed to her to trigger in contemporary spectators.*

Alfred Simon: In the eyes of the public, the last ten years of the Théâtre du Soleil – with its great trilogy of collaborative work, *1789, 1793, L'Age d'Or* – have been about collective creation. Then suddenly Shakespeare, six Shakespeares in a row, which requires a mobilisation of two years at least – what does this mean? Is this the end of collective creation at the Soleil?

Ariane Mnouchkine: What you're talking about concerns only collective creation in writing, because *Richard II* is one of the productions we have worked on most collectively. This postulate of collective work was adopted right from the beginning, and has stimulated everyone. In terms of the staging, the actors' input has been just as important as in the other productions. It's something you must understand clearly. In the past, the collective writing occurred on stage; we have never written a play as a group. The only written play was *Méphisto*, for which I was responsible. This did not prevent a degree of collective work, although it was too limited in my opinion. But in the Shakespeares, we have gone very far in the direction of collective creation. Since the beginning of the Théâtre du Soleil, this is the first time that actors are actually fabricating the things they use, that they are truly working with technicians, who are really in charge of overseeing the projects. This [aspect of collective creation] had been lost to some extent, it cannot be denied.

As far as collective writing is concerned, the fact that we have decided to stage the Shakespeares in no way means that we have abandoned the idea of inventing our own productions. It's what we have done for the past ten years, thirteen years. After thirteen years we wanted – let's say I wanted – to reread Shakespeare, faced with a certain writing difficulty I had encountered in creating wholly contemporary characters (that is, after all, the aim of our work: to manage one day to tell the story of our times). And all of a sudden I thought, 'we need to go back to school.' As a director, I ended up wondering whether I still knew how to direct. With the Shakespeares, I wanted once again to be stuck with a real director's production.

So I wanted to go back to school: myself, as a director, as a writer, the actors, everyone, especially the new members of the company, we needed a school that would be immense and that would surpass us. To put the bar at a very high level, to fix a goal which, in any case, we would never be able to attain fully. And the demands of this goal, its somewhat megalomaniac quality, has provided all of the young actors who had joined us, as well as the older ones, with a will, a desire, an appetite to surpass themselves.

All sorts of things come together in this decision. First, a love for Shakespeare, Shakespeare who is the source of everything. Then there was the pleasure of staging Shakespeare. And finally this moment for the company, which was like a second birth for the Théâtre du Soleil. At a certain moment there were many departures, which I took very badly, and which I'm only just beginning to digest. There were two choices: either these departures would bring about the dissolution of the company, which seems to have been the opinion of those who left, or there would be a new encounter, new attachments, new loves. I chose the second alternative and the others followed.

S: The renewal of the company was a bit hard for you . . .

M: What was difficult was the end of the relationship with those who were here.

S: Was this a crisis for the Théâtre du Soleil?

M: Yes, I think so. Well before *Méphisto*, [Jean-Claude] Penchenat left. Subsequent departures involved people who had joined us more recently. We could perform *Méphisto* with the resources we had, but not Shakespeare. Ultimately the project was to not be able to produce with the resources we had, so as to necessitate a renewal.

S: If one looks at what the people who have left the Théâtre du Soleil are doing, one has the impression that they attempt to continue on the path of collective creation, of improvisation, both for the large-scale works like *Le Bal* by Jean-Claude Penchenat and for the solo actors' numbers like Philippe Caubère who, in the end, simply adds a sketch to *L'Age d'Or*. So those people carry in themselves nostalgia for the Théâtre du Soleil and for collective creation from which you have taken a certain distance, at least in the form in which you have practised it for the last few years. In any case, what is marvellous in this Shakespeare is that it is collective. [. . .]

M: What Georges Bigot has contributed as the King, or Maurice Durozier as Northumberland, or Odile Cointepas as the Queen, or Philippe Hottier as the

Duke of York, is entirely comparable in richness and theatrical contribution to our earlier productions. If it hadn't been, we would never have succeeded. Alone, as a director, I don't claim for a moment to be capable of producing six Shakespeares in a year and a half. One needs actors on-stage who are full of images and rich in experiences, in many experiences.

S: And *Molière* was already at a distance from collective creation and the theatre you had practised. And above all there was this important thing: you became an author on that occasion. Since *Molière* and *Méphisto*, you have confronted the problem of writing, and the fact that you translated *Richard II* shows that you will not be able to elude it.

M: I will not be able to elude it, but I direct a company and the company cannot wait on my author's moods. I am well aware of this. We were unemployed, for financial reasons, and I did not want the period of unemployment for the company to extend beyond the period absolutely necessary. At a particular moment I understood that we would start again, but that I would not write a show. I don't think a theatre company should be entirely devoted to the works or attempted works of a single member of the company. I had a moment of anxiety for two months, realising that I was not moving forward in my project. And that's when I thought of the Shakespeare plays, which I first thought of using as study exercises and which have become the object of a production. After all, even Molière staged other people's plays when he wasn't staging his own. This is perhaps the one area in which one matures, a flexibility that wasn't there before. I could have insisted obstinately on doing a contemporary project, made the actors wait, left them on unemployment for six months, in panic, and spent a year preparing this production. We would then have found ourselves in a situation we came close to with *L'Age d'Or*, paralysed by the attempt to create a production on something that surpasses us, whose difficulty is beyond our resources.

S: Without a framework, without a central idea?

M: I disown none of *L'Age d'Or*, but it's true that at that moment, rather than being collective, *L'Age d'Or* had individualised the creation of each actor to an extreme point, to become something that for certain people was a form of hamming.

S: But there was no risk of that in the project you evoked [on contemporary history]: it was something enormous, the death of cultures, the death of history . . .

M: But I think the work on the Shakespeares will lead us back to this. The group needed to be better equipped to tackle that old project, which I haven't abandoned.[12]

S: I'd like to develop this question of the text a little, not by suggesting deceitfully that the return to Shakespeare is the return to texts, which is to say that the Théâtre du Soleil had finally understood that one can't do theatre without texts. I'm thinking instead of a phrase that a newspaper accredited to you where you spoke of 'the extraordinary chemistry by which an actor transforms a text into body and gestures'.

M: What I said was that the theatre is metaphor, metaphor of gesture, of the word, and that what's beautiful in theatre is when an actor transforms a feeling, a memory, a state or a passion. No one sees pure passion unless the actor transforms it into performance, that is to say into a sign, into a gesture. I quoted Pavese's phrase: 'Poetry began when an imbecile said of the sea that it looked like oil.' It's true that theatre begins when you say of an actor it looks like he's dying, but he's not really dying, it looks like he's walking, but he isn't walking. Because if he walked in life as he does on-stage, it would look like he's dawdling.

S: I would even say that theatre is corporeal, gestural alchemy, in the same way that, for Rimbaud, poetry was verbal alchemy.

M: With Shakespeare, it's both. In our work, we could never have that ambition. When people asked us: why don't you put on plays? I always responded that for the time being, our ambitions lay elsewhere. If you're working on a master-piece, you can make a reasonably accomplished production. But if you're trying to write the theatre of our times, you know you'll never succeed. [. . .]

S: The people who asked you why you didn't stage plays no longer ask the question, because a Shakespeare like yours is unimaginable in a company that hasn't done the kind of work you have done for the last ten years [. . .] One day [. . .] you said, 'if I were really sure that theatre cannot represent the world, I'd give everything up and I'd go raise sheep in the Ardèche.'

M: I don't remember that and I think it's not only to represent the world that one does theatre. With Shakespeare, this has become a bit more clear. Shakespeare doesn't only represent the world, he adds something to the world – he adds *himself* . . .

S: It's like Picasso's phrase: 'The tree exists, but so does my painting.'

M: Or even Malraux's, when he said: 'The artist doesn't copy nature, he rivals it.' In Shakespeare, that's precisely what you're confronted with. He participates in the world, but he also practises metaphysical alchemy, he transforms the vision of evil into a lesson in good.

S: You talked somewhere about modern art's complacency towards failure and death.[13]

M: More in relation to stage directors than creators. I think that at this moment there's quite a bit of floundering in the dark, the shadows, renunciation, collective suicide.

Whereas in Shakespeare, the death of Richard is a moment of the love of man such as I have rarely felt.

S: Do you think Bolingbroke loves Richard at that moment? Do you think that he's sincere?

M: When he takes him in his arms?

S: You wanted that *pietà*?

M: Yes. I think he loves him, that he loves the impossible; he would like to reconcile power and purity. And I think that a man who puts the act of murder in the hands of a madman [Exton] who believed, who read Bolingbroke's unconscious, and makes himself into its instrument – this is more than representing the world, or representing it to such a degree of depth, it is opening it up.

For me today, the idea of theatre as mirror is insufficient. That's what it was for a while, but in the present time that is no longer enough. I think the aspect of surgery, autopsy, the opening of a man, is what is most important. If you open man, this is what it gives, our Shakespeares. At this point it's more than a mirror. The mirror is to say to man: 'Look at yourself, how ugly you are.' But theatre can also say to him: 'Look at yourself, how beautiful you are'; or else: 'Look a bit at the other person that you don't know at all, those who come from the antipodes of time or of space, or of the spirit; look at how he is, he concerns you.' The other evening I was haunted by this idea: the spectators come in, what the hell has this got to do with them? This medieval King in England, performed by people drawing on an Asian theatre form? What will the difference of all of this [from their own lives] do for them? Well, it was not the difference that came into play, but the resemblance. [. . .]

When you're producing *Richard II*, if you arrive with all sorts of aprioristic assumptions about the play in your suitcase, either you quickly leave them at the cloakroom, or you ruin the play and reduce it to your own dimension, whereas it's in Shakespeare's dimensions. So I don't think I had any other choice with *Richard*. But the fact that I chose *Richard* means that there is also the other movement, which is to say that I wanted to confront myself, to confront us with a more metaphysical play, less 'lowbrow', without necessarily renouncing anything – neither *L'Age d'Or*, nor *Méphisto*. There were things in *Méphisto* we haven't managed to surpass, and which I would like to surpass in future productions. And we're spending time with Shakespeare precisely because we want to get a glimpse of someone who knows how to do things, and to see what we could draw from it. [. . .]

I think that the theatre is a place of experimentation for many things. I sense only that it cannot, that it should not be the place of one single experimentation per production: I sense now that I will no longer satisfy myself with a production that's only political, or only one thing or another. I don't think we have ever been satisfied with a single dimension at the Théâtre du Soleil [. . .]

S: But is it possible to perform at the same time the individual and his passions, society and history, the cosmos and the divine? In *Richard II*, through the mediation of Kabuki, haven't you in fact swung completely over to the other extreme, to the cosmic aspect? For my own part, I think that this play's primary dimension is liturgical.

M: Perhaps we have swung a bit, but it was voluntary. Having said that, there are people who think the opposite, that we've remained too much at the level of history, which was not our intention at all. I even stopped my historical research into the period very quickly. But I do think that, within the spectators, there are some archaic fibres that react to this play, something ancestral. Because I'm astonished all the same when very young girls or boys come and see me at the end, with tears in their eyes, to tell me it is extraordinary. What is it that they have in common with this play?

It's a bit like a dog who turns in circles before lying down, because ten thousand years ago he turned in circles to flatten out leaves. It's my impression with this play that there is something from which people have been liberated, but also something that they've lost. [. . .] In relation to this play, I think an audience of 1981 resonates with things, reacts to things that they no longer know normally, consciously. So if one looks from a certain historical point of view, one can say that they have been liberated from them, but one can also say that they no longer know them and have lost them. For me there is a dimension of loss and of liberation in the feelings this play stirs. Perhaps that is the contradiction of the sacred. I have the impression that spectators react to this production with organs inside them that are like the gills of some bygone age.

From Alfred Simon, 'Les dieux qu'il nous faut: entretien avec
Ariane Mnouchkine', in *Acteurs* no. 2, February, 1982.

3.5 SHAKESPEARE IS A MASKED TEXT
From an interview with Georges Bigot and Philippe Hottier by Jean-Michel Déprats

> There's a link, a reverberation between inner and
> outer space [. . .] I indicate passions in space.
> Jacques Lecoq[14]

In the following interview, two of the Soleil's core performers in the Shakespeare cycle reflect on the genesis of the codified gestural vocabulary used in the production of Richard II. *They discuss the work's relations to Asian theatre forms, and describe the central generative notion of the performer's 'state'. The work of both of these performers (as of others at the Soleil at that time) might be characterised in terms of the* generosity of their expenditure of energy – of the 'gift', in *Hélène Cixous's sense,[15] that they made of live performance.*

JEAN-MICHEL DÉPRATS: How did the rehearsals for *Richard II* start? With the search for a codified and ritualistic theatre form, inspired by Japanese theatre? Through preliminary work on documentation relating to Kabuki, Noh and Balinese theatre?

PHILIPPE HOTTIER: When the work begins, Ariane deliberately does not give details of her intentions because she worries that actors will imagine less if she talks too much. For *L'Age d'Or*, she simply told us, 'Once upon a time in China, three thousand years ago . . .' Here, she simply said, 'These are samurai.'

GEORGES BIGOT: She didn't say that. She provided us with images of that world. Much later on, we watched two films, one on Kabuki and another on Noh and Bunraku, but not at the beginning. At the beginning, our primary concern was to work on the characters. Our starting point was in a vision of our Middle Ages, but we soon lapsed into the imagery of Ivanhoe or Thierry la Fronde. Personally, I very quickly felt the need to tranpose with my body and my voice, intuitively taking as my inspiration whatever I knew about the *commedia dell'arte* or Japanese theatre.

H: What guided work on the characters was the notion of the breath of the story. There is the movement of wars and conflicts, and the characters themselves are the storytellers of their own passions. They speak all that they feel. They reveal their inner landscape and articulate it in a poetic form, for these are things one can't articulate in a rational way. The character is the narrator of the movements of his soul. Shakespeare reveals the character's interiority straight away.

For me, Shakespeare is a masked text. It's a text that says everything, just as a mask says everything when one knows how to use it. I understood this when I abandoned the techniques of *L'Age d'Or* in order to focus myself on the text, to really take it on board, to enter into the flood of words. Little by little, the character's gestures were elaborated. But I often felt I was telling the story only with my mouth. This is where the search for the character's *state* intervenes.

D: This term is part of your working vocabulary. Can you define it?

H: There are two things: the character's base state, and then the successive states he traverses. I would say that the base state is the attitude to life. Arlequin doesn't have the same base state as Pantalon. An actor will only begin to animate the character of Arlequin when he's found Arlequin's attitude to life – his perpetual jumps in perception, the state of curiosity and alertness that characterises him. Once this base state has been found, he will inhabit it successively in joy, anger, aggression, etc. The base state is modified through the secondary states.

Moreover, this particular mental state in which a character finds himself has a form. There are thousands of different kinds of anger. One speaks of veiled, violent, repressed angers. This vocabulary describes a movement of anger. So the actor has to show this internalised movement of the feeling, of the passion that occupies the character, he must draw it out in space and in gesture. The movements the actor makes, the quality of his voice, will show what kind of anger it is. Every word he utters will be suffused with the particular electricity that is the character's state at any given moment. What allows the state to be defined is obviously the words he says or the situation in which he finds himself.

B: You must take the character's passion absolutely literally. When he says, 'I'm in pain', you must show this suffering in a total fashion. If you were working in a psychological manner, you would play the sub-text: 'I'm in pain but I don't show it, I resist the internal suffering.' In psychological performance, you also look for a gradation: 'I'm beginning to feel pain, I'm in increasing pain . . .', whereas in Shakespeare, there are distinct successive states, in discontinuity: 'I feel pain/I no longer feel pain.' In order to be able to transpose this succession of strong states, of primary passions, one cannot remain in a register that's psychological, everyday, naturalistic.

D: At the beginning of the interview, Georges, you seemed to disagree when I talked of a 'ritualistic and codified form' to qualify your gestural work and your diction.

B: Because this form, this transposition of the ritual of the play, wasn't derived from a pre-existing theatrical language. We created it entirely. Each movement, each gesture was invented by the actors.

D: Nonetheless there's a code, a core vocabulary for the ritual: the caracoling entrances, the bent leg positions, the hands on the thighs, facing the audience. This isn't a naturalistic gestural practice.

H: That position is a transposition of deified man, of God-man. The King and those in power in the kingdom constitute a sort of Olympus, with a Richard II–Jupiter, a York–Chronos. There is a ritual and a code, even if this code was invented by us. I'd like to come back to the genesis of the theatrical language we created. We invented our costumes, our gestural forms, our characters, taking as our point of departure the idea one can get of Japanese theatre, much more than its real forms. In the course of the rehearsals, in the breaks, we played around together with martial arts. I have no knowledge of martial arts; but, starting from an intuitive vision of what martial arts could be, I understood that the characters of *Richard II* were kinds of combatants of the mind and of the body, that they were animated by warrior attitudes, both with regard to others and with regard to themselves. But these warrior attitudes are *within* them.

D: Georges, how do you see the evolution of your character?

B: For me, the narrative dimension is always present. At the beginning, Richard, the storyteller Richard, talks about his own political, regal and divine dimensions. Then the character becomes embroiled in a conflict, he loses his royalty, and finds himself confronting his suffering, his anguish as a human being. The storyteller Richard then talks about what a naked man is, and perhaps of what man stripped of his divinity is. The beginning of the performance is steeped in ritual; then the staging and the form evolve with the text. Gestures and physical attitudes leave hieratism behind, and produce a more carnal and sensitive transposition. But it's always a narrative.

D: What about you, Philippe, how do you see York? As an opportunist? Or as someone with a sense of the State, of the continuity of public service?

H: He's a rather complex character. With the exception of Richard, he's the most described character in the play. He's one of the only figures with a 'character'. I think he's sincerely respectful of traditions, of the status of those with power in the kingdom, and of the dignity and function of the monarchy. He is very attached to Richard, on a personal level, not only to his function. But it's true that he has a realist, opportunistic, I would even say hypocritical, side to him. When he notices that the flux of history flows in the other direction, he goes with the current. There's one phrase that summarises him admirably for me: it's when he says 'irremediable things are indifferent to me.'[16] Part of his function is as concrete reality in this play. Furthermore, he's a pivotal character. He has the role of mediator between adversaries in the play, and he also has that function of mediation in the relationship between the stage and the audience. He often calls the audience to witness. [. . .]

D: The music is an integral part of the production, and it plays an essential role. Did you start working with the percussion straight away?

B: The music didn't arise immediately, but it was introduced fairly quickly when we worked on the entrances. When a new character arrives, he presents himself to the audience. In order to make these entrances, we needed a rhythmic support. Then the musician looked for different sounds for each character, just as we looked for different colours for our costumes. The performance state implies an internal rhythm, a music that Jean-Jacques [Lemêtre] tried to transcribe. In general, when an actor entered with the right state, the music was right. This musical support helped the actor to perceive his own rhythm.

The role of the music became more important once the characters had been found, and we had begun the vocal work of transposing the text. In any case, from the beginning the relationship between music and acting was one of simultaneous invention and mutual influence.

From Jean-Michel Déprats, 'Un texte masqué',
Théâtre/Public 46–7, July–October, 1982.

3.6 THE ENTIRE BODY IS A MASK
From an interview with Ariane Mnouchkine
by Odette Aslan

In these comments recorded in December 1982 after the production of Richard II, *Ariane Mnouchkine locates mask work as the cornerstone of the Théâtre du Soleil performers' preparation – even for roles in which the mask itself is ultimately abandoned in performance. In terms of its formal, physical and emotional imperatives, mask work remains the one constant in the training of the actors, crystallising the recurrent ideals of legibility and presence in an inhabited 'state'.*

[In 1975] I said that the mask is our *core discipline*, because it's a form, and all forms constrain one to a discipline. An actor produces a kind of writing in the air, he writes with his body, he is a writer in space. Now, no content can be expressed without form. Many different forms exist, but in order to obtain some of them, there is perhaps only one discipline. I believe that theatre is a back-and-forth between what exists at the deepest, least known levels inside us and its projection, its maximal externalisation towards an audience. The mask requires precisely this maximal internalisation and externalisation.

A certain type of cinema and television has made us accustomed to the 'psychological', to 'realism', to the opposite of a form, thus to the opposite of art. Actors are placed in a setting, but the stage no longer really belongs to them. Whereas with the mask, they create their universe at every moment [. . .]

At the Théâtre du Soleil, we have worked extensively with expressive masks; for us, mask work constitutes the *essential training* of the actor. As soon as an actor 'finds' his mask, he is close to possession, he can let himself be possessed by the character, like oracles. Some of them are literally stifled by it, are without voice, without eyes, without body, annihilated by the mask. The others cross through, and this crossing is painful. They are asked to be 'visionaries', to give flesh to poems, images, visions. They have to take into account the external world – within which the play and the performance take place – and their internal world, that of their character. It is an exhausting task, which leaves neither their bodies nor their souls intact; an athletic task, for the body, the imagination, the heart and the senses.

The task is even tougher for the actresses. Men have more physical strength, and are accustomed to using their bodies, to climbing, jumping, falling; women are still conditioned by the corsets that were worn by many generations, a bit like

Chinese women whose feet were bound for a long time. All of this evolves quickly, and certain actresses succeed very well under the mask, but at the beginning they confront and overcome more difficulties than the men.

A masked character is in a permanent state of *crisis*, whether it's dramatic or comic. Nevertheless the actor can operate with non-masked partners who have a more discreet, more attenuated acting style. If this same actor performs without a mask in the next production, initially he will overstress the relation to the audience, but this tendency will decrease after a few days. For a masked actor, the relation to an audience is essentially frontal. A writer like Shakespeare, moreover, makes his characters speak to the audience. If we were to stage a Chekhov play, we would use the discipline of mask work differently, but it would still exist. The carnival masks we used in the film *Molière* were completely different. Carnival is a transgression, it carries a germ of provocation, but it must conserve a minimum of ritual and order; if it goes past the limits, it disappears. In a city, a village, it is important that the people come together, that they spend a year redoing the masks from generation to generation and prepare themselves long in advance for this day of transgression. For the actors, the mask is on another plane, within a form of communication.

In theatre, the entire body is a mask. Whatever the production we're staging, from the very beginning we always rehearse with elements of costumes put together by the actors, with whatever they find in our wardrobe stock. Ideas come to them, from performance, from the inner character; sometimes they find things that would not occur to a designer working with models. Subsequently Jean-Claude Barriera and Nathalie Thomas establish harmonies and volumes, affirming the lines traced out by the actors.

One cannot say that the fact of wearing a mask entails a particular rhythm. It is the masked character who acquires his own internal rhythm, which is susceptible to variations according to the state or emotion. Neither can one say that wearing a mask imposes any particular head or neck movement. One constructs the masked character overall, and then decides on the way he will express himself in particular situations. To perform anger, for example, will he only require one hand to tremble, keeping the rest of the body impassive? Will he make an enormous leap, a sudden convulsion of the entire body? Will he only emit a powerful breath, or will he strike a terrible blow? He can show anger in a thousand different ways. He can move nothing but the tip of his little finger. It is up to him to choose what will be most effective, both for the production and for himself, to know where to direct his energy, emotion, passion.

Since the hinged masks Erhard Stiefel created for *Richard II*, we have become very fond of wood: paradoxically, this material seems closer to flesh than leather – perhaps because it's furthest away. Stiefel had to avoid any resonance or alteration of the voice. If there is vocal modification, it must stem from the actor, not the mask. We will use masks in our next Shakespeare production, the two parts of *Henry IV*, in which two worlds meet: that of the Court, entirely hieratic and ritualistic, and that of the people. But undoubtedly we will have the feeling once more that we are starting again from zero. We never see ourselves as making use of some acquired knowledge in the domain of mask work. The greatest knowledge one can acquire is to know that there isn't any.

From 'Le masque, une discipline de base au Théâtre du Soleil',
in Odette Aslan and Denis Bablet (eds),
Le Masque: du rite au théâtre, Paris: CNRS, 1985.

3.7 REINVENTING A TRUE MUSIC FOR THEATRE
From an interview with Jean-Jacques Lemêtre
by the editors of *Fruits*

> Music is primitive because it's created manually and corporeally,
> with the same instruments as the actors: body and breath.
> Sophie Moscoso[17]

Virtuoso multi-instrumentalist Jean-Jacques Lemêtre first worked with the company on
Méphisto. *Since then, his eclectic musical sensibility and inventiveness have assumed a central
role both in elaborating productions and in performance itself. In this interview about his work on
the Shakespeare cycle, recorded in February 1984, he describes the creation of instruments, the
composition and notation of music, and the organic interrelations of actor and musician, of score
and improvisation.*

JEAN-JACQUES LEMÊTRE: One day we amused ourselves by counting the
instruments. There are 310 of them for the three productions, including the
little contraptions that are used once to make: 'pouet, pouet', 'king, king',
'crac'. And they must come from 37 different countries. There are Asian
instruments, African ones, French ones, European ones, some from the Middle
Ages, the Renaissance, modern ones . . . We even amused ourselves by making
a copy of a Greek lyre from the 4th century BC, using a metal bowl, a goat's
skin and some broom handles.

FRUITS: Are the instruments you create copies of instruments that exist or have
existed, rather than ones you invent?

L: It depends. It entirely corresponds to the form of work here. When an actor
comes on-stage, I have various elements at my disposal: my reading of
Shakespeare, what I hear from Ariane, what she says to the actor, what I
make of that, what I've read in the text, the ideas I have, the atmosphere of
the scene, what the actors provide me through their characters, the specific
situation of the characters in the scene we're working on. My first job is to try to
hear the timbre internally. From there, either it's the timbre of an instrument
that already exists, and I figure out how to get it or order it, or else I have to
construct it. And all of the instruments we've made have been invented, except
for a few drums (you invent nothing in a drum: it's a resonance chamber with a
stretched skin and cords). Although it's not pure invention; the principle already
exists, but it hasn't necessarily been made before.

The first analysis I do is an acoustical, technological analysis of the instrument. In other words: it's made in this way, so it works in this way, with strings, a skin, it is struck, scraped, with the fingers, with a plectrum. From there, I'm able to play instruments whose technique I'm not familiar with at all, and I don't care, because my goal isn't to make 'Oriental' music.

F: Do you do this in consultation with the actors?

L: No. Sometimes an actor comes to tell you 'I enter in this way and I want this music', but that never works; because at this level, everyone has their own work. An actor comes to the theatre to do theatre, and I come to make music for theatre. These are totally different notions. I support the actors, I help them, I am the support for the text.

F: If one follows the music and the performance, one gets the impression that you're a sort of conductor.

L: Yes, but I am both the conductor and the student. They [the actors] are the ones who provide me with the tempo of the scene. For example, in *Richard II* there is a clear difference between gestural and vocal elements. There are instruments for entrances and exits, instruments which correspond to particular characters. In *La Nuit des Rois*, since these are structured as themes, you follow it right away; the advantage of a theme is that we can play it before the actor arrives. Which means that after a while the audience knows very well who is going to enter on-stage. Whereas in *Richard II*, the character makes his entrance with the music, never before. Subsequently the music changes, because it performs his speech. In *Richard II*, the music is the punctuation of the text. In effect, I replace the commas, the full stops, the question marks, and I am a support for words like 'Richard' or 'England', the principal words in the text. Whereas in *La Nuit des Rois*, I create the atmosphere: the garden, the moments of anguish. In *Henry IV*, it's something else again. *Richard II* is rhythmic, *La Nuit des Rois* melodic, and *Henry IV* is both. In fact we are recreating the actual development of music: *Richard* is rhythmic in its primitive state; subsequently, just like the evolution of music, there are melodies, voices . . .

In any case I am never a soloist, I am always counterpoint, counter-melody, harmony . . .

F: Except when you sing in *La Nuit des Rois*.

L: When I sing the Prince's theme, to me it's no different from an instrument. For me, the voice is a musical instrument. But I don't use my voice like a traditional opera singer; I use it because after having tried all the instruments, I found the voice to be the best.

F: Doesn't the music function as the essential reference point for the actor?

L: Yes, of course; on that level, music possesses much greater power than any actor. I can indeed force someone to go more quickly or more slowly. It's a power relation, but if I abuse it, I work against the theatre. It's a double-edged sword. It's true that I can do what I want with the drums. For example, at the beginning of rehearsals, we discuss, we search, we work, and all of a sudden, we begin. If you have a couple of drum beats in your head when we start, right away the actors have the reflex to get themselves into position, because the power of music is very strong.

F: Could you talk about the composition of the music?

L: [. . .] The genesis of this music stems first of all from my own musical culture. I have the advantage of being able to play various different instruments spontaneously without too much difficulty. If I was only a saxophonist, I probably wouldn't do much with the Shakespeares. I think that it's my own research, and the work I did before coming to the theatre, that brought me to change my thinking. The principal idea is that in Western music, apart from some great experiences I've had and some very great teachers with whom I had the opportunity to work from a very young age, classical musicians bore me. I always want to do something different, both on a human and on a musical level. I have no desire to compartmentalise music. For me, playing jazz or classical is playing music; I don't want to be a specialist in a particular style of music, I just don't want to work like that [. . .]

Clearly, I was lucky to come here; it has allowed me to search for what I really wanted to do. And I have discovered that what interests me is accompaniment. There are many ways of doing music for itself, [. . .] but it's much more difficult to do music with other arts: theatre, dance, mime, cinema. The problem is that I believe that theatre music practically does not exist, or in any case no longer exists. It has often been anecdotal, either musical support, or 'effects', or collages: pure theatre music has not existed since the Greeks. [. . .] What interests me here is to totally recreate a true music for the theatre. It's a trap at the same time, because very often in rehearsals I fall into cinema music. Music here must say something and at the same time be something, and not exclusively 'music'.

F: Could you tell us how the creation of the music for the Shakespeare cycle developed?

L: Let's begin with *Richard*. Ariane had come to ask me if I was interested in doing the music at the Soleil. I said yes. It was a change for me, because *Méphisto* had been an interesting experience, but somewhat limited. I taught the actors to play the music I had written, then rehearsed them, and afterwards it was finished because they went off on tour. I only played chords from time to time. I told Ariane that what interested me now was to perform the music. When we started work on *Richard*, we thought: a primitive side, a bit warrior-like, and so let's begin by looking at percussive possibilities. What's more, the text often refers to fanfares, drums. So we took our lead from what was in the text.

We started with contemporary percussion, but this posed a number of problems. The first of these was that when you play an instrument which has the same pitch as an actor's voice, everything is cancelled out, the music and the actor. Contemporary timbres are made for a typical conception of a certain form of music. So very quickly you lapse into rhythms that are typical of that kind of instrument. And here it was a mistake. Nevertheless this music does possess an 'oriental' resonance, which stems from the tonality of the instrument: if I played the same theme on a clarinet, there would no longer be anything oriental about it.

Some people say the music for *Richard II* sounds Indian, but there is one Indian instrument for fifty-six others that aren't Indian. And for two Japanese instruments, people say it's Japanese music. But no Japanese person who comes to the theatre says to me: 'you are really skilled in Kabuki or Noh theatre.' For them, this is not their music, it's something else.

So there was a certain amount of work first, and gradually the contemporary instruments were removed and replaced with traditional instruments. They require different techniques and have different possibilities which seem more primitive, more simple, but correspond better to the actors. We tried everything; there were some instruments that didn't work, and then things became clearer and the music-space was reduced to exactly what was essential. It was at that point that we decided to really punctuate the text. To do so, we used the way a particular kind of Balinese music is conceived; it consists of supporting the text exclusively on the level of its punctuation and of providing the pitch in relation to the words. Which is to say that each vowel constitutes a note: for example 'a' is 'doh', etc.; we simply had to transpose it into another form.

We decided on percussion for the nobles and the warriors, and, in counterpoint to this, string instruments for the women. I know that there aren't many in *Richard*, but nevertheless each of them has her own string instrument with a melodic theme. [. . .] And when characters are in dialogue, we mix the instruments. There's only one musical duty, at the prison: in the text, Richard is supposed to hear music coming from outside. So we worked on melodies over the Balinese percussion.

For *La Nuit des Rois*, on the other hand, there was a lot of work on the themes. By watching the characters, I imagined the timbre of the instrument, then the melody, in relation to their movements, to what they recounted. There are also the garden themes; we invented an entire garden musically, and Olivia's entire house, with birds, shells, Indian string instruments which produce an airy resonance. In the same way, the entrances of characters are made to their own themes. And then there are certain narrative instruments which accompany the characters on a sort of journey.

In *Henry IV*, the music has a slightly different role. It acts as support to the narrative, but in a given *place*: it places the person in a desert space, and it makes the play move forward in time (that's the function of the dampened, very distant drums), like a caravan in a desert. There are also some echoes from *Richard*, and the comic prose scenes which are the most difficult for me. This is one of the areas that are still rather unclear to me on the level of the music–theatre relationship. In Chinese or Japanese productions, the music stops during the comic passages. I find verse very easy, there are caesuras, real punctutations, respiration; whereas the rhythmic structures of prose are much more complex.

F: Once you have found the music, do you write it down?

L: I don't use bar measures; this would give the music a mechanical quality which would close the actor in. Having studied Gregorian chant, I've learnt how to work with phrases rather than measures. It's not a problem if the actor gives me three steps, more or less. The actors give me the tempo through the way they move and the speed at which they speak; I'm constantly 'synched' with them, because they are the ones who give me the break-down of my beats, of my quavers, of my crotchets.

F: Do you note it afterwards?

L: No, I codify, otherwise I would have a monumental thing to read.

F: So you have your own code which allows you to play the same thing again each time?

L: My codification is the name of the instrument, plus a rhythmic codification; the rest is memory. I'm fortunate to have a very good memory: it enables me to invent. If an actor takes off, when he finds something new, I can invent an accompaniment there and then, and two days later I'll still remember it. I don't have a single note on my score.

F: You know the music of the three plays by heart?

L: The music is at once simple and very complicated. When I'm playing, it probably seems as though I know the instruments perfectly, which is not true. I manage to tune them according to my own tones. When I recreate a Finnish, Chinese or other instrument, I look at the way it's put together, I listen to the harmonies, I tune the strings, and then I play. But in the beginning, I have tuned it in the way I want. If I tuned it in the traditional way, I'm sure it wouldn't work at all. What I try to achieve is a unity. In *Henry IV*, for example, all of the instruments are tuned in relation to the gong, which is completely broken. That's my reference note. From there, all of the instruments have a sort of harmonic cohesion, although if you take each one individually, they are all out of tune.

F: You have been making reference to your culture, your history, could you tell us about it?

L: Yes, I am lucky to have my origins: my mother is gypsy, and this has allowed me to get to know certain musics and certain cultures without any problems. I have been able to play with Eastern and Far-Eastern musicians without even understanding what they were doing. [. . .]

F: Do you play any instrument in particular?

L: No. I tend to be more of a melodist by training. Being gypsy, when I make a melody, it is rhythmic, more so than for a Frenchman. When you speak French, you speak on four rhythms; if it's Ancient Greek, you use 736 rhythms; if you do English pop, it's sixteen rhythms. This is why French pop is often in English. French is a pale and impoverished language.

F: Has it always been?

L: Yes. These are the four rhythms in the French language. You can't go against them. Hence the work we did with Georges Bigot and some of the other actors in relation to the metrics of languages. We worked on tonal pitch of the spoken voice: Georges is on the edge of the singing voice, although he doesn't sing. We invented a new system of metrics which doesn't exist in French: double-long syllables, double-short syllables, and caesuras that one doesn't make naturally; this produces Georges' bizarre way of speaking in *Richard II*. I gave him technical, theoretical solutions, which as an actor he assimilated and transposed. He invented his own system from all of the basic material we gave ourselves. I worked by ear, listening to the melodies he created, and I gave him criticism on his melody, but not on his acting.

From 'Mesure pour mesure', in Anne Berger *et al.* (eds), *Fruits* 2–3 June, Paris: Presses Universitaires de Vincennes, 1984.

3.8 ONE MUST TRY NOT TO LIE
From an interview with Ariane Mnouchkine
by the editors of *Fruits*

In the following interview, recorded at the Cartoucherie during the season of Les Shakespeares *in April 1984, the editors of* Fruits *attempt to examine with Mnouchkine some of the company's shared language, the metaphorical vocabulary that constitutes a kind of shorthand underpinning working processes. So, for example, they address the words or notions of* 'évidence', 'the state', 'play' *and* 'pleasure', *and their roles in elaborating a poetry in and of the theatre. The humanist discourse is familiar in French physical theatre training and pedagogy, in particular Jacques Lecoq's. However, in this context it assumes an amplified sense of ethical and political responsibilities to the group as a web of dynamic interrelations, an organic 'culture' requiring continuous individual and collective renegotiation and reinvention.*

FRUITS: There is a language proper to the Théâtre de Soleil, a theatre language with a particularly rich metaphorical dimension, and which unites those who participate in this adventure. We're interested in going back to the sources of this language with you. For example, in relation to the theatre work itself, which seems to engender an entire idiom: it is less a question of drama-turgy or *mise en scène* than of a 'path', and 'adventure' as you and the actors put it. What can you tell us about this adventure?

ARIANE MNOUCHKINE: The Théâtre du Soleil is an adventure in many respects. First of all, doing theatre is an adventure, because one doesn't know what it is. In a certain way, one only knows what theatre is when one *sees* it, when it bursts forth on stage. But at this moment of revelation perhaps the wisest position is to admit to oneself that one doesn't know what it is, any more than one really knows what childhood is.

Like any artist, an actor is an explorer. It is someone who, armed or unarmed (more often unarmed than armed), goes into a tunnel that's very long, very deep, very strange, very dark at times, and who, like a miner, brings back pebbles: from amongst these pebbles, he will have to find and cut a diamond. I think that's what the actors call 'the adventure'. In any case, it's what I call the adventure. The first part of the adventure is to descend into the soul of beings, of a society, and then to return. The second part is the cutting of the diamonds without shattering them; finding the original form of the diamond in the pebble.

And then there's the adventure of this 'ship', our ship, the *Soleil*; it's an adventure because it's very beautiful, because it's very hard, and because it's very fragile. [. . .]

F: Other recurrent terms, other key-signifiers designate the theatre space: for example the term '*évidence*' [something obvious, self-evident]. Relationships that are established, discoveries, advances – you call these '*évidences*', even in everyday exchanges. An actor will say, 'So-and-so found such and such a role, because it was "*évident*"'.

M: The performer didn't find it 'because it was *évident*', but everyone saw it and accepted it *because it was évident*. One of the central anxieties for the actors is the question of who will perform what. It's normal. It's more pleasing to play the king than the person who enters and says, 'Monsieur le duc, the king is here!' [. . .] It's a moment of tension for the group as a whole and for each individual. When we say 'Georges plays Richard because it's evident that he's the best Richard', it is everyone, and not only me. It's no less cruel for those who will not play him, but it's more fair.

When we're looking for a scene, when we set out on the adventure of a scene, either we have found the right path all at once, and it's evident, or we lose our way. It seems evident, and a week later, it no longer is at all. We realise that the love at first sight was tied to a spectacular aspect (what we call 'badaboum!'), but that what is essential was not played. When the essential aspect is not played, fortunately alarm bells are set off, because it doesn't hold up.

F: The '*évidence*' is a metaphor; at the same time, in the literal sense of the word, it's a bringing into light, which signifies lighting up, the Sun perhaps [*le Soleil*], as if theatre depended on clarity of vision.

M: That's absolutely right. I believe that theatre, the work of the actor, are dependent upon the clarity of a vision at every second. For an actor to be able to perform, he must have not a clear view of things, but *clear visions*, in the visionary sense of the word, not only in the 'project' sense (of course one also needs a clear project). But the actor is always in the present; he must play the present of the character at every instant. That's the way in which we work. An actor must have the strength and the imaginative musculature to *receive*, to generate visions; then to transform them into clear images for the others. He can only do this if he know how to receive visions, states, emotions of great clarity.

The actor can and must only play one single state at a time, even if he plays it for a quarter of a second, and in the next quarter of a second there's another state; that is what happens with Shakespeare all the time. Shakespeare is extremely versatile in terms of passions; there can be consuming fury in one half of a line and blissful euphoria in the next.

F: Where does the term 'state' come from? How did you formulate this notion? It has a very generic ring to it: one thinks of the state of the world, a state of mind [*état d'âme*].

M: In any work, there are certain words that become indispensable. We could question them, perhaps we could say 'passion', or 'emotion' . . . The word came one day when I said to one of the performers, 'Watch out, now you're in a right state, but it is not a state'.[18] The term 'state' must be in Stanislavski, we didn't invent it. But it's certainly connected to *état d'âme* [state of soul]; an *état d'âme* is not only a melancholic state, or a desire to laugh, or uncontrollable laughter. It is also a state of the soul. We also speak of 'internal landscape'. [. . .]

F: In general the director is associated with technicity, virtuosity; it's clear that this is not the type of work you do . . .

M: [. . .] It is true that I am not at all a virtuoso. I have the feeling that I must work a great deal. I am always asking myself: 'What is theatre? How do you do it? What's in it?' I do not know at all. What I do 'know' is that it's mysterious. I think we don't know how to do it. [. . .]

F: What's the source of your passion for theatre? Is it the love of what is human? the love of stories? of images?

M: In theatre, there are always several stories being told. There are no theatre productions without a story of the theatre within them. And even when a production recounts the story of a catastrophe, an odious story describing the darkness of the human lineage, the very fact that this play exists and that human beings are performing it means that there is already Hope in Humanity. It's impossible to make theatre if one's not conscious of this. There are people who can think that 'there's nothing to be had from human nature'; but their presence here contradicts it! The fact that the Théâtre du Soleil exists contradicts it. The fact that we will disappear after twenty or thirty years doesn't mean that we have not existed. This means that at every moment, people have accepted to pay the price, which is quite legitimate, for art.

There's always a very hefty price to pay for art. Sometimes there can be – and there has been – disagreement; the disharmony that is engendered when someone is going to leave often relates, in fact, to the evaluation of the price to be paid, when for someone, this price is excessive.

F: Does that mean that to be committed to serve art is an act of faith towards Humanity? and towards Life itself?

M: Absolutely; it's evident for all the arts, I believe [. . .] Even for the most bitter of poets, their poem constitutes an act of faith towards humanity. [. . .]

F: You have said that you 'recognised' Shakespeare in Kabuki theatre, that it was a very Shakespearean theatre, and hence, more or less, your idea of transposing the history plays into an Asian register. What's the difference between a textual analysis and a theatrical 'analysis' which leads to the 'hatching' of a scene?

M: I would tend to say that the mission of textal analysis is to try to explain everything. Contrary to the tendency of recent years, I believe that the role of the actor and of the director is *not* to make everything available to understanding; their role is to illuminate, of course, not to obfuscate, but spectators must be left with things to discover. There are waves, resonances: an actor strikes a gong or drops a pebble in water, but he won't try to fix all of the waves that will be emitted, to freeze them so that everyone can clearly count the number of rings that are released. What is important, on the other hand, is that this actor *does* drop his or her pebble, in just the right spot, so that all of the emotional, philosophical, metaphysical, political resonances are produced. But as soon as he privileges one of these rings, it makes the others disappear. Textual analysis takes place at a different time, it can enumerate. An actor does not enumerate: at every moment he must produce the essential chord. The spectators probably receive what is destined to them, according to their levels and tendencies.

F: When you read a scene, what counts for you is vision and reception, more so than enumeration, the attempt to synthesise into an understanding?

M: I don't know. There are so many plays in a play! I'm a bit like everyone: first I read the first play that is apparent, then the second play, then suddenly I say to myself: 'Oh my, there are still eighteen more! So let's act!' In the course of rehearsals, there is a process of widening, of complication, and at the same time one of simplification, because we return to what is said, to accepting and believing what is said, at least with Shakespeare. Accepting the flamboyant clarity of Shakespeare.

We tend to say, *Richard II* is a play about power. Now if Shakespeare ended up writing a play about power, first of all he wrote 'the story of Richard II'. And we must perform the story of Richard II; and the audience, depending on its level of receptivity, receives a play about Richard II, a play about power, a play about voluntary deprivation. The more 'cultural' one wants to be, the more restricted one becomes [. . .]

F: You have said that you are looking to avoid the decorative and to go towards what is essential: what does the essential comprise? Could you talk about your own trajectory, of the evolution of theatricality? [. . .]

M: With *Méphisto*, we reached a point which, for me, was right on the brink of error. Not that I'm disowning *Méphisto*, it was a very important production for us; but it was a time when we placed such an emphasis on the décor that it affected the very functioning of the company: through the enormous costs incurred, through the time spent because of the growth of the technical aspect. And then because I suddenly realised that I had fallen into the trap: we had created an 'official theatre', which was very beautiful, in order to denounce an official theatre. Even so I had an official theatre and I had to make do with that, and with the limitations of a proscenium stage: everything I detest! In fact, what the theatre needed was a *splendid emptiness*. Now, a splendid emptiness is also expensive. It's much more difficult to create. We have all sorts of references for full splendour, whereas Emptiness always needs to be invented.

F: This search for the essential seems to lead you towards dramaturgical choices, like the absence of sets in the conventional sense of the word, and the modulation of spaces, their immensity. There's also an increased emphasis on working on the movements and expressions of the body.

M: At the Soleil, that's a constant; it's almost a matter of people's nature. Actors really love moving, or should love moving; if they are actors, they write with their bodies. A body without passion is a dead body; so they must animate it from within. It's not a question of wriggling about. To condemn an actor to immobility or fix him, or to define his placement before knowing what his passions are: these are errors to be avoided. [. . .]

F: You say that theatre is also poetry, and that what's fundamental is 'the Poet and the Actor'. In a literary context, the poet is often someone who works on minute subtleties, on the nearly invisible. Are theatre men and women poets of the visible, of full-scale vision?

M: The poet makes the invisible visible, makes the forgotten perceptible, makes things concrete. Theatre's the same; I can see a difference of means, but no more. Theatre makes suffering visible, makes love visible, makes fear, questioning, death, hate, power visible. [. . .]

I don't accept everything one finds on stage as theatre. *Les Clowns* is not theatre to the same degree as Shakespeare.

I think the Théâtre du Soleil has a sort of duty: to stage Shakespeare, because we need it, because it's beautiful, because it's a lesson, because it does us and others good; and we also have a duty to look for ways of making theatre about our times, about the histories of our own times; we must confront this problem. But it seems evident to me that the things we have done up until now, whatever their success, don't all attain the same degree of theatre. When people tell me '*1789* was much better than the Shakespeares', I know that, unfortunately, it's not true. It's a nostalgic vision. I'm not disowning anything; all of the productions have been essential in our trajectory, and have responded each time to our needs and the audiences' needs. Of course, it's not that something is better because it's contemporary; it will be better the day it's better! On the other hand, it's a necessity: we cannot get away from this. After the Shakespeares, we have to confront a contemporary project. How will it turn out? What will be the level of satisfaction? I have no idea; however I do know that we'll learn other things.

F: So it's a perpetual apprenticeship?

M: Absolutely. Every time we prepare a new production, we start again from zero. People say to us, 'That's not true: you know things.' Yes, perhaps we know a little better how to search. [. . .]

F: It would probably be more valuable to talk of a maturing of constants, rather than of an evolution; for example, in the position you have taken against a certain 'psychological', 'realist' theatre.

M: These are not 'positions' we've 'taken'. People ask me questions, I reply, I say what I think, what I feel. I don't go off to battle against the other theatrical forms. The best guarantee of fertile research is the freedom to do all kinds of research, including those that lose their way. I would be terrified if suddenly there were only research like ours. I think it's great that there are lots of mistakes all over! It keeps all virtualities open: you have the choice each time. It's not my fault if each time a magnet draws me back to the theatre I look for.

F: Why has the mask occupied a fundamental place in your work from the very beginning?

M: Because it is the very sign of theatre, because it is transformation, because it is an object which is like the human face, because it leads the actor, when he lets himself be led, because it forces him to go very far in himself, to un-mask himself, because it's truer than nature, because it puts the body into question. For me it has become the core discipline, even if the subsequent production is to be played without masks. The mask precedes the non-mask, not the other way around.

F: It's a fundamental element of theatrical performance [*jeu*]. To what extent is theatre play? One talks all the time about 'playing' in theatre: what does that mean?

M: It means playing! Playing the king, playing the queen, it means going to meet the king, looking in oneself for what is king, what would have been king in oneself if one had been king, what would have been dethroned in oneself, and furthermore, what was dethroned and what is dethroned every day. What is it in oneself that is assassin? And what would have made you an assassin if you had been an assassin? Even the furthest away, even the unimaginable: what is it in oneself that is bishop? What does one have within oneself of a Greek peasant or a Roman centurion? What does Julien Maurel have in common with Hotspur, five-hundred years ago? For Julien Maurel can only play Hotspur with Julien Maurel: he went to meet him, he went to look for a man who is buried in a stone tomb in Shrewsbury; and he recreates him, he brings him back to life. If he doesn't allow himself to be possessed to some degree by the soul of this man, he won't be able to play him. Of course it's a process of imagination, but in the end that's what possession is! He'll only be able to let himself be possessed by this soul, by this character, if he resembles him, if he finds what it is within himself that resembles him.

F: By asking about play and the use of the mask, [. . .] I'm wondering if it isn't absurd to separate tragedy and comedy, whether, in the theatre process itself, in the distancing, there isn't a comic essence. In Shakespeare, for example, even within the heart of tragedy, the irony of the story is so powerful.

M: It's the opposite: there is a tragic essence in everything. True comedy, magnificent comedy is tragic: it's only really comic when it's wholly tragic. The essence is religious and tragic [. . .]

F: One senses an intense emotional relationship between you and the whole company. Do you feel you have a maternal role?[19]

M: That's something that I denied fiercely a few years ago. Unfortunately I now think I can no longer deny it, but I think – I hope – it's not exclusively that. It also depends on the others. With some people it fluctuates, at times it can also go the other way around: some people are sufficiently mature to take me a bit under their wings when I'm not going so well. That also happens! Some of them, even some of the young ones, sense those moments when perhaps it's up to them to look after me a bit. It's very complicated. In any case, one can say that a group is always maternal to some degree. What would it be if I were a man? It would be paternal. Jean Vilar says some very beautiful things about that. Frankly I can't see how it's avoidable. It would be a refusal of responsibility on my part.

F: You say it would be 'paternal' if it were a man. We have often gotten a non-response when we asked the question of sexual difference, which doesn't seem to have much meaning in the company. It's not a question for you either? There's no difference between a male and a female director?

M: Yes: I think I direct the company like a woman and not like a man. On the other hand, if you come up against a non-response, that's because the men of the Théâtre du Soleil, aside from exceptions, are not very macho. Not only are they men who have a feminine side in them, but they need this feminine side to create, and they recognise it, work with it. When you ask them the question, they say 'I see no difference' because it's not a problem for them. Those for whom it's a problem must resolve it themselves. [. . .]

F: The Théâtre du Soleil stands out through its ethics and its socio-political commitment. Are theatre and the aspiration to justice interconnected for you, and in what ways?

M: All human activity is interconnected with it! I obviously think that when, in addition, one's profession is to communicate stories, human History, one must make one of two choices: either we are false witnesses, or we are witnesses. The fact of making theatre, of simply being an artist, increases the responsibility tenfold, one hundredfold, one thousand . . .; one does not have the right to lie. Since one cannot completely avoid lying, *one must try not to lie*. If I were in charge of a small carpentry business, I would think the same way. [. . .]

F: You always say that the centre of the work is the actor. When you began you were an actress?

M: I performed a little but I was not good. I knew very well that I would not be an actress; I knew I'd be a director. Did I already know that I would think what I think today? I don't know! [. . .] I would be capable of performing . . . but I would need a director! I too would need someone to help me be born, and I couldn't help myself be born alone because I would not be in a watching position.

F: Would you like to add something?

M: There is perhaps a question I'd like you to ask: a question people ask me each time: 'Why do people leave the Soleil?' Here is my response: 'I am very sorry when they leave'. It's a great pity, but people leave for a thousand reasons I've spoken of: when one no longer gets anything out of it: either one thinks one no longer has a place, or one simply wants to go elsewhere, or one wants to found a company . . . or we no longer love each other. I must admit this, once and for all: what surprises me is that love can become extinguished. I never believe it, but it's true.

From 'Le théâtre ou la vie', in Anne Berger *et al.* (eds), *Fruits* 2–3, June, Paris: Presses Universitaires de Vincennes, 1984.

NOTES

1 Mnouchkine in Colette Godard, 'Shakespeare at Vincennes: passion and fear', *The Guardian Weekly* 125: 26, 27 December 1981, p. 14.

2 Bertolt Brecht, *Brecht on Theatre: the Development of an Aesthetic* (trans. John Willett), London: Methuen, 1964, p. 276.

3 Mnouchkine in Catherine Dégan, 'L'acteur est un scaphandrier de l'âme', *Le Soir*, 20–22 July, 1984.

4 Originally, Mnouchkine planned to stage a cycle of ten Shakespeare plays; soon this was reduced to six, as here. Plans for the second part of *Henry IV* and *Henry V* were cancelled in the wake of the departure of Philippe Hottier (Falstaff). So *Les Shakespeares* became a trilogy: *Richard II, Twelfth Night* and *Henry IV Part 1*. A production of *Twelfth Night*, with an all-women cast, was abandoned only after several weeks of rehearsal.

5 The word *écorché* (literally, 'flayed' or 'skinned') is used in both English and French to refer to representations of anatomical figures, animal or human, with the skin removed to reveal the muscles, organs, etc. Probably the best known *écorchés* are by the 16th-century Flemish anatomist Andreas Vesalius.

6 The reference is to actor-director Charles Dullin's book *Ce sont les dieux qu'il nous faut*, Paris: Gallimard, 1969. Mnouchkine has paraphrased Dullin's words on many occasions. Cf. for example: 'We need actors, nothing else. We need actors who can suddenly become so great and profound and tragic that they can make us believe in gods. They become gods. So we no longer have to lower the rafters or have them emerge out of the mist, because in an actor's simple gesture or step or look lies divinity.' Quoted in Anne Tremblay, 'A French director gives Shakespeare a new look', *New York Times*, 10 June 1984.

7 Thierry la Fronde ('Thierry of the catapult') is a sort of French cousin of the English Robin Hood, reputed to have fought the rich in favour of the poor. *Très Riches Heures du Duc de Berry*, illuminated manuscripts created by the Flemish Limbourg brothers early in the 15th century, are associated with a Late Gothic court style of decorative elegance.

8 Cf. Jean Alter: 'Mnouchkine's actors were not Kabuki, but signs for Kabuki actors and the Cartoucherie a sign for a Kabuki stage: a theatre-within-a-theatre strategy carried to the extreme.' From 'Decoding Mnouchkine's Shakespeare', in Michael Issacharoff and Robin F. Jones (eds), *Performing Texts*, Philadelphia: University of Pennsylvania Press, 1988, p. 82. For a perceptive account of Kabuki as 'an imaginary theatre form', 'a Utopian fiction' in the Théâtre du Soleil's Shakespeare cycle, see Georges Banu, 'Le kabuki du Soleil' in *L'acteur qui ne revient pas: journées de théâtre au Japon*, Paris: Aubier, 1986, pp. 64–5.

9 *King Lear*, IV, vi. For an account of the paradox at the heart of this scene between Gloucester and Edgar, see Jan Kott's influential essay '*King Lear*, or Endgame', in *Shakespeare our Contemporary*, London: Metheun, 1967, pp. 112–20.

10 A 12th-century French narative poet, author of Arthurian courtly romances.

11 For details of Guy-Claude François's spatial design, as well as of Barriera's costumes and Cordier's lighting design, see Bethany Haye, 'Ariane Mnouchkine's Théâtre du Soleil: astonishing audiences with grand spectacle', *Theatre Crafts* 18: 9, November–December 1984, p. 83.

12 The impulses for this 'contemporary show' about colonialism and genocide in South-East Asia eventually crystallised in the play the company commissioned from the writer Hélène Cixous, *L'histoire terrible mais inachevée de Norodom Sihanouk, roi du Cambodge* (1985). Cf.: 'During rehearsals [for *Richard II*], I realised there was something there I wanted to say about genocide, and about the life force. It's a force which manages to surmount the impossible, which drives Shakespearean heroes in a world where death is easy and murder one solution among many; it's a force which isn't only ambition [. . .] they have a frenzied, greedy pride in living'; Mnouchkine in Colette Godard, *The Guardian Weekly*, op. cit., p. 14. Mnouchkine had also considered working on the Russian invasion of Afghanistan.

13 Mnouchkine in Catherine Clément, 'Shakespeare ne supporte pas qu'on apporte en plus son manger', *Le Matin de Paris*, 10 December 1981.

14 Lecoq quoted in Jim Hiley, 'Moving heaven and earth', *The Observer*, 20 March 1988.

15 For further details of Cixous's conception of the 'gift-that-gives' and of a 'feminine economy' of expenditure and exchange, see for example her 'Sorties', in *The Newly-Born Woman*, (trans. Betsy Wing), Manchester: Manchester University Press, 1986, pp. 85–7. See also David Williams and David George, '"Listening to images": pleasure and/in the gift', in *Australasian Drama Studies* 28, April 1996, pp. 63–78.

16 'Things past redress are now with me past care'; *Richard II*, II, iii, 170.

17 Sophie Moscoso, 'Notes de répétitions', in *Double Page 32* (*Le Théâtre du Soleil: Shakespeare 2e Partie*), Paris: Editions SNEP, p. 10.

18 Mnouchkine's pun is difficult to translate. She told the performer 'tu es dans tous tes états, mais ce n'est pas un état.' The idiomatic French phrase, 'être dans tous ses états' (literally 'to be in all one's states'), means to be all worked up, beside oneself with rage or anxiety.

19 Cf. the performer Hélène Cinque: 'Ariane is really the mother bearing us, supporting us, the one who gives us the start [. . .] she opens the way for us [. . .] she teaches us, she makes us learn things, she transforms us, she gives us passion.' In Anne Berger *et al.* (eds), 'Voir 1: En plein soleil', *Fruits* 2–3, Paris: Presses Universitaires de Vincennes, pp. 22–3. It is interesting to compare this articulation of interrelations between director and performer with Susan Letzler Cole's account of the 'maternal gaze' of certain practitioners: a mutual, interactive and supportive 'regard', part of a collective 'witnessing' and 'birthing'. See Cole, *Directors in Rehearsal: a Hidden World*, London: Routledge, 1992, pp. 5–6, 62–3. Although this discourse of the maternal appears to essentialise Woman as Mother, its recuperation of critical feminist rereadings of psychoanalysis and of *écriture féminine* (e.g. Irigaray, Cixous) provides a range of provocative analogies for the processes of an ethical inter-subjectivity, and an interactive creativity, as an economy of exchange.

CHAPTER 4
A MODERN PASSION PLAY
L'Indiade, ou l'Inde de leurs rêves
(Hélène Cixous, *The Indiade, or the India*
of their dreams)
(1987)

I have always thought that History could only be treated poetically in texts (unless one is a historian), that it had to be sung, that it should be an epic like the *Iliad*. History with its human face: Destiny. But does the epic still have its citizen's rights today? In the Theatre, yes. The epic still exists there, it is a place where what one might call 'legend' still exists.
Hélène Cixous[1]

History, like trauma, is never simply one's own [. . .] history is precisely the way we are implicated in each other's traumas.
Cathy Caruth[2]

I would hope that even in the most extreme exile there will be a force greater than everything, a force which continues to sing: what [Paul] Celan called the *Singbarrest*, the singable remains.
Hélène Cixous[3]

4.1 MEDUSA AND THE MOTHER/BEAR: THE PERFORMANCE TEXT OF *L'INDIADE*

Judith G. Miller

In this essay, Judith Miller provides a context for reading the performance of L'Indiade *in the light of Cixous's earlier writings on* l'écriture féminine. *Taking theatre as a site for the actualisation of the Other, Miller discusses the transformative potential that permeates the Soleil's performance of Cixous's play. She focuses on the maternal metaphors embodied in the 'unlikely theatrical trinity' of the pilgrim Haridasi, the she-bear Moona Baloo and Gandhi. Judith Miller is Professor of French at the University of Wisconsin-Madison.*

In her prose fiction, essays and theatre, Hélène Cixous teaches her public to question the terms by which the world is represented and, therefore, to examine how human beings see both this world and their place in it. In 1975, for example, in her oft-cited essay 'Le Rire de la Méduse' ('The Laugh of the Medusa'), she re-visioned the terrifying monster of Greek legend and Freudian analysis.[4] Rather than continuing the litany of castigation directed at Medusa's powers to turn onlookers into stone (or men into impotent masses), Cixous transformed the gorgon's deadly tendrils into positive signs of feminine energy. As fashioned by Cixous, the Medusa's laugh became the rallying cry of the liberated female creator. In 1987, in a somewhat less polemical if no less violent vein, Cixous asked that the beast within the human heart be reconsidered. To demonstrate its innocence as well as its savagery, she dressed this creature in Mother/Bear's clothing, and, in her play *L'Indiade*, had it dance under New Delhi's skies.

By juxtaposing Cixous's multiform Medusa with the equally complex scenic image of the Mother/Bear as this protean figure informs *L'Indiade*, it is possible to suggest how her earlier call as essayist for *l'écriture féminine* ('feminine writing') has been transposed and realised in her recent work as dramatist. It would seem that Cixous has found in the Théâtre du Soleil the embodiment of her aesthetics of transformation and fluidity. Likewise, Ariane Mnouchkine and her troupe have encountered in the writer Cixous an unqualified partner in their quest to develop a modern mythic theatre.

In addition to advancing notions of excess and transgression, which Cixous's female Medusa, with her pullulating phallic locks, incarnates, 'Le Rire de la Méduse' denotes a theatre practice relying on constant transformation. For example, Cixous's celebration of women's capacity to be conscious of, accept and incorporate the Other, thus their ability to grow, multiply and 'be infinitely dynamised by an incessant process of exchange',[5] can be read as a major instance of this process of metamorphosis. Calling for women to come to writing, Cixous moreover portrays feminine being as unending, continuous and transformative development. Finally, and connected to the concepts of excess, transgression and metamorphosis, throughout 'Le Rire de la Méduse' Cixous proposes maternal images, metaphors in which she establishes the 'force which stands up against separation'[6] – a force which, while enabling metamorphosis, also prevents rupture.

Translated into theatrical terms (and setting aside considerations of 'masculine' or 'feminine' for the moment), Cixous's Medusa essay can be understood as implying a theatre which refuses causal logic and linear development; which privileges ambiguous characters whose psychological motivation and gender identification are not easily classifiable; which explodes a mimetic time and space frame; and which balks at foregrounding dialogue as the most important basis of communication. Her assertion of maternity as non-separation, however, also indicates a non-fragmentary and non-dislocated theatre, one which ultimately unifies its public.

Most of these characteristics have been fundamental to the Théâtre du Soleil's practice since the mid-1960s. Furthermore, in its functioning, the Théâtre du Soleil has endeavoured to abolish hierarchy and – like the unselfish, limitless woman of whom Cixous also speaks in the Medusa essay – has 'shattered the framework of institutions'.[7] By sharing tasks, collectively developing its productions, and entering into financial partnership with its public,[8] the Soleil has disrupted the institution of theatre itself. So it is hardly surprising that the troupe's literal fleshing out of Cixous's *L'Indiade* has reinforced and developed the concept of transformation which permeates her text.

In *L'Indiade*, Cixous creates a sweeping panorama which telescopes the crucial decolonisation period in India's recent history (between 1937 and 1948) into a five-hour drama. She confronts in heady debates the members of the Indian Congress Party – Nehru, Azad, Patel, Badshah Khan and Sarojini Naidu (Plate 4.1) – with members of the Muslim League, notably its leader and chief strategist Mohamad Ali Jinnah. While the predominantly Hindu Indian Congress Party seeks to establish a socialist, secular and independent India, the Muslim League struggles for both independence *and* partition. Jinnah adamantly claims the creation of the state of Pakistan to be the only solution for India's Muslim minority. The intransigency and careless politicking of both sides, as well as the haughtiness and, later, haste of India's British rulers, lead to a bloody civil conflict pitting Hindu against Muslim against Sikh. In shorter, more pungent, and ultimately bloody scenes, the people pay physically and emotionally for their leaders' inability to come to terms. Squabbles among rickshaw drivers, for example, make palpable the fragile veneer of community; profound and dangerous fears about religious and caste differences surface at the merest hint of insult.

Positioned in the centre but also above the debate is Mahatma Gandhi, accompanied almost everywhere by his wife Kastourbai – even after her death. Gandhi himself rather magically appears on stage at crucial moments to strategise with Nehru, wash the feet of an untouchable, mingle with the rickshaw drivers,

Plate 4.1   L'Indiade. Sarojini Naidu (Myriam Azencot) leaves on a rickshaw pulled by Inder, an 'untouchable' (Mauricio Celedon); in the background, Gandhi and the Congress leaders with Sir Archibald Wavell (Christian Dupont). Photo: Martine Franck/Magnum

plead with Jinnah, and preach by example his dual message of non-violence and universal love. Although allied with the Congress Party and linked especially to Nehru and to Badshah Khan, Gandhi is prepared to eliminate the Congress Party's political leadership if this would serve to preserve a united India. His death ends the play at the ironic moment of renewed peace. Gandhi's final hunger strike has momentarily halted the carnage caused by independence and partition, but an outraged Hindu, unable to accept the Mahatma's magnanimity, has killed him.

This straightforward account of the narrative of *L'Indiade* not only belies the concerns expressed in 'Le Rire de la Méduse', but also distorts the experience of the production itself; for the Medusa vision enriches its every aspect. In fact, the ensemble of *L'Indiade*'s features can best be apprehended through the lens of transformation. In particular, the treatment and development of theme, setting, register, acting and music illustrate the ways in which the concept of transformation guides the performance.

Thematically, the notion of truth reworks itself throughout the play, the debate never settling on one position regarding India's possible future. Both the Congress Party and the Muslim League support their opposing verities with years of experience as well as conviction. And even Gandhi's ideal of universal love, when tested by the realities of distrust and greed, fails to be entirely convincing. Cixous shows its shortcomings in the episodes concerning the peasant Rajkumar, who waits patiently (and non-violently) for Gandhi to find time to counsel him about how he should treat his rapacious neighbour. He ceases waiting, however, when the neighbour claims for himself Rajkumar's home, all his belongings, his wife and his daughter. Taking up the sword in his turn, Rajkumar kills his neighbour's son. Consumed as he is by his personal tragedy, Rajkumar cannot make sense of Gandhi's admonishments for peaceful coexistence.

Scenically, the space is also forever changing. Between scenes, the 'people of India' surge on to the central playing area to establish the contours of a particular India, usually through the unrolling of rugs and the plumping of pillows. For example, the debate begins in the starkly elegant whiteness of the mats and throws of the enemy political camps. The Congress Party and the Muslim League occupy their separate spaces as if immured in them, just as they are imprisoned in separate ideologies. Later, 'the people' invade the space again. Dressed in gloriously coloured saris, turbans, veils or skull-caps – their head-coverings signalling the various religious identities – they lend new class dimensions to the setting simply by their physical presence. As silent witnesses, they suggest the profile of other Indias. In three major parade scenes, the stage space again bursts with energy as the scarlet-clad rickshaw drivers pull their prestigious charges across the playing area – now the streets of Delhi.

Textually, and correspondingly in terms of delivery, the linguistic register also shifts ceaselessly – from, for example, delicate lyricism to commonsensical aphorisms. As an instance of the former, Gandhi's lament after the death of his dearly-loved wife images their separation in terms of an unholy rebirth:

> *What luck we have had. You – mother and child to me, – me – child and mother to you. For sixty-two years, each nourished at the other's breast. How sad you were departing yesterday, leaving me behind sad and abandoned. I pass through death at present, and crying out I shall be born to the survivor's chilling fate. My soul trembles from the cold as I face the flames which soothe your soul.*[9]

While such poignant and emotion-laden passages tend to dominate, earthier and more piquant remarks frequently lace the dialogue. Typical of the people's wisdom, for example, is a Bengali pilgrim's rejoinder to Jinnah. Jinnah has just protested that the Hindu-dominated Congress Party will oppress India's Muslim citizens. Haridasi, the pilgrim, counters with a parable from nature: 'Never does my Mother, the Cow, step on the little chick. Cow turds, yes, little chicks, no!'[10]

Like the linguistic register, the notion of truth and the performance space, the actors are also in constant transformation. Most play several roles, changing from one to the next with astonishing speed. And while the actor is transformed to a greater or lesser degree in all theatre work, in *L'Indiade*, the original transformation takes place at least partially in front of the spectators, who are thus changed as well. Upon entering the theatre, the audience members are invited to watch the making-up process. This ritual – and the actors' concentration and environment make clear that this *is* a ritual – both maintains the audience's awareness of the play of the real and also, paradoxically, entices it into the Soleil's dream of India.

In fact the actors interact with the spectators as though the latter were a group of tourists wandering into an Indian city. It is as if a life-sized, pastel and geometrically-patterned Indian genre scene had come to life before one's eyes. Consequently, the spectators themselves are transformed into 'European interlopers'. And before the debate begins (but not before the play begins) Haridasi directly addresses various members of the audience, asking them their names, posing for pictures and introducing spectators to each other. All the while, untouchables and various street people drift into the playing area where they begin to sweep and polish the marble floor. They smile eerily at the spectators, again helping to position the audience members as Western 'guests'.

Finally, one might speak of the changing or transforming locus of communication. In L'Indiade, communication is never centred for long in the spoken word. In addition to gestures, glances and movements, music in particular refocuses communication in non-verbal aspects of the performance. Verbal and musical elements bleed into and transform each other. For example, the steel drums which introduce Gandhi throughout the second part of the play become a musical metaphor for his moral stance as well. As events grow increasingly out of control and the mood approaches hysteria, Gandhi's rather tranquil if quizzical musical theme reminds the audience contrapuntally of a different way of being in the world. The drums, then, interfere with and transform the ways in which the reigning ambience affects the spectators.

Of all the features of L'Indiade which can be read through the concept of transformation, none is more intriguing or central than the associative cluster which in this essay has been termed the 'Mother/Bear'. This figure includes three apparently separate characters who all, in fact, work together to establish a dominant maternal metaphor which posits as a possible solution to the seemingly endless conflict an encompassing yet non-stifling 'mother love'.

The first among them is Haridasi, the Bengali pilgrim, a character who extends both Gandhi's aura and his philosophy of non-violence. Witness and commentator, she links the audience to the play just as Gandhi connects the various social classes and political camps to each other. She is omnipresent and conciliatory, never giving up hope and even, in the imminency of Gandhi's death, entreating the spectators to believe in mankind.

The second is the dancing bear, Moona Baloo. The Bear, like that other méduse, the jellyfish, is completely alive to everything passing around her. She reacts instinctively to the growing tension in the second half of the play. Only Gandhi, who shares her innocence, keeps her calm. Together they gambol about enthusiastically and awkwardly, both of them 'babies', as Haridasi laughingly tells the audience.[11] But as people grow violent around her, Moona Baloo too becomes a 'beast'. Like Gandhi, she must also be sacrificed, for she turns into a killer, her innocence unable to withstand the blood-letting. As Cixous explains, this parallels humankind's refusal to acknowledge the divine in the human and to accept the yearning for compassionate exchange:

How we love the innocence of living creatures, how we long for Paradise, and how we scratch at God's gate each time we caress the Bear. But, of course, if by misfortune, we are able to translate that bizarre tenderness into nostalgia for our own goodness, we will waste no time in placing the Bear in a realm below the human. That the human should be defined by the love of the other is something we ordinary Westerners hardly ever think of. Because that does violence to our customary violence.[12]

The third and chief figure of the Mother/Bear cluster is Gandhi himself. He is the true Medusan hero: beyond gender, both mother and lover, infant and old man. According to the character Lord Mountbatten, Viceroy of India, Gandhi is 'the last proof of the existence of the gods and of their impotence to impose their prophets on our political times'.[13] Unafraid to humble himself ('humbling oneself' being a notion he does not, in any event, comprehend), immortal (reborn twice within the play and again by the very existence of the theatre performance itself), Gandhi, like the mother in the Solomon tale, knows that love precludes the struggle for mastery. He is the embodiment of the sum of all the maternal metaphors from 'Le Rire de la Méduse': an empowerer, a nurturer, a person who laughs freely and whose laughter sets free.[14]

It is therefore Gandhi who delivers the message of love which, despite the ugly quarrelling between Nehru and Jinnah, despite the terrifying massacre and pile of corpses in the penultimate segment of the play, weights and infuses the entire production. Indeed, he speaks to Jinnah as if to a reluctant beau:

There's no love without fear. And even, sometimes, no love without a kind of disgust, yes, repulsion. We human beings, Hindus, Muslims, masculine, feminine, we're so different. We are bizarre. There facing me is the other, and nothing's like me! For example, you and I, could anybody imagine [people] more different? You, with your handsome hair, your fine tie, your suit, your polished shoes and all your teeth. And me without. Without everything. Without hair, without suit, without teeth, and with all my toes forever chewing on the road. What attracts us in this world? Mystery. The other sex, the other religion, the other human being. There's a tree, two leaves aren't identical but they dance to the same breeze: it's the human tree. Let us give human things time to germinate, to ripen.[15]

Gandhi, Haridasi and Moona Baloo are the three terms of Cixous's unlikely theatrical trinity, what might be entitled a 'Medusan head', or – for the purposes of this discussion – a 'Mother/Bear'. All three partake of the same argument for literature and writing, which here also assumes the form of an argument for love. Cixous has been developing this argument since the 1970s when she wrote that women must open up and allow themselves to be traversed and changed by what seems, or has been deemed, foreign. Only then will they discover all their hidden beauties; only then will the 'beast' within – Medusa or bear – reveal its possibilities. These days, however, immersed in the exceptional theatre that is the Théâtre du Soleil, Cixous has reworked her concepts in such a way that the liberating 'feminine' is no longer understood as that which must be conjured up and released but rather, that which the theatre is capable of realising. 'Tout est femme au théâtre', writes Cixous;[16] 'in theatre everything is woman'. And this 'woman', far removed from all conventional definitions, this 'mother' who is beyond gender yet can birth the world, encourages the spectators of the Théâtre du Soleil to find the holy and the heroic in themselves.

From Judith G. Miller, 'Medusa and the Mother/Bear: the performance text of Hélène Cixous's *L'Indiade*', *Journal of Dramatic Theory and Criticism*, Fall 1989.

4.2 A LONG PASSION

Hélène Cixous

The following extracts from author Hélène Cixous's programme notes for the production of L'Indiade *provide elements of a historical context for the Partition of India. Cixous details her particular concerns here: an intertextual and epic passion play of civil war, with constellations of mythological associations; the ethical integrity of an array of characters, affording a polycentric dramaturgy; the 'difficult joys' of independence; and the production's indebtedness to the plurality of India, of which her play remains no more than a 'footprint'. Cixous's language is epiphanic and poetic throughout, her rigorous historiography at the service of a richly metaphorical 'mythology'. The India she conjures up is the site of possibility in an exploration of the ethics of alterity, the site of the imaginary.*[17]

'If you don't mind, I will speak to you of love . . .'

TRIUMPH AND MOURNING

On 15 August 1947, India is born. For thirty years the Indian people have fought to bring about this day that had been so longed for. Thirty years, through bondage, prisons, great waves of non-violence.

A long passion. Thirty years of anger and of dreaming: 'When we are free, from the old India will be reborn a young India which . . .'

At last this blessed day comes, freedom comes, up goes the saffron, white and green flag. But the sky is black and this day of joy is a day of mourning. The smiles have dried on the lips and bitterness inflames the eyelids.

For destiny has played one of its tragic tricks on India. The day of birth is also a day of farewells and tearing apart.

On 14 August 1947, Pakistan is born. Carved out of the great body of India, torn from the breast of the continent by an implacable operation, this new country emerges from India in a torrent of blood. Everything is separated, people, villages, rivers, communities. Punjab in the west and Bengal in the east are sliced alive down the middle.

And the Indian soul writhes with grief and rage.

For a long time, knives have flown. Never has History lived such a great exodus. In one day, ten million people are uprooted. Death is innumerable.

So, was this the celebration you prepared for us? This Partition? And yet, through the tears, a sad joy nevertheless, since we are independent.

Why this division? How? By what mistake, madness or necessity?

Everything had begun with one single hope that united and carried 400 million Indians of all religions, of all castes, towards the same goal. Then little by little the ark starts to fissure, division strains the immense body, cracks its joints.

An adverse dream arises and opposes union. The dreamer of this dream of division is a haunted, powerful, inflexible man. A man cast in will power, Mohamed Ali Jinnah. And so it is that he gathers part of the Indian Muslim community around him, so it is that Jinnah the atheist calls Indian Islam towards a Promised Land, Jinnah, who does not believe in Allah. Destiny juggles with sincere hearts.

A second story now intervenes in the struggle for Independence. The fighters stumble as they advance. Their own brothers attack them. And it is a fray that moves gasping towards the goal.

If at first the dream didn't quite believe in itself, it soon gains assurance. In 1940, it enters History and is called: Pakistan. Now it has a name, all it's missing is a land.

And despite the desperate efforts of the great Indian leaders (Hindus, Muslims, Sikhs, Christians, atheists . . .), everything helps it to realisation: the Second World War, the hazards of politics, the British, only too happy to weaken the Indian Congress freedom-fighters by using Jinnah's Muslim League. In the night of war, Jinnah takes great strides.

So when the world conflict comes to an end at last, the hour of the 'Meeting with Destiny' that Nehru spoke of approaches.

Yes, India comes at last to the Indians, but in what a state: divided against herself, wounded, gangrenous, wild with hatred. And, in order to save her, people believe only in amputation.

One man alone is opposed to the vivisection: Gandhi.

He, the mother, cries out to King Solomon: 'Don't cut the child in two, give it living to he who claims it at all costs.' But there is no Solomon. The sword falls.

A TIME OF BLOOD, BUT A TIME OF THE HEART

The story that bears the fated name, Partition, is in truth an immense story of love. Love is what it was about, beyond politics and religion.

Can one speak of love today, publicly, aloud, in public and political spheres? Can one speak of love with love, and without derision in the television-era? No, today love is relegated to narrow, private intimacies, forbidden in high places. Let us love one another, what head of State can allow himself to say that?

Well the Indians were constantly speaking of love for thirty years, and right to the highest levels of the State. The glorious entry of love into the *res publica* in the middle of the twentieth century, such is the gift India made to the universe through Gandhi.

And since love had the right to speak and to exist, thanks to the Mahatma, it went to town wholeheartedly. All of the political battles took place on the very stage of love – for some, whether they liked it or not. People loved one another, unloved one another, searched for one another, found one another, separated from one another, lost one another, clung to one another, with love. The great rendings had the convulsed faces of hateful lovers.

The separations, the regions cast out of India, the party alliances, the agonies of the populations, the promises made, kept, broken, the events appear with the moving and familiar faces of our passions. Storms of the heart, gratitudes, disappointments, rancours, repudiations, reunitings, it is all there, only lived on the magnificent scale of India. Yes, at that time, barely yesterday, when the West was tattooed by Hitler, people were burning with love in Asia, and a part of humanity was living a sublime epoch on this very earth.

THE KNIGHTS OF THE ABSOLUTE

The unprecedented aspect of this story is that right in the middle of the twentieth century, living near us were human beings who belonged to spiritual eras that have been over for us for centuries and millennia.

Men like Gandhi and Abdul Ghaffar Khan are biblical, comparable to Abraham; their interlocutors are men and their Gods. And as in their earthly lives they comply with heavenly law, they are sometimes as incomprehensible as the stars.

And Jawaharlal Nehru, Abdul Kalam Azad, Sarojini Naidu, Vallabhbhai Patel, all inhabit an exalted region of honour. To follow their adventures is to find oneself in front of an Indian Round Table. None of them is lesser nor greater than the others. O golden age of loyalty and respect!

But when these figures, with their souls formed from the stuff of myth, encounter reality, what is the outcome?

Gandhi's saintliness crossed with political calculation? Nehru's idealism with historical contradictions, what is the outcome?

COMBAT, NOT WAR

Those who fight for freedom, also fight for Truth, each according to his stature.

For our heroes, all is combat. Combat, not war. And the first combatant of all, the untiring one, who girds his loins at four o'clock every morning, is Gandhi, the divine warrior. His so virile soul is nourished by the *Gita*,[18] that bible of the Kshatrya – the warrior in the caste hierarchy – which reveals the mysteries of an athletically sublime morality. Yes, Gandhi is a warrior. His bow is love. His law: disinterested action. Do or die is his motto.

To do or to die: to live or to die. And what doing! A doing that is satisfied with its own movement. To live, it suffices to do. Action is its own reward, its fruit.

Victory or defeat, all the same, in a certain way, all is victory.

But which of our heroes hasn't been beaten once or many times? Beaten, but not vanquished. For there is victory in defeat for whoever has understood the message of the *Gita* and of Gandhi.

And exhaustion? All have known it. These are human beings. Gandhi is only a human being. That's why he is so great.

It is a demanding morality, which promises the effort and not the fruit. But it is joyful, because it undoes defeat.

Gandhi is cheerful. Those around him laughed a great deal, and tried not to cry.

This play was born of India. It is not India, it is only a molecule of India, a footprint.[19]

It is a play about the human being, about the hero and dust, about the struggle of the angel and the beast inside each of us.

There are all sorts of human creatures here, angels, saints, women, men, the small, the great. And souls change in stature depending on the adversity.

But I shall never finish saying all that this play could not bear on its human back.

There are not
  the camels that pass like dreams
  the cow asleep in the middle of the road
  the little baby goats of Durgapur that caper about in the heart of the highway hell
  the vultures on the dome of the tomb of Lhodi Garden
  the sleepers like countless dead on the pavement in front of the Calcutta station and some are dead
  the three hundred starving people jostling like birds around the soup pot in Nizamuddin who show us what human hunger is
  the rats that cross through the exultant cadences of the Qawali's song
  the legless child who runs like the wind on his crutches on the esplanade of the Red Fort
  the miserable regal women carrying pyramids of bricks on their little heads up there at the trembling top of the bamboo scaffolding
  the mysteriously beautiful children who are like tears fallen from the eyes of the miserable gods up there
  the ravens as numerous as the Indians
  the passenger in the train from Bolpur who asks: and you, tell me, where do you think God resides?
  the guru of the Bauls in the ashram planted amongst the Bengali rice fields who has really understood Gandhi's thoughts
  the very old man sitting at the corner of a Calcutta side-street so small that you don't see it, in front of a single can of polish so small that you don't see it, and who is waiting for a god to send him a shoe to shine, it will happen or will not happen, and the old man is not begging because he's working, waiting, he is working waiting for nobody or someone

But all that is not said here is nonetheless silently here, I hope. Nothing is forgotten. 'What really exists cannot cease to exist.'[20]

All that doesn't figure here has become the murmuring and multitudinous earth in which this play has taken root and breath, in order to rise then, inch by inch, up to the stage.

From Hélène Cixous, 'Si vous le permettez, je vais vous parler d'amour', a preface to
L'Indiade, ou l'Inde de leurs rêves, Paris: Théâtre du Soleil, 1987.

4.3 AS IF THERE WERE A LIMIT TO HISTORY!
From an interview with Ariane Mnouchkine and
Hélène Cixous by Gilles Costaz

In an interview published two days before the opening of L'Indiade, *Mnouchkine and Cixous discuss the relevance of such a historical project in contemporary France, then describe the play's relationship to the Shakespeare cycle and the production of* Sihanouk, *as well as to India – particularly in terms of its decentred, multi-vocal dramaturgy.*

GILLES COSTAZ: Two years ago at the Théâtre du Soleil, you staged a play about Norodom Sihanouk and the history of Cambodia. Now there's *L'Indiade*, a play about India and its partition – the years 1937 to 1948 [. . .]. Aren't you looking for your subjects a bit too far from the preoccupations of French audiences?

ARIANE MNOUCHKINE: As if there were a limit to History! As if India weren't my affair! As if South Africa weren't my affair! I am French, but I belong to the world. If India is not our affair, it risks becoming so. A few years ago, who would have thought that Iran would be our affair?[21] I know that once again people will write that we've made a historical production. But in reality we're talking about what concerns us. We ourselves did not know to what extent we would be talking about ourselves, about our times, our divisions, our intolerance, our hatred.

GC: *Sihanouk* was a contemporary story recounted in a form inspired by Shakespearean chronicles. Is this the case with *L'Indiade*?

HELENE CIXOUS: One is very blind when one writes. One does not formulate genres. The form is imposed by the story. In comparison with what I have written before, this play contains an entirely new freedom which was dictated by India. India requires being multiple, being a multitude of singularities. I had an enormous notebook of terms and conditions of the Indian people! Right away, when I began the play, there were fifteen, twenty, twenty-five characters, which are not at all walk-on parts. I can't put more than five characters in one scene. I wrote as if I was on a boat on which I came and went to bring the characters over and back. I have had very particular relations with them. I crossed the leaders first. The small ones came later. Our Baul [Haridasi], the woman troubador who doesn't make history, who hears it and transmits it throughout the play, with her knowledge, I came to get her last . . .

AM: After *Sihanouk*, *L'Indiade* is part of a diptych, unless it's a triptych – how can we know what we'll do next? Sophocles, perhaps. But I'm astonished to see the degree to which this new play is different. *Sihanouk* was the child of Shakespeare, this one is the child of India. Instead of a centre which attracts all the characters, as a magnet attracts iron filings, here there is a multitude of leaders, men and women, and a people, and all of them, within themselves, are also multiple and divided. And since there is in them such searching, such metaphysical and moral ambition, these ambitions imposed themselves on the whole company, much more so than we had thought. We are making even greater demands on ourselves.

GC: In a text in the programme,[22] Hélène Cixous writes that this is a story of love but that it's also the story of a hatred. How is this conveyed?

HC: My good fortune is to have been faced with very different historical characters; having them together in a tragic play is an ironic gift made to History. I'm thinking in particular of Abdul Ghaffar Khan,[23] the giant of virtue who never faltered, a Muslim whose faith was also fidelity to Gandhi; of Nehru, a prince of the planet who travelled the entire earth with a world consciousness that Indians rarely have; and of all those people who were carried by a thirst for freedom, as Indians still are today. History has played new tricks on them, but their despair contains hope. Forty years after independence, it is heart-rending.

AM: We were not able to say everything. We could be reproached, for example, for not having spoken about the castes, but it would be absurd. India is so vast that our intention is never anything more than to translate a fragment of India, magnificent and terrible. Cambodia was a sparrow crushed between two hippopotami. Here it's a herd of animals, enraged ones, gentle ones, regal ones, abject ones, whose dreams we understand. The play is subtitled 'the India of their dreams'.

When Mohamed Ali Jinnah, who fights for the foundation of Pakistan, intervenes, we don't detest him. His dream seems to me to be one of division, but we love him.

GC: Did you go to India to prepare the play?

AM: Yes, we went back twice. We pursued people who had lived through this period. But the Indians have buried it voluntarily. There was a film on the subject, *Les Enfants de minuit*, but no theatre. Indians themselves say that they haven't had the strength to dare look closely at that period. But they think it's indispensable. It might indeed be time for them to remember.

It was very enriching to talk with people in India. Their perspective isn't the same. Looking is authorised, one has the right to be curious. And in conversation they are very voluble. After their initial questions, they come to God, to the meaning of life, with a passion as intense as that given over to soccer in some other countries. They believe in thought, even if they are excluded from knowledge. They also believe in listening. They listen so avidly that one gets the impression they're angry. They consume speech with their eyes. Each production has its little laws. Their attention has found its way into our production, it is one of its laws. Listening is an activity here.

HC: For *Sihanouk*, I very nearly didn't go to Cambodia. I didn't need to. But I absolutely needed to go to India. I was missing the 'dough' of the language. During my first trip I didn't hear the language of ordinary people. How does a rickshaw man, or a peasant, think? One doesn't find it in books. In the course of the second trip, at the beginning of this year, at last I was able to hear the heart, at the roots of the language, thanks to two women – a Bengali and a poet, who translated responses word for word. It was only very late, and after a major period of anxiety, that I was able to get half of my characters to speak.

GC: At the time of *Sihanouk*, you felt a sort of responsibility with regard to the Cambodians. Do you have the same feelings in relation to the people of India?

AM: No, India and its eight hundred million inhabitants don't need us and aren't waiting for us. But they are watching us. When we put a rickshaw man on stage, there are five million people who risk being misrepresented if we transpose him badly. And one must not insult the great figures. We need India, she does not need us.

GC: In the staging of your Shakespeare cycle, you referred to Asian theatre, and in particular to Indian theatre. Have you returned to this style in directing *L'Indiade*?

AM: The problem didn't arise. The temptation I feared never cropped up. Shakespeare returns all the time, because you ask yourself: what would he have done here? Sometimes you tell yourself he wouldn't have done this act, and that it's up to us to figure it out. But as for the Asian forms, they are here, completely internalised. Perhaps this production is not a descendant of Shakespeare, but a 'mother production'.

HC: As I've said, when I write, I don't see anything, I only hear. When I interrupted the writing of a book about Mandela[24] to write *L'Indiade*, I proceeded blind. I need to be blind. In order to write, one must not see. Ariane, on the other hand, is a visionary. To be a director, you must be an architect and a musician. Ariane hears every note in Jean-Jacques Lemêtre's music, in the places where I don't hear a thing. And she possesses the music of space. It's wonderful to see space being born.

The play has a freedom that is a constraint for Ariane. The aesthetic order of the production must contain a certain Indian dis-order. What she and the Soleil actors have created is very beautiful. The map of India resembles an enormous heart. People will feel this enormous heart.

If I write theatre, it's because I think one must have several pens and use them in relation to each other. But the experience with characters is overwhelming, it has brought me to states I do not experience when I write a literary text. In literature I have pleasure, but in writing for the theatre I give myself more exaltation and love. The theatre is an art so seldom frequented that people often speak about it badly. Few understand its violence.

From Gilles Costaz, '*L'Indiade*: un troupeau d'animaux furieux',
Le Matin, 28 September 1987.

4.4 BETWEEN POETICS AND ETHICS: AN EPIC APPROACH TO REALITY
From an interview with Hélène Cixous by Catherine Anne Franke and Roger Chazal

In the following interview, Hélène Cixous discusses Sihanouk *and* L'Indiade, *the two contemporary historical chronicles she wrote for the Théâtre du Soleil in the 1980s. She describes her first contact with Ariane Mnouchkine in the context of agitational street theatre, before articulating the profound impact of Shakespearean dramaturgy, in particular in his history plays and tragedies; she talks above all about the central role of tragic irony in her own plays. In a discourse marked by her interest in psychoanalysis and a contestatory politics, she foregrounds her recurrent concern for theatre as the site for an ethics of alterity, focusing in particular on the relationship between writing and acting as processes of transformation. She also describes her pleasure in the transformative process of her texts' embodiment in performance, celebrating the abandonment of the 'authority' of authorship. Finally, she recuperates and rereads Aristotle's conception of catharsis in terms of an ethics of compassion and a political imperative to 'speak' contemporary history. The interview was conducted in Paris in June 1988.*

'A CERTAIN KIND OF FREEDOM': WRITING FOR THE THÉÂTRE DU SOLEIL

CATHERINE ANNE FRANKE AND ROGER CHAZAL: Could you first speak a bit about how you came to work with Mnouchkine, about the genesis of that artistic venture, and about the genesis of the two plays you have written so far for the Théâtre du Soleil, *Sihanouk* and *L'Indiade?*

HELENE CIXOUS: How I came to work with Ariane is kind of novel, it's a short story in itself. I've known her for a long time; I met her because I went to see *1789*. I was struck by the strength of this work. At that time, I was involved in a kind of action with Michel Foucault. This was a small movement called GIP – Groupe Information Prison – which dealt with prison conditions. I went back and told Foucault about Ariane's work, and suggested to him that we should meet her and ask her to work with us. So I took him to the theatre. I didn't know Ariane at the time, but we spoke together and immediately came to both a kind of sympathy and agreement. She made a very short play for us that lasted about four minutes and we started doing it in the streets. It was a kind of caricature of prisons and police, performed by some of the actors from the Théâtre du Soleil. We tried to perform it in front of prisons, but I think it almost never succeeded, because before we could finish the police were there, and at that time they were extremely violent. Once I was even knocked out, in Nancy, in front of a prison. From that time on Ariane and I remained friends, and we did other political work together, in the women's movement for instance, but we never worked together theatrically. And then one day she asked me if I would try to write something for the Théâtre du Soleil. I was really surprised because I thought we were very far apart as regards art and the way I write; I didn't think she would find anything that would please her in my work or make her think that I could write for her, because my work was so different from hers.

F/C: And how did you see the differences at that time?

C: There are, from my point of view, only differences. And I think that what inspired Ariane was a kind of trust she had in me for reasons I don't know. She should speak about that. But I tried. She asked me to try, and it wasn't clear at all that I would succeed in doing anything. I had never done any work of this kind before. That was in 1983, and it took us two years to get to the performance stage. Ariane had a great dream to do a play on contemporary history. She had many ideas, and she was already rooted in a continent that was the source of all her inspiration: Asia. We came around fairly rapidly to Cambodia. What decided that it would be Cambodia was the character of Sihanouk. Yet I was afraid to deal with the present, with people who are alive. I think it's impossible to do that. First, have you got the right? You can make huge mistakes, you can mistreat people, you say things that will hurt them. To do that would be a kind of sin, unless you can find a posture that is delicate enough, tactful enough not to hurt the other. But you can never be sure of that. [. . .]

F/C: Can you talk about the differences you perceive in writing for the theatre? What is different about writing for a space, for an audience?

C: These things are decisive. Writing for the Théâtre du Soleil means writing a large play, in a tradition which is mine too, that is, an epic way of approaching reality. And writing for them gives me a certain kind of freedom. They have all the necessary means, they have imagination, they have a spirit of adventure, they are not afraid. For instance, writing something for fifty characters seems mad. I would never have attempted it on my own. Dealing with history means you have to have many characters in the play. Alone I would have been afraid, but when I asked Ariane, 'What are you going to do if there are twenty, fifty characters?' she didn't care, she can invent them. So there's no limit, and I've written without limit.

F/C: Do you and Ariane choose the subjects for your plays together?

C: No, we choose a direction, a global general subject, for instance the history of Cambodia. We open the door, afterwards I have to find the subject, because I have to write the story. You can write history from so many points of view, and choose different levels and invent different characters, since half of the characters of course are fictitious [. . .]

'WRITING UNDER THE SIGN OF SHAKESPEARE'

F/C: You said during your recent trip to California that you find you're becoming more tolerant, and that you know this to be dangerous. What is the danger?

C: I was alluding to the fact that when you write for the theatre, and particularly when you write history, you have to deal with people who belong to the type called the 'villain' in Shakespeare. There are for instance the Khmer Rouge, people whom I despise. In order to create their characters on stage, one has to reach a point of understanding, even of sympathy in relation to them. One has to understand Iago, whereas I don't like Iago. Shakespeare had to identify with Macbeth, with a potential and a real murderer. When I say that it's dangerous, I mean that you always have to make the distinction between the world of art and the world of reality. That is to say, in art you have to forgive Macbeth everything, and give him every chance to survive critical judgement, otherwise he won't exist at all. But if you meet Macbeth in real life, on the political scene, you must not forgive. So you must separate the two scenes. It's difficult.

F/C: Since you mention Shakespeare, could you continue a bit and talk about his influence on your present theatrical works?

C: I wrote *Sihanouk* under the sign of Shakespeare, I worked across and through Shakespeare in order to write it. The textuality of *Sihanouk* can be said to be worked by a Shakespearean symbolicity. His influence in my text has to do with the kind of political gestures across history which his texts exhibit. In a fundamental and founding way, it's true that Shakespeare is like the ground for my text. It's more like the ground on which I walk than like a tableau which I would try to decipher. I have an originary biographic rapport to Shakespeare. Shakespeare is for me like the Bible. It's one of the most ancient texts in my memory. I'll say that right away, before any reflection: I have always read Shakespeare. I don't remember a time when I didn't read him, in the same way that there are other texts which make memory for me, which make ground for me: for example, Greek as well as Germanic and Sumerian epics, and then the Bible. These are my 'bibles', my invisible organisers, so incorporated in my memory that I no longer distinguish them from myself. They're there, these bibles, when I need them, unconsciously. I'm conscious after the fact for instance, but not during the work, that the *Indiade* is inspired not by Shakespeare but by the *Iliad* and the Bible, whereas *Sihanouk* is nourished by, is rooted in Shakespeare. [. . .]

For me, Shakespeare comes before everything, he is always already there before any writing, be it fictional or theatrical. After which comes the situation of my theatrical enterprise, and in particular the fact that I started to write plays which sought to recount contemporary history. At which time it seemed to me that all historical theatre, which Shakespeare called Historical Plays, is inevitably in direct descent from and ancestral relation to Shakespeare. For me, as soon as one attempts to do historical drama, one is in a Shakespearean space. Shakespeare and no one else is synonymous with historical drama. So there is in my work a return to Shakespeare, a call-back to and across him, in the way in which I play with contemporary history – that is to say, in the same way the text of Shakespeare used to play with history.

Sometimes spectators ask me what my relationship to Brecht is: it's non-existent. I'm not familiar with him, probably because I don't feel a need to be, because he would not take me where I want to go. It's Shakespeare who is the conduit for everything, and I know why: it's obviously both libidinal, and the fact that Shakespeare's is an epic theatre. His drama places theatre in the realm of legend which, for me, melds with what I want to hear and make heard in a work of art.

F/C: Could you give further examples of the nourishment that your recent plays have taken from the Shakespearean tradition?

C: Well, one Shakespearean trait which I didn't borrow from Shakespeare, but which I sense is in an echoing rapport with the Shakespearean tradition, are the moments of pause in my plays, which I adore. Theatre gallops, it has to go at a rapid pace, that's one of the laws of the dramatic genre in relation to the audience. A theatre which wastes its time, starts to drag its feet and make poetic meditations, becomes intolerable to the audience. There must be action, things must move forward, this is the law of theatrical pleasure. History is like that also. When we tell a historical story, we also move from act to act, from action to action, and we are struck by all the *coups de théâtre*. So I say from time to time, let's stop history. At such a moment, I inscribe an *arrêt*, a scene which is a scene of stopping, of stopping history, in the same way that we say in French *un arrêt de mort, un arrêt de vie.*

During certain moments then in my plays there are these pauses, that is to say, no history. These moments when history stops are to me very poignant, because in fact history doesn't stop, that would be impossible. But from time to time we want to stop it, we want to sit down and look at the stars. It's as though, through these scenes, I were trying to inscribe the nostalgia on the part of human beings for eternity. If we could stop history, then there would be a constant peace, a constant rest, whereas this is not the case, there is no rest, there is only war.

In Shakespeare there are moments of suspension like this, and in his universe these pauses usually happen before a battle. For example there is a magnificent pause in *Julius Caesar*;[25] it's Brutus's night. Brutus is all alone, and he's speaking to Lucius, his servant who is sleeping, everyone is asleep, and Brutus is there, he's sitting up with the night. It's a moment before war and before death and I have always found this scene to be magnificent, because all of a sudden the theatre stops and we see a man. There's no more theatre, no more action, just a man all alone on the earth. I'm very sensitive to these moments of absolute solitude, when nothing moves, when the audience itself is no one or the gods, the silence, and a thought passes. In these moments we interrogate ourselves, and we speak our fear, and our indecision.

Lastly I'd like to mention another trait haunted by Shakespeare, a trait which is very important in *Sihanouk*, and that is the existence of tragic irony, which for me is one of the most important elements of dramatic writing. The characters on stage are blind, they think they can see, they act, but at the same time they are seen by us as not seeing what is going to happen to them, not suspecting that which is being prepared for them, they're late in relation to the announcement. Whereas we are in on the secret, the spectator is in the know about what's going to happen to the character. I call this the representation of human blindness.

We the spectators are also blind. We see Sihanouk's blindness, we see that the Cambodians are blind to what's going to happen to them, which we the audience can see rising up to meet them. What this should inscribe is that we, the audience, don't see what's going to happen to *us*, only someone behind us sees it, God sees it, maybe you see it. That's the secret, we don't see our own blindness.

The play which represents this in the most fabulous manner is Shakespeare's *King Lear*. King Lear is surrounded by people who are all telling him 'you don't see, you don't see what you're doing, lift the scales from your eyes'. And the tragedy of the story is that the blind man says, 'No, as a matter of fact I see very well.' This is the height of blindness. But that's us. That's one of the strengths, one of the most beautiful elements in Shakespeare, which is infinitely more poignant and heart-rending than its equivalent in Greek tragedy. There is a blind man in Greek tragedy, it's Oedipus, but Oedipus doesn't interest me at all, because his blindness is not a function of the unconscious. Oedipus simply *cannot* know what he's doing, whereas King Lear *could* know but he doesn't see. His is self-blinding, and that is our blindness, we blind ourselves. We're not blinded by circumstances, or by a fate which exceeds us, it's a lot worse than that. It's our human impotence which in Shakespeare dazzles us by its magnificence. Tragic irony, the mark of our human weakness, of our human unhappiness, has always upset me.

The most important scenes in my own plays in this respect are the scenes in which we are shown what could have not happened. Consider for example the moment in which Sihanouk must decide whether or not to return to Phnom Penh. He's in Paris, and he's receiving loads of telegrams, and he becomes the plaything of those telegrams, which are like the gods. The gods are telling him: 'return, no don't return, return', etc. It's at this moment that we see the tragic machine starting up. We wonder why Sihanouk doesn't open his eyes, and we know it's destiny, it's Sihanouk, it's blindness. And, as twentieth-century spectators we can also add, it's the unconscious. We know this, this is the word we've added to Shakespeare. Shakespeare knew about this, but we can actually use the term 'the unconscious'. [. . .]

F/C: In a contemporary universe where the gods no longer exist as they did at the time of the *Iliad*, where would you now locate the superior forces of which you speak?

C: They still exist but are now interiorised. They are unleashed on-stage and in our hearts in the form of drives, with a force like that of nature. Maybe I believe that human nature has its resources, its provinces, its nerves, in the same way that nature does, its climate, its winds, its skies, and I don't know how to write without that. I don't see how writing can write itself without the wings of wind.

F/C: You've spoken about uncertainty. I see in your plays a kind of contemporary knighthood, people who are on a quest, in search of the truth.

C: On the one hand there's knowledge and on the other there's belief. This year I'm talking a lot in terms of faith, but I realise that this is something to fear. It's a term one must use with caution, because above all I wouldn't like to fall into religiosity, pseudo-mysticism, etc. I 'believe', and I insist on believing. I insist as well on a certain number of values. When I work, I situate my work between poetics and ethics. I express myself poetically, at least I hope so, but I think in relation to the world. This is a state which is at the same time historic and cultural. Cultural because of what I heard, what I understood when I was young about the position of my family in history and of my family as Jewish. Not that there was a religious message in our home, but more because my family belonged – and I'd call this my good fortune – to those who have been persecuted, oppressed, massacred. They aren't any more, the Jews are no longer the massacred of today, we've changed our objects of persecution, but I was born into a universe where my family was persecuted. When I say this is my good fortune I really mean it. I feel sorry for those who haven't learned about persecution from suffering it, those who have not learned about human pain, who have been deprived of the experience of unhappiness. I think it's necessary to have met with unhappiness, in the same way that we have to have met with evil in order to understand goodness. Of course, too often the meeting with evil can destroy all belief in goodness. But sometimes there is the opposite effect, and this is what I learned in childhood: that goodness is fragile, that the human being is fragile, that life is fragile, and that the political powers of evil in the universe are of an awesome strength. One of the first messages I retained is that it's possible to eliminate a people from the face of the earth. It was in the first years of my life that I saw how it's possible to uproot an entire people from the earth, as though it were a potato. At which point I also learned that there is a world which exists and which cannot be uprooted, and that's the world of the text. As long as we haven't burned all the libraries in the world, there would always be a book, and that book could traverse all the hells, with it we could tell stories and sing songs and recite poems. I understood that there was something that was always saved. It's this combination of death and evasion via writing that founds all I've done since then. Poets were my first knights, those who with their words defend the soul.

I love knowledge. It's a succulence of the mind, something to be savoured. But I've never liked it when knowledge erects itself as master, when it declares itself as final. I don't believe in final knowledge. I believe that knowledge goes from ignorance to ignorance. There's nothing I hate more than someone who thinks he knows. I think knowledge should go hand in hand with its own incertitude, its own vacillation. It should meet its own limit and then go farther, tripping. When knowledge believes it knows, this is a sign of its profound weakness. All masters are vulnerable people, who erect themselves, who grab on and use knowledge as a crutch, because they're afraid of not knowing. I'm not afraid of not knowing.

'MODERN PASSION PLAYS': *SIHANOUK* AND *L'INDIADE*

F/C: Do the two texts you've done for the Théâtre du Soleil, first *Sihanouk* and now the *Indiade*, seem very different from each other to you?

C: I feel so. I think that I have been able to inscribe more of my own philosophy of life in *L'Indiade* than in *Sihanouk*. Of course, this is because of the subjects themselves. In *L'Indiade*, there are many characters who say things that I think. There's no one character with whom I can really identify, but there's a little bit of what I feel or think in six or seven different characters. [. . .]

One of the themes of *L'Indiade* is the question, who's going to be faithful to whom? And there we have all the paradoxes of fidelity. It's a magnificent question. In *L'Indiade*, everyone is unfaithful to everyone else, and yet the only desire on everyone's part is for fidelity. We could say that Gandhi is subjectively faithful, objectively unfaithful, if we insist on one's word as if it were a notarised contract. But Gandhi wasn't a notary. He could say one thing one day and then say the opposite the next, because in the mean time life had transformed the ground on which he was advancing. Fidelity is almost an abstract value. It's of the order of the heart. It's not keeping one's promises, because after all no one ever keeps his or her promises. Fidelity rather is not lying, day after day, moment after moment. Fidelity contains infidelity. Gandhi knew this, and it's in this way that he was tragic.

F/C: Could you talk more specifically about the figure of Gandhi? You say in one of your texts on the theatre that he is for you like an angel.

C: I prefer to say that he's a naked bird, an angel without feathers.[26]

F/C: What for you is the importance of the figure of Gandhi? Did the actor's interpretation of that role contradict in any way the Gandhi you had envisioned?

C: For me, Gandhi was not more important than the other characters in my play. I think he's a familiar figure, but equal to the others. Of course he's more remarkable, he's more original. I realise that for many people he seems to be enigmatic, because he belongs to the level of the absolute, and I realise that people don't like to sojourn in that type of country because it's difficult. But for me he doesn't seem enigmatic because a journey to the country of the absolute is not difficult for me. Not that I'm a prophet, but as a poet I very often go there.

Seeing Gandhi on the stage is quite different however, but that's because there are two moments to a play. You write the play, which is something quite personal and subjective, it's your own emotions. And then when it is performed, it becomes the work of others. This is different. For instance, you realise you're going to cry at points that didn't make you cry when you were writing, and vice versa. Or things that I didn't realise were comical make me laugh when they're embodied. There's a new kind of freedom in the new interpretation. When my feelings change, I'm not the writer any more. I'm almost the creation. I don't care any more about what I've written, what I really enjoy is the work of the actors. You know, I hate sports, but it must be like someone who watches a tennis match and who notices every move made by the players. I enjoy watching every 'move' made by the actors.

F/C: There is a higher degree of what could perhaps be called realism in *L'Indiade* than there has been in other productions by the Théâtre du Soleil. In your texts on the actors, there is also an insistence on virtually becoming the other.[27] Could you discuss this?

C: Yes, but I wouldn't call this an insistence on realism, I'd call it an insistence on truth, which is just the opposite of realism (Plate 4.2). Realism for me is the worst thing in the world; it's television, it's documentary, it has no soul. Realism is only facts, and facts are nothing. What the actors have achieved in *L'Indiade* is beyond realism, it has to do with truth. Realism doesn't touch anybody. You can watch a massacre on television without realising it's true, that people are really dying, suffering, etc. If you can catch the truth of it, then you start crying. [. . .]

F/C: You've written quite a lot about the actors, can you tell me why?

Plate 4.2   *L'Indiade*. 'An insistence on the truth' (Cixous). From left to right: Goulam, a
Pathan (Zinedine Soualem), a Sikh soldier from Simla (Asil Raïs), a Hindu
soldier from Simla (Bernard Martin), Tughlak, a Pathan (Jean-Louis Lorente),
Rahman, a rickshaw-wallah (Mahmoud Saïd), Bahadur (Mahmoud Shahali) and
his bear Moona Baloo (Catherine Schaub). Photo: Martine Franck/Magnum

C: I write so much on the actors because I know they have to take the same route
that I take as a playwright. I don't know what the director does. I don't know
how Ariane works, I don't see the path she follows. Suddenly something comes,
and I don't know how it has come to the surface. Whereas with the actors I feel
I can trace the very strange and deep itinerary they follow, because it's my own,
except that they don't write. They write with their bodies. I do the same type of
thing, it's very vertiginous. We both become somebody else, it's a maddening
experience. So I recognise all the signs of that kind of transformation. I also
recognise it when they are not there. You have to live another life. You have to
get up, and instead of putting on your own clothes, you put on the body and the
story of someone else. It's very strange.

F/C: You've also written that in order to create fifty voices in a play, you have to do
a very subtle work of identification with each character; you have to arrive at a
set of metaphors that are those of each character.[28] And each play seems to have
its own overriding metaphor as well. I'm thinking of the bicycle in *Sihanouk* and
the she-bear in *L'Indiade*. Are these metaphors which occur to you at the moment
of writing, or do they come as images when you begin rehearsing the play?

C: They are part of the writing, part of the general imaginary scene. They are at
work in the play. In *Sihanouk*, for example, there are all sorts of threads, all sorts

of metaphors, dealing with transport. The whole play *L'Indiade* is a kind of history of a she-bear. The bear herself is a metaphor for the play, for innocence and guilt, for innocent guilt, for guilty innocence, for intelligence and wildness.

F/C: And your own identification with each character, do you feel that it's an identification which resembles that of the spectator who goes to see your characters, or that of the actor who embodies them?

C: When I write I identify with each character, and I realise that I resist some of the characters because I have no sympathy for them; as I've said, I have to fight that. I have to be sympathetic even with those for whom I have no sympathy. This is a real work on my own unconscious. But when the play is finished, I become a spectator, and then I begin to identify with the actors, with their work, with their very strange adventure that is the quest for the character. I'm in a very strange position. It's true I'm probably not an ordinary spectator. I'm the spectator of the actors and of the acting process, since I watch the rehearsals. I suppose that the regular audience members are spectators of the characters, but I am a witness of the actors, of the actor working towards a character, working towards that very special type of ideal.

F/C: You've said that in the theatre you 'tell stories of modern passions', and that 'although passions are always classical, what makes them modern is when they are looked at with a humorous eye.' How do you see the relationship between tragedy and comedy in your plays? Certainly *Sihanouk* is more comic than *L'Indiade*. [. . .]

C: I think that *L'Indiade* is humorous, but maybe we're so tense, maybe the story is so tragic that we don't perceive the humour. The character of the beggar-woman Haridasi, the universal character in *L'Indiade*, is constantly funny. But I realise that sometimes when she's funny, like at the very end of the play, people don't laugh, because at that moment they want to cry. I realise that at that moment, people are so tense, they know something horrible is going to happen, and they can't afford to laugh. This is very interesting, because it means that in our own life, when there is a struggle between tragedy and comedy, tragedy always wins.

F/C: Do you see a difference in genre between *Sihanouk* and *L'Indiade*? There seems to be a purity, a classical quality to *L'Indiade*, whereas *Sihanouk* seems more like a tragi-comedy in the Shakespearean mode.

C: *L'Indiade* is much more tragic, of course [. . .] The partition of India is one of the great tragedies of contemporary history. But I don't write thinking I'm going to produce something tragic or something comic. I write thinking I'm going to write something true to human life.

'SINGING AGAINST HELL': TOWARDS AN ETHICS OF ART

F/C: Why then do you think that in human life the tragic always wins over the comic?

C: I don't think it always wins. I don't believe in that. This is the common lot of people, but I myself am not like that, I don't think of tragedy as the winner. I think poetry wins. I think there's something stronger than tragedy. It's not happiness of course, it's thinking, it's thought which is stronger than everything. That's why I've talked about Etty Hillesum.[29] She was a young Dutch journalist. She wrote in an extraordinary, powerful, hopeful way, from within the precincts of despair. She was already going to Auschwitz, and she knew about it. And she's not alone. Milena[30] did that, all kinds of people did, particularly women. It does mean that in the worst kinds of hell there is something stronger than hell, the singing of human beings against hell, in spite of hell, through hell. [. . .]

F/C: In terms of the question of innocence and guilt, you've spoken of a moment when one is going to be guilty, but one could choose not to be. [. . .] You've said that the theatre can best capture this precise moment in a human destiny. Why?

C: Because you witness it in time. There is a space of time which is limited. You're there, and you do live in your own body, in your own consciousness of time. That very strange moment when things may not happen, or happen, in the theatre it is actually one instant. It's not artificially elongated as it is in a book. It really lasts one moment and then it's done. In Shakespeare you have this in a wonderful way. I've always felt it very strongly. For instance, in *Antony and Cleopatra* there is a small moment when the spectators see Antony who, instead of going ahead during a decisive battle and fighting his enemies, changes direction because he has seen Cleopatra fleeing and he decides to do the same. People in the audience shout, they see that he's losing the universe. That's extraordinary. That's theatre. If you were to read such a moment it would be quite different. It would be slowed down. The theatre has to be sharper, and much more active and rapid than writing. This is the advantage of the theatre, but it's an ambivalent advantage. When one wants to treat a slow-going thought, then the theatre is at a disadvantage. [. . .]

F/C: What do you think happens to the spectators of your plays when they leave the theatre? Do you think a cathartic process is operated?

C: I don't know. It's a day of emotion. One day of emotion. One day out of indifference. What I can tell you from my own experience is only that they are moved. I see five or six hundred people stopped in the meaningless race of life and listening, listening to others, and accepting to be hurt or happy. I see that they cry, or refrain from crying, and I think that's something important. It's very important.

Theatre only exists because it procures for us a bonus of pleasure, it's even I would say made for that. There is a secondary advantage taken from spectacle, which Freud speaks about. Maybe we should admit that there is a tragic pleasure, and that the fact that such a pleasure exists is a good thing. We can laugh at the theatre, but we can in an equivalent manner take pleasure also from the tears we shed. Spectacle first strikes, seduces, carries away, charms us, in such a way that we can forget that it's the golden and magnificent costume clothing terrible massacres. It's a paradox, but it's made to be one.

I think that 'spectacle' doesn't destroy profound emotions, and that perhaps this charm, this seduction, this pleasure permit us to tolerate the intolerable. What would the naked intolerable be? It would be the vision of charnel houses, the naked charnel houses, bones, the grimace of the concentration camp. These are things which the individual must go on a solitary pilgrimage to contemplate. One must go to Auschwitz, or to what remains of the Cambodian charnel houses and wrap ourselves up in meditation on these remains. But this is without language, it's obviously done in silence; and it's not art. Once there is art, of whatever kind, there is transposition, there is metaphor, and language is already metaphor. Theatre is another kind of metaphor. But this is not only a question about theatre, it's a question of art in general. And it's the question of the word placing itself on that which would otherwise be only silence and death. It's a huge problem, it's the problem of the poet. Can a poet permit him or herself, and does s/he have the force to speak about that which has been reduced to silence? Wouldn't this be blasphemy? Isn't it a necessity? Isn't this exactly what we must attempt to do, knowing all the while the paradox, knowing there is a price to be paid on both sides: something is lost but something else is safeguarded. This is the question I am always asking myself. My choice has been made, after all I've decided to try to speak about that which takes our breath away. Because more than anything else I'm suspicious of silence. There is such a thing as a respectful silence, there can be a silence which sings, but I'm suspicious of human silence. In general it's a silence which represses.

From Catherine Anne Franke and Roger Chazal,
'Interview with Hélène Cixous', *Qui Parle* 3: 1, Spring, 1989.
Translation by Catherine Anne Franke.

4.5 YOU MUST KNOW WHO WE ARE, AND WHAT WE BELIEVE

An open letter from the Théâtre du Soleil to the people of Israel

Shortly before departing for Israel to perform L'Indiade *as part of the Jerusalem Festival, the members of the Théâtre du Soleil wrote the following statement to their hosts, explicitly criticising the Israeli government's refusal to negotiate with the Palestinians. This remarkable open letter is both credo and interventionist claim on a reconciliatory, pluralist future. The text details the intercultural status of the company, and its determination to use theatre as cultural and political intervention; it invites parallels with the divisive violence of events represented in* L'Indiade, *a cautionary tale in this context. The full text was published on 15 April 1988, a month before the company's arrival, in the following Israeli newspapers:* Ha'aretz *and* Yediot Ahronot *(in Hebrew),* Al-Ittihad *and* Al-Fajar *(in Arabic), and* The Jerusalem Post *(in English). A week later, it was also printed in* Le Nouvel Observateur *in France.*

You have invited us and we have accepted your invitation. But before we cross the threshold of your house, you must know who we are and what we believe.

We, authors, actors, musicians, technicians and director of the Théâtre du Soleil, originate from twenty-two countries (France, Portugal, Chile, Belgium, Italy, Brazil, Algeria, India, Cambodia, the United States, Tunisia, Turkey, Armenia, Lebanon, Iran, Spain, Germany, Switzerland, Argentina, Guatemala, the Dominican Republic, Togo). We are Christians, Muslims, Jews, Buddhists, Hindus and atheists, we are white, we are black, we are yellow, we are from countries which, in the course of their histories, have taken the roles of the colonised and of the colonisers, of the oppressed and of the oppressors, of the occupied and of the occupiers, from countries which have all known, and know, their hours of pride and shame, of progress and decline, of dignity and indignity, of humanity and inhumanity. That is who we are.

And now what we believe:

– We believe that the appropriation of territory by force is inadmissible;

– We believe that the killing of children, whatever the circumstances, and whether they be Palestinian or Israeli, is a monstrosity;

– We believe that the killing of unarmed civilians is a violation not only of the Geneva Convention but above all of moral law;

– We believe that a nation that oppresses another cannot be an entirely free nation;

– We believe that it is madness to try to destroy by force what no military force can ever destroy: the love of the homeland, the spirit of freedom. The body can be broken, but the soul of a people cannot be crushed. And of all the peoples, the Jewish people have proved this for thousands of years;

– We believe that the Palestinian people is right to revolt against the Israeli occupation and that its cause is just;

– We believe that the Palestinian people have an inalienable right to self-determination and to a Palestinian State;

– We believe that the State of Israel has an imprescriptible right to exist here, in peace and security;

– We believe that there are two peoples in this Holy Land, and that it should be shared and its borders negotiated. In the hope that, later on, once time has fulfilled its function in forgetting and forgiving, an association will arise;

– We believe that there have been enough stubborn heads, obstinate in error, in crime, and that there have been enough blind eyes and deaf ears;

– We believe that the leaders chosen by the Israeli people should agree to negotiate with the leaders chosen by the Palestinian people, even if these leaders are not to their liking, and whatever their strategies have been in the past;

– We believe that it is now time for the right of the stronger camp to give way to the duty of the stronger camp; and that since Israel is the stronger, it must take the first step. The biggest step. Is Israel incapable of this? Could Israel be more afraid of peace than of war?

– We believe that by refusing to see those Palestinians who hold out their hands, Israel runs the risk of one day being confronted with those who only know now to brandish the dagger;

– We believe that Israel and the PLO should come to a mutual and simultaneous recognition at the moment negotiations begin; then the whole world will breathe and hope once more.

We have hestitated about coming; we have talked, we have consulted a fair number of you, and we have decided not to add a facile refusal to so many criminal refusals. Nothing will persuade us to despair of the strength of words, to renounce our faith in humanity and also in art. We shall never renounce them. We are coming for the sake of peace and of those who defend it, out of admiration and fraternity with all those in both camps who, sometimes risking their own lives or braving some absurd law of their country, attempt to 'cross the bridge', to meet and talk together – whether in Paris, Brussels, Beirut, Bucharest, Budapest or Tunis, on one bank or the other.

Our visit is an homage to all of those in Israel – members of the Knesset, intellectuals, writers, artists, lawyers, journalists, citizens – who, tirelessly and for decades, have been weaving the fabric of peace which irresponsible leaders obstinately insist on tearing apart. We are coming because we believe that people change, that they have already changed, that many Palestinians have changed, and that if Israel fails to change, it will lose not only blood and lives, but the honour of internal peace. For we fear that the blindness of some is driving all of the Israeli people towards the massacre that engenders massacre and civil war.

We are telling you all of this because one must not enter the house of a friend with a heart full of unspoken suffering and secret reproaches.

From Le Théâtre du Soleil, 'Lettre aux Israéliens',
Le Nouvel Observateur, 22 April 1988.

4.6 A LESSON IN THEATRE: A MNOUCHKINE WORKSHOP AT THE SOLEIL

Josette Féral

Josette Féral, Professor of Drama at the University of Quebec, was a participant in a workshop at the Théâtre du Soleil after the season of L'Indiade: *one of a series of open workshops Mnouchkine conducts free of charge every year. In this article, Féral records her impressions of Mnouchkine as teacher. Her account reflects on the demand for an ethical integrity and rigorous discipline, and the prioritisation of mask work in the preparation of the actor. In addition, it includes transcriptions of detailed advice and criticism offered to the student performers.*

Ariane Mnouchkine's annual workshop at the Théâtre du Soleil's Cartoucherie is unannounced, its dates passed on among friends. People wait a long time to get into this renowned programme. Many candidates apply from all over the world, over 1,000 in 1988. Mnouchkine sets up preliminary interviews with each applicant to determine who can stay. Nothing fundamental is said during the few minutes of interview – just the reasons why each applicant wants to take part in the workshop. Undoubtedly Mnouchkine detects a certain sincerity, sensitivity or expectation that tips the scales. The candidates themselves are often incapable of saying what might have determined the final decision.

We were 220 at the end of this stage, from 42 countries. More than 200 for a workshop lasting seven days, perhaps ten; we overheard the trainees say that sometimes Mnouchkine extends the training and everyone began to hope that she might do it this time also. When we asked, Mnouchkine answered that she didn't know yet, that it depended on a lot of things, especially on us trainees.

THE RULES ARE GIVEN

We arrive at 9.10 a.m. the first day. With the help of Sophie Moscoso, Mnouchkine reads off our names and hands everyone an attendance card. At the end of the call, Mnouchkine retains the late ones and berates them vehemently. The first rule of the actor is punctuality. Latecomers in the future will be crossed off the list.

Other rules are imposed very quickly: absolute respect for masks and costumes, absolute silence in the hall, attentive observation of everything that happens on stage (apprenticeship involves looking as much as acting, Mnouchkine sharply reminds us at various moments). Also, the hall must be cleaned at the end of the day. However, despite these strict rules, actors keep going in and out during improvisations, costumes always end up in a heap on the floor at the end of the day, trainees sitting on the bleachers aren't always as attentive as they should be. The cleaning is reduced to a team of a few volunteers who put the hall back in order every night. Only the masks hold everyone's respect. The initiation to an ethics is difficult! Mnouchkine is outraged.

Overcome and discouraged by so much laxity and lack of goodwill, she ended the third day of work by announcing that she would interrupt the training and everyone could go home. The training had really started off very badly; the level was too low this year; there had been no effort toward real collaboration. Mnouchkine's dictum was like a cold shower. Confronted with this unexpected blow, we woke up and tried to make Mnouchkine change her mind, but she resisted. After two hours of discussion, the workshop was allowed to start up again. But this time everyone understood that we would not be given the three extra days we'd all secretly hoped for.

Never did Mnouchkine say that she offered this free workshop out of generosity, out of love for theatre and for actors. (Of all the workshops she gives, this is the only one that costs nothing.) She does it because she is very worried about the future of theatre acting, a practice that is waning and must be saved. Besides, from the beginning she was very clear: 'There are perhaps twenty actors among you; if such is the case, this would be very good. We will try to do theatre together then; and if we are able to have a few minutes of theatre during these few days, only a few minutes, then it would be fantastic.'

It turned out that Mnouchkine was right: during those seven days, where everyone improvised an average of two scenes in groups, you could count at most one short half-hour of intense and exceptional theatre. This half-hour was not delivered in one block of time, but in fragments of a few seconds or sometimes a few minutes, when spectators witnessed the emergence of a story and the exceptional osmosis of a character and an actor.

'MASKS THAT TRAVEL VERY WELL'

'I would like to remind everyone that this is a workshop. Seven days we will share together. It is not an audition. If you come to the carpet [i.e. the performance space] to show yourself, or to show *me*, you will not be showing anything. It is not a training to prove yourself. It is a training for theatre.'

The warning that Mnouchkine begins with is important. The actors, some of them present for their second or even their third workshop, know that this is where Mnouchkine recruits her actors. It happened that way for *L'Indiade*, and before that for *Sihanouk*. That is why some are hoping, while others attend simply for the pleasure of participating and learning under Mnouchkine's merciless eye.

Sitting in the first row, she follows all of the improvisations – even the most pitiful ones – with total attention and a great listening power, searching with determination for a sparkle of theatre. If the improvisations go on without genius, Mnouchkine does not show any less respect for an actor's work as long as that actor brings true desire for creation to the stage.

She can sometimes be strict, or even ferocious, which paralyses even the bravest beginnings. 'There is not even a minimum amount of sound needed,' she says before an actor can leave the stage. But her judgement is always right, without complacency. Her gaze is precise, her attention intense. She is in search of theatre in all of the bits of improvisation which are presented to her during the course of the day (from 9.00 to 5.00, interrupted by two brief coffee breaks and a lunch hour). She also looks at all gestures and even behind the masks. She may abruptly interrupt an improvisation after a few seconds, or have the actors leave the carpet, or forbid an actor to enter the stage because his appearance shows lack of respect for the costume and for the mask. Everyone ends up accepting these moments; they are never arbitrary and are compensated by remarkable times when direct dialogue and interaction emerge before everyone's eyes without mediation between Mnouchkine and a character. And so during the most productive moments of the workshop, Mnouchkine singles out one group of actors or an isolated actor with whom she works to try to give birth to a character. She assigns a trajectory, which opens a vast imaginary world, animating the actor with a certain wind, giving her depth and projecting her forward.

As is her custom, Mnouchkine makes her actors work with masks. It appeared during the course of improvisations that masks from *commedia dell'arte* and from Bali marry well and adhere to the same theatrical laws. We made our acquaintance with Pandeba, Rajissan, Pucci (baptised during the workshop). 'I will not give you the characteristics of a mask, otherwise I would reduce them,' Mnouchkine said to begin with. 'Some have names, others not. This one is Rajissan, for example. They all have greatness. They have a complete soul. Do not look down on them. Do not caricature them if they are uncultured. Contrary to the masks of the Noh theatre that we embalm so well that we cannot find them, these are human. But they are sacred too. We called this one Punta. This other one has eyes, it dances; it is very difficult, it doesn't have a name. This one is Pandeba. The mask is heavy, but be careful, he is light, very light. This one also; do not make him out to be more of a simpleton than he is. This one is complete. He has buttocks and a hole in the butt. It's obvious that the best thing that can happen to you is to love one of these. To love it means to recognise it, to have known it. You will see, they travel very well. They are surprised, but they adapt themselves very well. It is the opposite for the *commedia dell'arte*. They are crushed by character traits, they die under characteristics. They are human beings.

These masks are made of leather and wood. They are very fragile. Erhard Stiefel made them. You can imagine what would happen to you if you break one.' We laugh.

'IN ORDER FOR THERE TO BE THEATRE, YOU ONLY HAVE ONE SECOND'S TIME'

After presenting masks and using them for the first time, we proceeded to teamwork: the choice of a character, the development of a scenario, the preparation of a costume.

Mnouchkine proposed a theme: occupation. Last year, the subject was invasion. Improvisations this time centred around collaboration, resistance, black market, fear, rivalry, cowardice, denunciation.[31] All Théâtre du Soleil costumes are at the actors' disposal: the clothes from the Shakespeare cycle, from *Sihanouk*, even those from *L'Age d'Or* and *1789*. Mnouchkine has a special taste for costumes. She likes them to be lively, rich, exact, finished. These preoccupations produced the splendour of the Shakespeare costumes, their extreme sensuality, the warmth of the *1789* costumes, the opulence of the velvet and lamés, still shining from the various shows. During the workshop, dressing became an important phase of the preparation, the phase that allows an actor to enter into her character.

Actors formed groups by affinity to develop scenarios for improvisation. One quarter-hour, one half-hour, sometimes three quarters of an hour of group consulting and conspiring for improvisations that often only lasted several minutes. 'It's too long,' Mnouchkine would sometimes say. The actors tend to lose themselves in the maze of a convoluted intrigue to the detriment of work on details of events and states of being.

'In order for there to be theatre, you only have one second's time. When you enter the stage, the story is already being told. I want so see a character right away. Where is he? Why does he arrive? Why is he there? The spectators have paid, you cannot tell them: wait until I get settled. We, the public, are there, and they, the characters, know that we are there. I know that you know that we are there. And you know that I know that you know that we are there. And we are there for them. That is the most difficult thing.'

SOME BASIC RULES FOR THE ACTOR

Mnouchkine incessantly repeats the same advice. It's simple, but always turns out to be difficult to put into practice.

Preparatory work and the scenario[32]

Do not make confabulations as though you are staging *Les Misérables*. Content yourself with three good lines of preface. The goal is not to get to the end of the story. Work together. What can you do all alone at home? Nothing. You have to learn together. Listen to yourselves. Take yourselves in. You must accept things from others. If that person proposes something to you, take it.

To imitate does not mean to plagiarise, it means to recognise. They have been imitating for generations in the East. It is not a question of imitating from the exterior but from the interior. Not to imitate what the other has done, but what he was. If it is impossible to imitate in this sense, then it is impossible to imitate someone else, a character. You have to have the humility to put your feet where others have left traces.

You also have to have imagination and secrets. Do you have secrets? [*Laughter*]

Could it be that in this workshop there are no secrets? You must learn the patience and humility of mystery. Do not try to be original at any price. I do not care about originality. Learn from others. When someone does something good, do it yourself a second time and bring it further.

Avoid falling into an idea; search for the true, not the realistic. The true is not realistic. To enter on to a stage is to enter into a symbolic place where everything is musical and poetic.

The mask and the character

The masks make terrible and unyielding demands. The costume is chosen on the basis of the mask and the character. The mask is not make-up. It is not a non-entity. Everything is at its service. If you use it incorrectly, it will denounce you right away. You are the one to yield to the mask, it will never yield. So you have to respect it, love it. If not, it is as though you don't recognise that these masks have a history, a past, a divinity. Instead of wishing to rise toward them, you bring the mask down toward you, you make them banal. You have to make a journey toward them. You do not use a mask in any which way. You do not use just any mask, either.

Our relationship to the mask is one of magnanimity. These masks come from far away, from another continent. The theatre is another continent. It seems as though you would like the theatre to come here. No! Theatre is not comfortable here. When you call a character, it comes with its world. It is complete. It is not a group of functions. Keep the autonomy of each character. Keep some air around them. No prettiness, no *coquetterie*. I want to see a character. I feel as though you are expecting instructions behind the mask. No!

The costume

Finish your costumes well. They can be your friends. They are your enemies if they are badly made, if they don't hold together. The brains themselves have to be made, covered, without hair. Bare skin is difficult to use with masks. Hands, feet – it all makes it too realistic. Do not become bizarre and ugly creatures. It is a sin not to believe that in every creature there is beauty.

The acting

Look for your little interior music that gives rhythm to your actions. Let your imagination come to you. The difficult thing is to let yourself do while doing. You are either *in doing*, which blocks you, or *in the letting yourself do*, where you do nothing.[33]

Use your imagination. The imagination is a muscle. It can be built up, enriched, nourished, by looking at others with mischievousness but without meanness. The actor is an active receptable; this is not a contradiction, but a difficulty. You must be concave and convex. Concave to take in, and convex to project.

Avoid moving around all the time. If you move constantly, I don't see you. You must find your stops and your rhythm. The stops give movement, the states of being give life. In order for me to see you, you must stop. Only do one thing at a time. If you jump for joy, good: so jump, then speak – but do not do both at the same time. Sometimes you acted out two things: your despair and your mistrust. You have not been able to act one thing at a time. So we haven't seen anything.

Complete your gestures. Take the time to finish everything. Do not stammer with your gestures. Complete your stops. Also, avoid slowness that tries to be profound. It's often too slow to be honest. Do not fall into true slowness. You have to act out this slowness, but at a quicker pace. Slowness is an enemy. After several seconds, there is nothing left of the previous illumination.

Avoid over-acting and being idea-filled. Verbiage is as gestural as it is verbal. Avoid decorating. Some people do not realise the physical exertion this demands. Do not adorn your acting when you haven't got the essential down. There are people who arrive and don't have anything in their bag. And others who arrive with many things in their bag, and it is worse. Proceed in a simple way.

You are so rushed that you explain yourself to us instead of living. Do not comment on your gestures constantly. The public is not stupid, it understands. You do not take the time to act out your desires and your anger. You are not in the *present*. You are here already and I do not see your desires. I want to know what you want before you get here.

One of your only weapons is action; but while you are in the doing alone, nothing can happen to you. You need states of being, presence. It is the state of being that justifies actions. The most important thing is to find your state of being. You need a *pure state of being*, a series of pure states of being. Is it enough to work on the state of being? Are you sure that if we work on a state of being the state will follow? No. A lot comes from what you believe or do not believe. But to *believe* is most important.

You believe that space is outside of you. This is wrong, it is in you. I can only take in space if I see you take it in. I only see this distance by your look. We are the ones who see you seeing. You must be visionaries; it is essential. As long as we have illustrative entrances, figurative ones, you cannot fly off. If you illustrate space, there is no stage, there is no theatre. You have to see to believe.

You want to create by intelligence; no. Give yourself time. The problem is a rapport between the interior and the exterior. If you are not able to translate this rapport, you do little things – instead of daring to tell us, instead of making signs. Signs ask the question. If you haven't at a given moment felt both the emotion and the externalisation by the sign, you haven't found it. Do not hide yourself, reveal yourself. You have to dare to discover. You are being figurative instead of metaphorical, instead of finding the sign.

Your problem will be to translate your state of being. Dramatic acting is a translation. Translate something immaterial, an emotion in a body. It is through the body that this emotion operates. The actor is a double translator, because his own translation must also be translated.

'THE MASK IS ESSENTIAL FOR TRAINING THE ACTOR'

During the course of the workshop it was shown that the mask is essential for training the actor, because it does not allow lies and it uncovers all the weaknesses of the actor: lack of imagination, knowing how to act more than how to be, lack of presence, lack of listening power, etc. By its very nature, the mask uncovers all complacencies, all weaknesses. It works against the actor who doesn't enter it and uses it to hide herself. Inversely, it can become sublime and bring forth theatrical moments of rare intensity. Behind the mask, thanks to it and its support, characters emerge and are led into extraordinary adventures.

It is true that the use of the mask imposes a certain form of acting, which other less typed theatrical forms do not. But it is evident that the rules of theatre which apply themselves to the mask are valid everywhere.

During the course of the classes, certain simple principles recurred again and again, although it was always difficult to apply them: the distinction between easy and simple, decorative and necessary, falsity and trust, big and little, solitude and listening, displacement and action, illustrativeness and state of being, exteriority and externalisation.

Some of the advice Mnouchkine gave to the actors ended up having the strength of maxims: find the true and precise little detail; look for the little to find the big; do not confuse displacement and expression, apoplexy and dynamism, slowness and depth; refuse moves for the sake of moves in theatre; do not act counter to the mask; do not accept a versatility during an improvisation; know when to give up what we had planned on, and accept what might present itself. But more than anything Mnouchkine untiringly stressed the importance of the vision we bring to things – the vision that teaches, listens and remembers. The necessity of apprenticeship by observation.

Despite the numerous failures, the rare successes, this workshop was a deep lesson in theatre. At the end, Mnouchkine reminded us that the laws of theatre undoubtedly exist, but during the night they hide and the next day no one knows where they have gone.

From Josette Féral, 'Mnouchkine's workshop at the Soleil: a lesson in theatre', *The Drama Review* 33: 4, Winter 1990. Translated by Anna Husemoller. Also published in French in Josette Féral, *Dresser un monument à l'éphémère: rencontres avec Ariane Mnouchkine*, Paris: Editions Théâtrales, 1995 and Montreal: XYZ Editeur, 1995.

4.7 BUILDING UP THE MUSCLE OF THE IMAGINATION
An interview with Ariane Mnouchkine by Josette Féral

The following interview took place in March 1988 at the Cartoucherie, during a performance of L'Indiade. *Mnouchkine reflects on some of the 'fundamental laws' governing performance, and on the interrelated roles of emotion, belief and imagination in the processes of acting.*

JOSETTE FERAL: I know right away that you're going to answer my first question by saying that there are no theories about acting.

ARIANE MNOUCHKINE: I don't know if I would say that. I know that I myself do not have any, maybe because I am not in the position to develop a theory on acting. I may not ever be capable of developing a theory on acting. Because in fact the idea of a theory of acting involves a written development of the theory of acting and a practice of acting. That is to say that we, directors and actors, put into practice the practice – we don't practise the theory.

I think that if there's no theory of acting, at least there are theoretical laws that we may find, curiously enough, in all traditions of acting. It is true that the term 'theory of acting' doesn't seem fundamentally wrong, but it always sounds somewhat imperialistic and pretentious. I prefer to use the term *fundamental laws*, laws which we sometimes recognise, but then sometimes lose and forget. It is only practice that can suddenly make law or tradition rise to the surface.

I will not say then that there is no theory of acting; on the contrary, there have been many of them. Of course, what interests me in these multiple theories are the essential laws that are common to all of them.

F: What are these laws?

M: Do you want me to make an inventory of them? How shall I tell you? They are so mysterious and so volatile. Sometimes we get the impression that a rehearsal goes by, and we've forgotten laws we thought we knew perfectly the day before. All of a sudden during a rehearsal, there's no more theatre; an actor cannot act, a director cannot help an actor any more. We ask ourselves why, and we cannot understand. It seems to us that we're respecting the laws, and actually all of a sudden we realise that we have lost the essentials: for example, *being in the present.*

I believe that theatre is the art of the present for the actor. There is no past, no future. There is only the present, the present act. When I see young students work on what they call the 'Stanislavski method', I am surprised to find out how much they go back to the past all the time. Of course, Stanislavski talks about the character's past: where does he come from? what is he doing? But the students are not able simply to find the present action. So they go back, and I always tell them, 'You enter leaning backwards, weighed down by all this past, while in the theatre only the moment exists.'

I think that the greatest law is probably the one that governs the mystery between inside and outside, between the state of being (or the 'feeling', as Jouvet would say) and the form. How do you give a form to a passion? How do you exteriorise without falling into exteriority? How can the autopsy of the body [*corps*] – I mean the heart [*cœur*] – be performed by the body. My slip of the tongue is revealing because the autopsy of the heart must be performed by the body. An actor worthy of the name is a kind of autoptist. His or her role is to show the inside [. . .]

'EMOTION COMES FROM RECOGNITION'

F: You talk about emotion from the actor's point of view, but doesn't emotion exist for the spectator as well?

M: The emotion is different in the two cases. For example, Indian theatre offers something very beautiful from this point of view. There are great theoretical books on the subject. There is Zeami, of course, but there is also an Indian book,[34] an enormous work that gives the theory of Indian theatre as a whole. It contains laws that I find extraordinary. For example, there are different words to define the emotion of the actor and the character [*bhava*], and the emotion of the spectator looking at the actor [*rasa*]. In Western theatre, in the acting style of certain actors, I find an ability to bring together what should be their emotion, which should be a part of the action, and what the emotion of the spectator should be. These are the good moments: when all of a sudden a spectator has tears in her eyes while what the actor performs is a moment of enthusiasm, happiness and laughter. Why do you suddenly start crying with joy or recognition?

F: Because you perceive at this very moment the exactitude of what is happening. It is the truth of the moment we experience, independently from what is expressed.

M: Exactly. The emotion comes from recognition. From the fact that it is true.
[. . .]

F: How do you help an actor to be in the present? Do you use a technique, or method? Is your method a form of listening?

M: I believe that there are no techniques. There are methods, and every director has one, maybe an unconscious one. I believe I have one, but I do not know it.

The last word you said is very important: 'listening'. I believe that I know how to do that well. I love to listen, and I love to watch the actors – with a passion. I think that's already a way of assisting them. They know that I never tire of listening to them, of watching them, but how do I help them? I don't know.

F: In one of your texts you wrote, 'One must build up the muscle of the actor's imagination.' The nourishment you feed the imagination is a form of assistance.

M: When I work with very young actors, one of the first questions I ask is, 'What do you think is the actor's most important muscle?' [. . .] It is the imagination, and it can be conditioned, worked on.

F: How do you proceed?

M: With sincerity, with emotion. By acting, by really acting. Not through memory, I don't believe in that. You have to be able to have visions little by little, to be a visionary – to see what they talk about, to see where they are going, where they are; to see the sky above them, the rain; to take in the emotion of another and to believe in it.

In reality, *the* essential theory is that you have to believe: believe in what you act, what you are, what you incarnate; and believe in what another incarnates; believe in the emotional turmoil, in one's strength, one's anger, one's joy, one's sensuality, one's love, one's hatred, whatever. But you have to believe in it. The common misinterpretation of Brecht is that we thought he said you shouldn't believe in it. Brecht never said that; he said you should not deceive.

I think there is something in the actor's work that obliges him or her, not to fall back into childhood, but to enter childhood. Actors must divest themselves of all made-up images which go against the work of the imagination; such images are clichés or crutches where there is no emotion [. . .]

'WE MUST HAVE THEATRE THE FIRST DAY'

F: Does work on character happen alone? In a group? In discussions?

M: Nothing ever happens alone. From the very beginning the work happens by acting. For us, there is never, never any work at a desk. We read the play once, and the next day we are already on the stage. The actors can decide to try all the characters they want for several weeks, even several months. They have old bits of costume at their disposal to disguise themselves, and they begin. And we act right away. We must have theatre the first day.

F: Do actors remember what they have done on-stage, so that the good things they have found during improvisation are retained? Or is it simply a period of exploration?

M: There is a period of exploration, but the good things remain when they are really good. This is what you were saying about the precision of gesture, what we call the *evidence* of gesture. The gesture is not what remains, because things are fixed much later; but we will know that such and such a character has that type of gesture, that he's a little like that. Then we will discover something else. Because one of our most important laws is to keep firmly in our mind the conviction that all of the characters – *all* of them – have a complete soul. We realise it's slightly dogmatic to say that each character in a play contains all the others. There is a little of Prince Hal in Falstaff, a little of the father in the son, a little of Juliet in the nurse, a little of the nurse in Juliet. Everyone is complete. Otherwise we do not progress. Which happens to us sometimes.

There were times when I realised that the concept of work on a character, the concept of character itself, could be very limiting, that we could often translate a character by limiting it instead of creating someone without limits who is always a surprise. There are character types, of course, but you always have to be able to go beyond the type.

F: Do you make a psychological study of the characters? I am asking you this because in *L'Indiade* we don't get the impression that the characters have a psychology. Instead the characters seem to be from the theatre, they are presented as theatrical constructions, with a complexity but without day-to-day psychology. They are emblems. They are motivated by signs rather than by psychology.

M: We flee daily life. We do not talk of psychology, but rather of the characters' souls. But they still have emotions, sensations; they are cold, hungry, proud, they want power, they don't want it, they're stubborn. Each one of them has their own way of being, their own world. Nicholas Boileau said, 'The truth is not always verisimilitude' – and verisimilitude is not necessarily true. This can be understood precisely in a historical play: that is, what happens, happens. These characters experienced it, oriented it, or made it happen. It was with their 'psychology', as you say, that the events took place.

But, and there's no question about it, the theatre is not supposed to represent psychology but *passions* – which is something totally different. Theatre's role is to represent the soul's different emotional states, and those of the mind, the world, history. In the Théâtre du Soleil, psychology has negative connotations; 'psychological' acting is a criticism. It means a performance does not reach truth; it is slow, complicated, narcissistic. Contrary to what we believe, psychology does not pull toward the interior, but toward the interior mask.

'ALL THEATRE IS ORIENTAL'

F: There is no tradition of gesture in the West. Many directors must look for this tradition in the East. You yourself in the Théâtre du Soleil have to find inspiration from Asian theatres. What are you looking for?

M: Theories that have marked all theatre people. Artaud, Brecht and all theatre people – because it is the source of theatre. I think that we go East to look for theatre. Artaud said, 'All theatre is oriental.' This thought goes very far. He doesn't say, 'There are oriental theories that are interesting for theatre'; he says, 'All theatre is oriental.' I believe Artaud is right. So I tell actors to look for everything in the East. Myth and reality, interiority and exteriorisation, and the autopsy of the heart by the body that we talked about.

We also go to look for non-realism or theatricality. The West has only given birth to the *commedia dell'arte* – and even this comes from Asia – and to a certain type of realism, from which great actors escape. It's true that great actors, even in a realistic theatre, succeed – and I don't quite know how – in not being realistic themselves. But it is difficult.

F: Is theatre in need of traditions?

M: It needs sources and memory. It needs to be worked on in order to allow the depths and origins to come to the surface. We have traditions. Lineages exist and they belong to us completely, even beyond national borders.

F: Why don't you put your theories about acting in writing?

M: First of all, my area is not writing. Also I sincerely think that everything has been said already and in an extraordinary fashion. Someone asked Jean-Jacques Lemêtre, our musician, if he invented instruments, and he replied: 'You do not invent instruments any more – you transform them, you rediscover more, but you don't invent them any more; they have all been invented.' I too reply that you do not invent theories of acting any more. The problem is that theories exist, but that they have been buried at the same rate as they have been pronounced. Let young students read Zeami, Artaud, Copeau, Dullin, Jouvet, Brecht as well. Everything is there. And let them make theatre. We do not need to say more.

From Josette Féral, 'Building up the muscle: an interview with Ariane Mnouchkine', *The Drama Review* 33: 4, Winter, 1990. Translated by Anna Husemoller. Also published in French in Josette Féral, *Dresser un monument à l'éphémère: rencontres avec Ariane Mnouchkine*, Paris: Editions Théâtrales, 1995 and Montreal: XYZ Editeur, 1995.

NOTES

1 'From the scene of the unconscious to the scene of history', in Richard Cohen (ed.), *The Future of Literary Theory*, London: Routledge, 1989, p. 12.

2 Cathy Caruth, 'Unclaimed Experience: Trauma and the Possibility of History', *Yale French Studies* 79, 1991, p. 192.

3 'Conversations', in Susan Sellers (ed.), *Writing Differences: Readings from the Seminar of Hélène Cixous*, Milton Keynes: Open University Press, p. 150.

4. 'Le Rire de la Méduse', *L'Arc* no. 61, 1975, pp. 39–54. The English translation used below is 'The Laugh of the Medusa' (trans. Keith and Paula Cohen), *Signs* 1: 4, 1976, pp. 875–93. [JGM]

5 *Signs*, op. cit., p. 883. [JGM]

6 Ibid., p. 882. [JGM]

7 Ibid., p. 888. [JGM]

8 Miller is referring to Mnouchkine's invention of the *billet-mécène* at about this time: a form of voluntary patronage, in the face of financial deficits, whereby audience members could pay more for their tickets – an explicit resistance to the double-binds of corporate sponsorship that represented a minimal denting, rather than any 'shattering'. By early 1988, the Soleil employed about sixty people, everyone receiving the same salary of 7,500 francs a month.

9 Cixous, *L'Indiade, ou l'Inde de leurs rêves*, Paris: Théâtre du Soleil, 1987, pp. 75–6. All translations from Cixous's play in this essay are by Judith Miller. [JGM]

10 *L'Indiade*, op. cit., p. 24. [JGM]

11 Ibid., p. 125. [JGM]

12 Cixous, 'L'Ourse, la Tombe, les Etoiles', in *L'Indiade*, op. cit., pp. 249–50. [JGM, translation modified]

13 *L'Indiade*, op. cit., p. 148. [JGM]

14 For a critique of what is read as Cixous's universalising humanism, and in particular her discourse of the maternal in this 'pantheistic liturgy', see Anne-Marie Picard, '*L'Indiade*: Ariane's and Hélène's conjugate dreams', *Modern Drama* 32: 1, March 1989, pp. 24–38.

15 *L'Indiade*, op. cit., pp. 81–2. [JGM, translation modified]

16 'The actor is always a bit saint, a bit woman: she must give life while withdrawing. What's more in theatre everything is woman: woman the director, birthgiver to the characters *and* the actors'; Cixous, 'L'Incarnation', in *L'Indiade*, op. cit., p. 265. [JGM, translation modified]

17 Cf.: 'Cixous's and Mnouchkine's ambitious endeavour is a historiography, a *mythography* and a *demo-bio-graphy*.' Anne-Marie Picard, *Modern Drama*, op. cit., p. 26.

18 The *Bhagavad Gita* ('The Song of our Lord'), a central section of *The Mahabharata*, is Hinduism's most celebrated and influential devotional work. It focuses on the Pandava archer Arjuna's discussion with Krishna about the necessity and propriety of war. See J.A.B. van Buitenen's *The Bhagavad Gita in the Mahabharata: Text and Translation*, Chicago: University of Chicago Press, 1982.

19 In an article on *L'Indiade* as confusion and subversion of mimetic theatre's purportedly 'objective' referentiality, Timothy Scheie proposes a reading of Cixous's footprint metaphor: 'The "real" India is an impression, a negative space, an absence which

the spectators, like the characters in the play, fill not with a truthful referent but with the contingent projections of their own imaginaries: the "India of their dreams".' 'Body trouble: corporeal presence and performative identity in Cixous's and Mnouchkine's *L'Indiade*', *Theatre Journal* 46: 1, March 1994, p. 42.

20 Cixous is quoting from the Sanskrit epic *The Mahabharata*. Peter Brook's CICT production of *Le Mahabharata* had premiered at the Avignon Festival two years earlier in July 1985; *L'Indiade* opened at the end of September 1987. According to Marvin Carlson, the 'goal' of *L'Indiade* 'may be considered the opposite of Brook's [in *le Mahabharata*] – instead of seeking a universal experience outside of history, *L'Indiade* seeks to place its material in historical consciousness and to provide for its audience an insight into the dynamics of the historical process, with a view, ultimately, towards making the results of that process more humane.' 'Brook and Mnouchkine: passages to India?', in Patrice Pavis (ed.), *The Intercultural Performance Reader*, London: Routledge, 1996, p. 90.

21 In the late 1970s, Ayatollah Khomeini, the Shi'ite mullah who led the revolution to overthrow the Shah of Iran, lived in exile in Neauphle-le-Château, a suburb of Paris. He used his base in France to send much publicised messages to the people of Iran.

22 See section 4.2 above, Cixous's 'A long passion'.

23 Abdul Ghaffar Khan was a Pathan leader from the North-West frontier who supported the Congress Party. His non-violent struggle for a unified India earnt him the nickname 'the Gandhi of the frontier'. Persecuted by the Pakistan government, he spent more than forty years in prison.

24 *Manne aux Mandelstams aux Mandelas*, Paris: Des Femmes, 1988.

25 *Julius Caesar*, II, i, 1–70.

26 Cixous, 'Et qui est l'Ourse?', in *L'Indiade*, op. cit., p. 251. It is worth noting the degree to which Gandhi's central ethical principles have echoes in Cixous's own discourse: most notably, non-violence (*ahimsa*), search for truth (*satyagraha*), love of the other, and non-violent civil disobedience.

27 For example, 'L'Incarnation' and 'Qui es-tu?', in *L'Indiade*, op. cit., pp. 260–6, 267–78.

28 'L'Incarnation', in *L'Indiade*, op. cit., p. 262.

29 Cixous has written in similar ways about the intersection of a number of artists within an oppressive history, including Paul Celan, Osip Mandelstam, Anna Akhmatova and Marina Tsvetayeva. For a brief account of Cixous's interest in these figures, and in Etty Hillesum, see Verena Andermatt Conley, *Hélène Cixous*, Toronto: University of Toronto Press, 1992, pp. 102–18.

30 Milena Jesenská was a Czech writer whose intimate correspondence with Kafka, in the early 1920s shortly before his death from tuberculosis, has become celebrated. She died in the Nazi camp at Ravensbrück in May 1944, after four years of incarceration. For further information see Jana Cerna, *Kafka's Milena* (trans. A.G. Brain), Evanston, Illinois: Northwestern University Press, 1993.

31 Evidently at this time Mnouchkine was already thinking about a possible performance on the French Resistance. To the present time, she believes the forms for this production evade her. See Alfred Simon's interview with Mnouchkine below, section 5.2, 'The space of tragedy'.

32 The following advice is compiled from statements delivered by Mnouchkine during the 1988 workshop. Sometimes she was speaking directly to an actor, sometimes her comments were general. They have been edited together here. [JF]

33 Cf. *siddhi*, the goal of a number of Asian psychophysical practices, which Phillip Zarrilli describes thus: 'a state of "accomplishment" in which the doer and done are one [. . .] a state of stillness in motion' [which] 'frees the martial or performing artist from "consciousness about", preparing him for a state of "concentratedness" [. . .] *doings in the now moment*.' Zarrilli, 'What does it mean to "become the character"? Power, presence and transcendence in Asian in-body disciplines of practice', in Richard

Schechner and Willa Appel (eds), *By Means of Performance: Intercultural Studies of Theatre and Ritual*, Cambridge: Cambridge University Press, pp. 131, 134.

34 Mnouchkine is referring to Zeami's fifteenth-century treatises on the art of Noh, and the *Natyasastra*, a 2000-year-old Sanskrit text on theories and codifications of performance.

CHAPTER 5
MYTH AND THE CONTEMPORARY

LES ATRIDES
Iphigénie à Aulis (Euripides)
Agamemnon (Aeschylus)
Les Choéphores (Aeschylus, *The Libation Bearers*)
Les Euménides (Aeschylus)
(1990–1992)

Sometimes one has to go very far. Sometimes the right distance is extreme remoteness. Sometimes it is in extreme proximity that it breathes.
Hélène Cixous[1]

What is passive, immobile, asleep in the heart creates a desert [. . .] The more our desert, the more we must rage, which rage is love.
James Hillman[2]

5.1 *ÉCRITURE CORPORELLE* AND THE BODY POLITIC: *LES ATRIDES*

Sarah Bryant-Bertail

The following extracts from a detailed analysis of the performance texts of Les Atrides *explore the production's exposure and critique of certain aspects of the Greek myth as self-serving narratives of legitimation that endeavour to naturalise the patriarchal ideology of an empire as it begins to define itself. Employing a critical vocabulary that draws on feminists Judith Butler*[3] *and Teresa de Lauretis,*[4] *as well as on Brecht, Barthes and Said, the author proposes a reading of the* mise en scène *of* Les Atrides *as contestatory and counter-discursive, above all in terms of 'the fateful intersection of gender and empire'. In particular, she details the destabilising gestic function of doubling/multiple casting and costuming. Sarah Bryant-Bertail is Assistant Professor in the School of Drama at the University of Washington, Seattle.*

Mnouchkine's commitment to a historically responsible theatre has taken her along a Brechtian route through a *Verfremdung* [defamiliarisation, critical distancing] achieved by borrowing from Asian theatre. In a seeming paradox, she explains that she can only seize the historical import of a work (i.e. its relevance for our times) by creating a distance. For *Les Atrides*, a cycle of four plays that adds Euripides' *Iphigenia at Aulis* to Aeschylus's *Oresteia*, this distancing is achieved through the filter of an imaginative context inspired mainly by Kathakali dance, make-up and costumes, and the colours and fabrics of India. The Atreus cycle is part of a long series of 'Orientalist' projects for which the Théâtre du Soleil has adapted Asian theatre conventions to stage Western texts [*Les Shakespeares*, *Les Atrides*], or created new works that depict the colonisation of the Third World more directly [*Sihanouk*, *L'Indiade*]. Both serve a necessary function in the Soleil's ongoing political and cultural critique, a dialogical engagement against and with the Western and specifically French theatrical tradition.

Like Barrault, Brecht, Brook, or anyone else who appropriates the art of another culture, Mnouchkine risks practising cultural hegemony. Nevertheless *Les Atrides* stages as *historical* the verbal, visual and aural discourses through which the West *embodies* the multiple Other as a non-Western, non-masculine, ultimately non-human 'oriental'. The historical responsibility taken on by Mnouchkine is an elucidation through theatrical means, above all that of *l'écriture corporelle*, or writing by the actors' bodies, of the fateful intersection between the discourses of gender and empire in this founding myth of the West, setting forth power relations that remain in force today [. . .]

For Mnouchkine, as for Brecht, the historically responsible theatre does not aim to reproduce a context outside itself. Neither ancient Greece nor India nor France is imitated realistically. The attempted reproduction would imply that history flows along everywhere else but on stage, unless theatre is forcibly transformed into history's channel. Instead, theatre is both a producer and production of historical consciousness, and Greece, India, Asia, and implicitly France and Europe, are shown as floating cultural signs. In short the *mise en scène* is semiotic, not as a formalistic structure but as a site where historical signs are *produced*. It is more than a theatre aware of itself, or an epic theatre with direct speeches to the audience, 'non-linear' time, montage space, separation of elements, songs and dancing interrupting dialogue, etc. Above all, *Les Atrides* is not a staging of the tragedy as inevitable, but as a history that didn't have to be.

The *Oresteia* has become so encased in canonical production styles and receptions that it appears to be suspended in a world sealed off from time. It is often claimed as the founding text not only of Western drama but of Western culture, and usually interpreted as the defeat of the old barbaric tribal law of revenge and the victory of the new rule of democratic law. However, a historical inscription of gender, race and empire underlies this idealised mythic reading.[5] Mnouchkine's prefacing of the trilogy with the rarely staged *Iphigenia at Aulis* strongly foregrounds the ambition, violence, misogyny and sheer political expediency of the militaristic patriarchy [. . .] By simply prefacing the *Oresteia* with *Iphigenia*, Mnouchkine opens the work to a feminist perspective. Indeed, she sees sympathy for Clytemnestra and a critique of the patriarchal Greek empire as already inherent not only in Euripides but even in Aeschylus – with the work of *Les Atrides* being to strip away layers of time and convention and let the text speak for itself [. . .]

The concept of the *mise en scène* as a historical construction site is evidenced in the theatrical space as soon as the spectators enter the building. On the back wall of the spacious *salle d'accueil*, or reception hall, and illuminated as the focal point of the whole hall, is a large political map of the ancient Mediterranean world, with a red line representing the voyages of Agamemnon.[6] Around the room on the walls, stands or tables are photos and books on Greek history and culture. At a long counter and from small carts, Greek food is prepared, sold and eaten on site [. . .] On their way to the performance in the adjoining hangar, spectators must walk along a path above what resembles excavation sites filled with life-size terracotta statues of people wearing the same costumes as the actors, facing in one direction and either standing alone or leading horses, recalling for many the famous army of ancient Chinese warriors. Sculpted by Erhard Stiefel, the statues have been affectionately nicknamed 'the crowd' by the company, and seem to be frozen in the act of walking up out of the earth.[7] The spectators, having crossed this 'excavated' transition space and taken their seats in the steep bleachers, wait a time, then the lights dim as the sound of a kettle drum rises to a thunderous roar; and suddenly the dancers of the chorus rush on with exuberant shouts in a whirling blaze of red, black and yellow costumes, as if the crowd of statues had returned to life and found their way to the stage.

According to Mnouchkine, the chorus is the key to achieving a historical perspective, of distancing what is too near and recalling the past to life. The stage-filling energy of the dancers with their bounding leaps, cries, richly elaborate Kathakali-like costumes and their faces an expressive circle of white make-up, black-lined eyes and curved red lips, is the most startling departure from conventional stagings of Greek plays. The physical presence of twelve to fifteen men and women of the chorus accompanied by the live percussive music of Jean-Jacques Lemêtre electrifies the theatre. Because it was crucial for Mnouchkine that the audience hear the text clearly, it was never sung and only chorus leader Catherine Schaub or other single voices spoke the chorus's lines. Moreover, the chorus never danced while dialogue was being spoken. The principal actors often joined them, either as characters or as anonymous chorus members. Convinced of the importance of choral dance to ancient tragedy, Mnouchkine aimed to restore its vital role, not by reconstructing it from iconic or textual evidence but by imbuing it with the still living energy of the Kathakali and Bharata Natyam dance theatres whose forerunners almost certainly had confluence with those of Greek theatre.

The space mobilised by the décor, music, light, and the voices, gestures and movements of the actors, all set up a historical writing, above all what Mnouchkine calls an *écriture corporelle*: a writing with the body, a gestic vocabulary of signs that reappear throughout the plays, not just delineating a style or illustrating the text but haunting the ongoing action so that there can never be the sense of a pure present. The performance space is the discovery site of a buried story. The bare simplicity of the set and scenography express this site as a cosmos waiting to be historically specified. The playing space has no curtains, flies or wings, but is a wide expanse of terracotta-coloured floor surrounded by a wall of the same material and colour, crumbling and seemingly blood-stained in spots, and broken by several recesses and by a double-doored gate in the upstage centre. The space of the Greek cosmos is defined as enclosure within enclosure: the terracotta wall encloses the stage, and this inner wall in turn is enclosed by a high wooden wall painted the bright blue of sky and sea, in the middle of which is a second large gate that opens at times to reveal darkness beyond. Suspended above the stage is a white canvas 'tent' roof decorated with Greek designs, through which bright sunlight (actually fluorescent) seems to shine. Several spectators have compared the playing space to a sunbaked bullfighting arena, connecting it to the matador-like costumes worn by several of the characters: Iphigenia, Clytemnestra and Orestes.[8]

For portentous entrances or exits, large box-shaped platforms on hidden wheels carry the main characters and define the locale. In *Iphigenia at Aulis*, a glide brings Iphigenia, Clytemnestra and Orestes to Aulis; a second becomes the altar of Iphigenia's sacrifice, and a third carries Agamemnon to war. In *Agamemnon*, it brings Agamemnon and Cassandra to Argos; and finally, in *The Libation Bearers*, it is the tomb of Agamemnon. Only these platforms, pulled by ropes that have no visible operators, pass through the outer wooden doors beyond the blue wall. Thus they alone seem able to traverse the space between life and death, the known and the unknown worlds. In the course of the productions, the gliding platforms come to signify the movement of a fate whose drivers remain a mystery.

The psychic and social space of the Greek world is also created by other scenographic signs. A sound of vicious dogs is heard at the end of three plays, and for two of them it is accompanied by a tableau of the murder that has just taken place. Each tableau is a mattress with life-size mannequins of the murdered couple [Agamemnon/Cassandra, Clytemnestra/Aegisthus] lying together as if caught in sexual embrace, and each time it is dragged with increasing difficulty on and off the stage by actors. Whereas the platforms glide seemingly without effort through the two sets of gates, the mattresses are always dragged through a central vomitorium from under the audience, emphasising their significance as deathbeds, all too human *vehicles of fate* connected expressly to sexual relations. The mattresses visibly replace the *ekkyklêma* used in Greek theatre for such violent and fateful tableaux, but their difficult manoeuvrability contrasts with our image of the rolling *ekkyklêma*, as it does with the gliding platforms[9] [. . .]

The production of *Les Atrides* underscores in several ways the tragic irony of Clytemnestra's murder of Cassandra; most importantly, Cassandra, Iphigenia, Electra and a leader of the Furies are all played by the same actor [Nirupama Nityanandan]. In *Agamemnon*, the chorus has just described the death of Iphigenia: how she struggled and tried to cling to the ground but was tied, hoisted up and held face down 'like a goat', gagged and silenced, then her throat cut with a sword. Listening to this Clytemnestra is doubled over, a signal gesture for pain that will be repeated by several characters. Just at this moment, Cassandra appears upstage at the outer gateway on a chariot-platform, and Clytemnestra hesitantly takes a few steps towards her as if she recognises her, but the chorus

Plate 5.1   Les Atrides: Agamemnon. The Emissary (Simon Abkarian) and the chorus. Photo: Martine Franck/Magnum

blocks her path and the moment is gone. Later the same platform is taken into what seems to be the palace grounds, and the two women have a moment alone. Clytemnestra tears down the red cloth behind which the girl is sitting with her back turned, unwilling to come out. Clytemnestra tries to speak to her, asks her to use sign language, and even climbs up on the platform with her, but finally gives up. Recognising Nityanandan, we sense that somehow it *is* Iphigenia, and that if she only turned around or spoke she and Clytemnestra would see it too[10] [. . .]

Mnouchkine's production of *The Eumenides* strongly historicises the text's depiction of the feminine Furies/Eumenides and by implication of women themselves as elemental irrational forces that must be tamed and submerged by rational 'male' forces. Through the striking addition of contemporary costume elements, the Furies are exposed as a constructed embodiment of demonic femininity, a monstrous foreign other against which the patriarchal state defends itself. When the Furies finally appear, they are revealed as the 'real' source of the sound of raging dogs we heard at the close of the preceding plays. The Furies chorus wear fierce dog-ape masks, snarl and move with an ape-like gait; and whereas in the preceding three plays the choruses were free to climb over, sit on or stand behind the inner wall, to retreat to its recesses and go in and out of its entrances, the openings are now blocked by metal grates behind which the Furies are trapped. The quality of anachronistic pastiche in the costumes is suggested by certain critics' comparing of the Furies to creatures from *2001 A Space Odyssey* or *Planet of the Apes*.[11] The three leaders by contrast wear rags and tennis shoes and resemble Brechtian characters – or in the words of one critic, 'Brechtian bag ladies',[12] with Nityanandan dressed like Mother Courage. As Clytemnestra's ghost, Carneiro da Cunha appears in a bloody karate-like white shirt and pants, reappearing as Athena in the same costume minus the blood. Similarly, Apollo's white robe resembles the Messenger's in *Iphigenia* – except that the blood is now gone. The repetitions in costumes and multiple casting create their own historicising comment. Carneiro da Cunha reappears as Athena to address Nityanandan, now a leader of the Furies. Through this *counternarrative* created by the discourses of casting and costume, and the anachronisms of the final scene, the unified image of the Greek cosmos is shattered, and along with it the discursive unity of the myth itself.[13]

We recall that two of the preceding plays ended with a violent tableau of two mannequin corpses lying in sexual embrace on a bloody mattress. In this context, the voices of attacking dogs gave a sense of recurrent *human* brutality in which both sexes participate. With all this preceding *The Eumenides*, it is difficult to believe our eyes when all the violence is attributed to the feminine elements gathered here, represented by Clytemnestra and the Furies. Textually, the winged hounds of Agamemnon are never quite forgotten, even though the Furies are set up as the source of the violent sound. As increasingly contemporary embodiments of violent feminine forces, they expose their semiotic function of *grounding* the patriarchal Greek state. Athena herself, recognisably the same actor who played Clytemnestra, ironically stands on another white mattress, a clean one this time, as if it were a throne or pedestal. When the Furies finally accept their new role as guardians of the hearth, Athena gives them the honour of standing on it. The stage narrative of the mattresses culminates in this last play. We recall that Aegisthus and Clytemnestra managed only with difficulty to drag the mattress off by themselves, whereas Electra and Orestes had to be assisted by the chorus. At the end of *The Eumenides*, Clytemnestra stands alone on-stage on her mattress, trembling arms outstretched, facing back towards the again-imprisoned Furies as if to restrain them. The gliding platforms of 'inevitable fate' never reappear here at all.

This staging of the women's final defeat does not totally serve the patriarchy, however, nor erase the threat it feels. The barring of the performance space by metal grates is only the final concretisation of a long historical process, the open admission of what the signs have told us all along: Greece is a militaristic patriarchal empire, and Athens a city state and an Idea whose borders must be policed [. . .] In the text, the threat of its 'others' literally goes underground, as the Eumenides are escorted to their subterranean home by a crowd of Athenian women and girls. In this production, Clytemnestra lifts the bars and the Furies are 'freed' temporarily to enter the arena, where they first rush towards the audience in their ape-like gait, screaming and gesturing from the edge of the stage, then gradually take a more human posture as they engage in a dance resembling those in the preceding plays. Then they are reimprisoned. Thus a kind of terrible peace is reached.[14] The *mise en scène* is a body politic closing in as it becomes visible.

When Athena embraces the leader of the Furies who is about to be led away, it is one more ironic sealing of the women's defeat. However, since we know that these two performers also played Clytemnestra and Iphigenia, the gestus of their closing embrace is a *mise en scène* with multiple meanings. The irony of both mother-daughter and goddess-demon trapped definitively in this system becomes even sharper. Yet at the same time the embrace is also very moving, because we have watched these two since they were a mother torn apart from her daughter in the first play, seen them pass by each other, each fighting her battle alone, needing and yet failing to recognise each other. Thus along with the bitter irony, there is a joy that they are reunited because this moment has been long in coming. (The stage image of ragged women embracing each other has recurred at the end of several of Mnouchkine's productions over the years, and has become a kind of signature.) The spectator's identification of the women's tie has become a performative act in itself, a counter-discourse to the master narrative that is inscribing defeat. As a whole, the *mise en scène* illuminates the violent theatrical scenario through which the City still inscribes itself as the dawn of democracy and the victory of civilisation, law and rationality over barbarism, revenge and irrationality [. . .]

In summary, through the signs of a fantasised Asian theatre, *Les Atrides* sets a double *Verfremdungseffekt* into dialectical motion; in attempting to keep the text 'as we know it' from dissolving into its new 'Oriental' context, we can hear it with new clarity. At the same time, the interlocking sexual and imperial politics are brought to light through many non-verbal stage discourses, so that we can retrace the familiar *Oresteia* story as a playing out and legitimation of a set of power relations that we recognise all too well because they still exist today. Although the multi-racial cast and the Kathakali-inspired dances, costumes, make-up and bodily language of gestus in *Les Atrides* do make the performance appear exotic, the East becomes a stage sign that is exposed as such – a repertoire of images used to write a story in the space-time of a theatrical arena. Yet in being written the unity of the myth is not shored up but visibly disintegrates. Signs of the East share this arena with signs from the West, from Greek theatre to contemporary film. In its cumulative effect the borrowing does not repeat the reduction of India or Asia to a colonised other, but illuminates this Orientalism as a borrowing of living traditions in order to retell and interrogate a founding story of the West. Wherever the colourful figures originated, and whatever their proportion of Eastern and Western ingredients, the abiding memory is that they unearthed themselves to walk up from the past, dance for us, and re-write the old new story of the house of Atreus.

First published as 'Gender, empire and body politic as *mise en scène*: Mnouchkine's *Les Atrides*', *Theatre Journal* 46: 1, March 1994.

5.2 THE SPACE OF TRAGEDY
From an interview with Ariane Mnouchkine
by Alfred Simon

In an interview recorded late in 1990, when work on the first two plays of the Les Atrides *had been completed, Mnouchkine discusses the implications of tragedy and the tragic today. With reference to* Iphigénie à Aulis *and* Agamemnon, *she compares the dramaturgies of Euripides and Aeschylus, particularly in terms of the role of the chorus. She explains the structure of the Théâtre du Soleil tetralogy, with Euripides' play placed at the beginning of the* Oresteia, *and the relationship with Greek performative forms and ideas – notably Aristotelian catharsis. Finally, she locates this project in terms of continuing research with the actors, as a pedagogical 'apprenticeship' in the avoidance of* psychologisme: *as with* Les Shakespeares, *a return to past forms as a route forward to theatrical representations of contemporary history.*

ARIANE MNOUCHKINE: Although I'm not a Hellenist, I decided to take on the translations because existing ones weren't good. I started with a word-for-word translation which Claudine Bensaïd, a teacher, had written for me. I had the *Belles-Lettres* bilingual text in hand, with Mazon's translations, on which people usually rely. I realised that the French and English translations contained enormous differences in meaning, stemming from copying mistakes reproduced from century to century. Translators had tampered with the original manuscript to such an extent that it didn't seem possible to reach the meaning. I sensed that things had been toned down.

   Then I came across a study by a great philologist, Jean Bollac, who has worked on the *Oresteia* for fifty years, verse by verse, so as to reconstitute the text and the meaning. I decided to pursue him. I met him. He gave me access to his archives, and when I realised that I would never finish the other translations, he agreed to translate *Iphigénie à Aulis* himself. Above all else, we wanted to make a very precise and exact translation, the opposite of Claudel's style of adaptation [. . .]

ALFRED SIMON: It doesn't bother you that, in order to present the story from beginning to end, you put Euripides first, placing his play before Aeschylus' trilogy?

M: It's true that we begin with the younger author, and that has certain consequences.[15] For example, one realises that the chorus in Euripides has nothing to do with Aeschylus'. In the latter, the chorus is womb-like. Everything comes from it. It's the central character. We sensed this very quickly. In Aeschylus, everything comes from the chorus. The characters are fragments of human beings, they're all the same, as if they didn't exist as people. In Euripides, on the other hand, the chorus is treated almost as a punctuation device, although it retains its Homeric qualities. Furthermore, in *Iphigénie*, the chorus is made up of young foreign women who, while of course concerned, are rarely active, and never wholly so. This is the opposite of the chorus of old men in *Agamemnon* and, to an even greater degree, the chorus of *Les Choéphores*, because they give their name to the tragedy [*The Libation Bearers*].[16]

When I started to reread the Greek tragedies, and in fact for many I was reading them for the first time, I realised that I understood nothing about them, and yet I was caught in their spell. When I read *Iphigénie à Aulis* for the first time, it struck me as being one of the greatest.[17] I immediately told myself that the whole story needed to be recounted, that this was the only way of understanding the *Oresteia*. For an audience as culturally removed from it as I was, it's necessary. Otherwise they wouldn't understand Clytemnestra at all, she would become a criminal monster. It's above all she who is concerned.[18] And that's how we decided to produce all four plays. We under-estimated the size and difficulty of the task. For the Théâtre du Soleil, Shakespeare and Aeschylus represent the same challenge; perhaps Aeschylus is even harder. It requires from the actors such a reconversion: such paring down, and such strength of exteriorisation, and at the same time such a strong and profound interiority . . . It's true that the obvious stylistic differences, the surprising inventions of Euripides precede Aeschylus improperly. But we benefit by witnessing the progression of the story.

S: What do you call the inventions of Euripides?

M: [. . .] In particular it's Euripides' dialogue that is innovative. It's more . . . modern than Aeschylus'. But I don't have a judgement of value or a hierarchy between the two.

S: Those who have become interested in Greek tragedy in the wake of Nietzsche, Claudel and Barthes, have often thought that the pinnacle of tragedy was –

M: – Aeschylus!

S: Yes, and in particular the *Oresteia*. And that the decline of tragedy and the misunderstanding of the tragic was heralded by Euripides.

M: I only partially agree with that idea. In the process of working with the actors, each time we come back to *Iphigénie*, we are more sensitive to the difference and our pleasure increases. This relates in particular to the chorus. And when we put on the chorus's costumes from *Agamemnon* again, something mysterious and even cruel happens. Now, if we're working on both plays at the same time, we discover analogous moments in *Iphigénie* too. It is wrong to claim, like Nietzsche in particular, that Dionysos is absent from the theatre of Euripides.[19] [. . .] At the Théâtre du Soleil, we were initially so convinced of that inferiority that it slowed us down a little. And then, during a particular scene, we understood that what it contained that was most modern was not a weakness. The chorus is somewhat diminished, but the characters assert themselves, Iphigenia in particular. The chorus is no more than an instrument that serves at least to lighten things up, if not as entertainment.

S: What you're saying relates above all to the writing of the dialogue.

M: But also to the construction of the play. The suspense! the *coup de théâtre*! The dramatic interest comes across in both. Euripides invents *coups de théâtre* which are very appropriate and poetic, *coups de théâtre* that are *coups de cœur*, that strike the heart. And what is tragedy if it isn't the palpitation of the organic heart, and consequently the tragic chorus? Why not accept the *coups de théâtre* in Euripides if we love them in Shakespeare? I'm not alluding to the providential intervention of a messenger at the end, or to any other *deus ex machina*. But for example Achilles arrives, unaware of what is taking place in his name. Then Clytemnestra arrives, and with three questions brings the message to light, without meaning to! Normally Achilles and Clytemnestra should not have met. Their meeting is a *coup de théâtre* [. . .]

During rehearsals, with Aeschylus, even more so with Euripides, we had the impression that the entire history of theatre was unfolding before our eyes. In the course of improvisations, sometimes Marivaux came to mind, but what was intimidating, even stifling, was that one feels one is really *at the source*. With Euripides especially, one senses how, later on, Marivaux will construct a scene. Chekhov, I don't know, he's too atypical. He's a theatre all by himself. In Aeschylus, the arrival of Aegisthus at the end of *Agamemnon* has a Shakespearean quality to it. It all depends on the spirit of the translation. I saw Antoine Vitez's *Electra*. He was looking for a modernism, the modern suit for example. That's not what we did at all. I try to inscribe tragedy in the nearest foreignness possible. The same goes for the music, the dance, the chorus.

S: What brought you to produce *Les Atrides*, rather than the production on the Resistance?

M: I wasn't ready. I wanted to create the production on the Resistance, and at the same time I was resisting it. It remained on the level of photography, or cinema for me. For example, I couldn't imagine the space. When it comes to mounting a production, I always need to imagine a space, even if that space will change later on. Without a spatial outline, I can't do anything. That's how far we had got. Hélène Cixous was in on it. Her writing was galloping along. There was theatricality in all of the scenes she wrote. But as for me, I saw one décor for one scene, a different one for another scene. I was swimming in full-blown realism. In the end what happened was somewhat analogous with what we lived through when we were working on *Sihanouk* before putting on the Shakespeare cycle.

S: So you had envisaged presenting *Sihanouk* before the Shakespeares?

M: Well, not *Sihanouk* directly, but Cambodia, the genocide in Cambodia. We called it the production about Cambodia, or, even worse, the contemporary production. Similarly, today we talk about the production about the Resistance. As long as we refer to it in this way, we won't be ready. In any case, I won't. Once we can call it the Jean Moulin production, for example, once it acquires some flesh, then we'll know that we can begin to work. That's my conviction. I think, by the way, it will indeed be a Jean Moulin production. At the time of the Shakespeares, I still believed that I would write the text myself. Now I know that I'm not capable of it. Translation, yes, adaptation, perhaps. But an original text, no. So at that time we went back to our studies, with Shakespeare. And the same holds true today, with the Greeks [. . .]

S: So it was a temporary inability at the level of writing that determined what you did?

M: No, not the writing. I said that Hélène Cixous had progressed in the work a great deal. She decided to stop, given that I was not ready. That's when I signalled to the actors that we were stopping the research on the Resistance. And I had noticed that they were all more or less in the same uncertainty I was in. All of them had 'contemporary' images in their minds, in the worst sense of the word, devoid of the mythic dimension which must exist within us to cross into theatre. And so I proposed the project on tragedy [. . .]

S: Is it the global character of the undertaking, the fact that the *Oresteia* is the only trilogy that survives to us today, that made you choose it?

M: I have always enjoyed telling a story in its totality. We had already come close with the Shakespeares. But it's true that I also wanted to produce once again a large production in several parts. However, what's most important is the splendour of this tragic story, one of the most beautiful of all. Other reasons played a part, although I was unaware of them at the outset. The role of the women, for example. At first I didn't realise how important the women were, and how much that meant for me. We recognised this during the rehearsals.

And after all, for a story of such scope, we only had the choice between the house of Atreus and the house of Labdacus (Oedipus' family). We chose the former. And who can really say why? There is necessarily something mysterious in a choice. Perhaps the balance of the definitive choice became apparent when I placed *Iphigénie* at the beginning of the four plays. The moment when I discovered a play I hadn't known at all and when I undestood that it *opened* onto the *Oresteia*.

S: Is this related to a feeling that in Aeschylus' *Agamemnon* the explanations of the watchman, of the chorus and its leader at the beginning of the play, are not sufficient to make us understand the mechanism of the tragedy?

M: With *Iphigénie à Aulis*, we witness the crime of Agamemnon at first hand. He sacrifices his daughter in calculated self-interest. If Agamemnon's crime and Clytemnestra's suffering are not represented, even if the chorus repeats it forty times, this won't exist for an audience unfamiliar with the myth. For us too this became concrete during rehearsals. On the other hand, as soon as this crime and this suffering are made concrete in *Iphigénie à Aulis*, the chorus in *Agamemnon* assumes its full importance! It denounces the messenger's lie at the end of *Iphigénie*[20] [. . .]

S: It's a great problem in theatre, erudite theatre, the first acts of exposition in the tragedies of Corneille [. . .] Is this the first time that *Iphigénie* has been performed at the beginning of the *Oresteia*?

M: Ah! Yes, I think so. And we did this precisely because we were aware that we're not scholars working for scholars. The more we progress, the more we think about the audience. In the contemporary context, given the cultural lobotomisation people have to endure, such texts are a gamble. It is so complex, harrowing and sensuous that one can have doubts. [. . .] Spectators must be able to accept *not* understanding at times. And at the same time one must do one's utmost to ensure that everything that is comprehensible is understood.

S: Were you tempted, not to reproduce them, but to draw inspiration from Greek theatre spaces, from the famous configurations in Epidaurus or in Athens?

M: Not at all! First of all, I wasn't familiar with it, and didn't want to be. I prefer to work by confirmation, to have my intuitions confirmed by documents after the event. Now that I know it, that famous configuration does not seem very good to me. [. . .] That sort of shed which served as a back wall! We don't know. So what's the point? What is necessary is to rediscover everything through the magic of theatre. These texts are so powerful philosophically, and as literature of course, but above all as theatre, that they ought to blind us. One cannot see something that is blinding. I think we'll be very close in spirit to the true space of tragedy.

S: Particularly since you've been very close to that space for years, since the Shakespeare cycle. For *Hécube*, [Bernard] Sobel seemed to take inspiration from the décor for *L'Indiade*. Is the notion of a 'Theatre of the World' [*teatrum mundi*] at all present in scenography of this kind? Is it an image that touches you?

M: It seems a bit too global to me.

S: I think it's more or less absent from Greek tragedies, although it's so present in Shakespeare.

M: The Greeks speak only of the soul. They speak of it biologically. The guts! As soon as that mysterious thing called theatre really occurs, it's always the Theatre of the World. When I'm looking for a space, I don't think about that. I ask myself: where does this take place? Where do these people return to, in order to perform this for us? The chorus, Agamemnon, Clytemnestra – when they re-emerge from their graves, where do they return to recount and relive like a passion what they have lived? Perhaps certain spaces sometimes succeed in becoming the Theatre of the World. So much the better. But that's not why I do it. I don't think one can start from there [. . .]

S: Has the presence of Jean-Jacques Lemêtre [. . .] played a role in your choice?

M: Not the only one, of course, but if Jean-Jacques hadn't been there, I wouldn't have thought of staging *Les Atrides*. Just as I would never have thought of introducing masks into the Shakespeare plays without Erhard Stiefel. There are decisive encounters. I don't know how one could stage a Greek tragedy without having a musician who loves theatre and the work with actors, like Jean-Jacques. All the more so in that we can't do everything the Greeks did. For example, make the actors sing. In the first place we don't know how they sang. Perhaps less than we believe. And we are not singers. Our chorus is very musical, but in fact more danced than sung. Furthermore, I want people to understand the text, and that's almost impossible in song. Jean-Jacques literally transposed song into dance. I don't understand how one can mount plays that were conceived with and for music without music. [. . .]

S: Is the music still based on rhythms and percussion?

M: Rhythms, yes. Not only percussion. Jean-Jacques does not do reconstructions, although he has worked on what we know of Greek music, and we know more about the music than other technical aspects of Greek tragedy. One must also take into account the resemblances between certain kinds of folk music, such as Turkish popular music and Greek paeans.

S: Were you inspired by what we know of Greek masks?

M: Absolutely not.

S: In *L'Age d'Or*, you wore masks of the *commedia dell'arte*. In the Shakespeares, of Chinese acrobats. And in *Les Atrides?*

M: It is violent make-up. As in Kabuki.

S: Did this provide an opportunity for additional work on masks, as at the time of *L'Age d'Or*?

M: Additional work, certainly! But on the mask, and especially on what it means for an actor to exist on a stage – I can't tell you yet. Work on what essence is, perhaps. The essence of presence, of existence. What makes the difference between an actor who enters, starts to speak and all goes well, and another who does all sorts of things, and all you want is for him to stop! Already in *L'Indiade* I felt this to some degree. I was always saying to the actors, 'Less, even less'. A mixture, a balance between more and less. On the one hand, always more economy; on the other, the maximum, all of *that*, of the 'that' which remains. The problem is that I haven't managed to know what this 'that' is, and yet I recognise it as soon as it's there. It has nothing to do with the academic cliché: the text, nothing but the text, yet all the text – that's all too facile, although the complete expression of the text also enters into the 'that'.

In short, there is a good *nothingness* that one must attain, and a bad *nothingness* one must eliminate. It's not a question of 'doing nothing' either, which some people take as praise for an actor, by saying that he does nothing or almost nothing. If someone does nothing, nothing happens, that's all. On the other hand another actor enters, he does something, it is nothing and it's everything. With tragedy at least there is something: acting, mythology, myth. And we believe it. Don't talk about impassiveness and immobility either. The characters are always saying: I'm crying, I'm suffering, I'm bleeding; they are always showing biological symptoms, translating a biological energy. But with economy. The body must not lie.

S: Nudity?

M: An extreme nudity, certainly. Nothing to do with supposed sobriety. There are so-called sober actors who are terrible show-offs.

S: And yet this has nothing to do with a philosophy of nothingness.

M: Nothing at all.

S: So what is the meaning of tragedy for you?

M: There are thousands of books that attempt to give the meaning of tragedy. The chorus in *Agamemnon* keeps saying, 'It was the gods who did everything. Man made the wrong choice. He will perish.' Zeus does everything but the unjust man must perish. That is where tragedy is: the wrong choice is fatal. There is destiny and there is choice. What can one do when the best choice, the fairest choice sometimes also leads to death? But the wrong choice leads to the abyss. And destiny leads to death, even with the right choice. How can one escape? To me, this palpitation of thought is magnificent, this kind of forwards–backwards, one step ahead, one step back. Their bodies palpitate, their hearts swell and contract with the rhythm of their thought.

The idea is fleshy for the Greeks. It is their great theatrical invention: giving flesh to questioning. Thought is always an action in theatre for everyone, but even more so with the Greeks. Thought is an activity of the body and a suffering. Often darkness and sometimes illumination. It is magnificent and terrible, terribly difficult for the actors.

Ultimately, tragedy is life, quite simply. It is the eternal contradiction between necessity, the 'detestable inevitable', and choice. One never precludes the other. Unfortunately the right choice does not preclude a bad destiny, catastrophe, and destiny does not preclude choice. [. . .]

I would add that tragedy is also apprenticeship. It's Agamemnon who affirms that, 'Understanding comes through suffering.'[21] That in itself is tragic. That progress must be paid for through suffering!

S: Does this imply [. . .] a love of pain, a complacency towards suffering?

M: The Greeks love the spectacle of pain in theatre, on stage, in fiction, yes. Indeed we all love pain, violence, blood, death in the theatre. The Greeks love sacrifice and slaughter.

S: Perhaps because tragedy has a sacrificial origin?

M: Perhaps it's also the true sense of the word *catharsis*. They understood that certain things, violence, must be expressed one way or another, and that it's better to express them on a stage than in reality. Even among the Théâtre du Soleil actors, this violence is sometimes censored. At the beginning of the rehearsals, in front of Iphigenia with her throat slit, they didn't dare admit to themselves that it was beautiful and voluptuous. One senses that Greek audiences were able to listen to such things for hours on end. And in the end we are too, with them.

S: Particularly in the plays of Euripides. His baroque side.

M: In Aeschylus too. The scene in which Clytemnestra returns with the bloody corpses of Agamemnon and Cassandra unites beauty and perversity. Clytemnestra not only wanted this murder, she also stages it to the very end. The word perversity is not appropriate, by the way. For the Greeks it's a matter of human nature itself. During the Shakespeares, we did not explore the question of catharsis in such a radical manner at the Théâtre du Soleil. With *Les Atrides*, it's impossible to avoid it. Violence is present from beginning to end. And anyone who does the same work we did will realise that everyone is permeable to it, everyone shares it. More than that, one must share it in order to be able to put on a Greek tragedy. If one stages it while censoring oneself, entirely repressing one's own drives, then I think that the essence of the tragic is lost.

The person who articulated this best was Nietzsche, all the same. In spite of its over-hasty judgements, which were scandalous to some, what is really dazzling in *The Birth of Tragedy* is that this man with no practical experience of theatre immediately perceived what was essential. In terms of the central question, 'What is it to perform a Greek tragedy?', what is essential lies in the relationship between Apollo and Dionysos, and this philosopher sitting at his desk, without any physical relationship to the theatre, went straight for it. It is all there. Greek tragedy attained its apogee in the balance between Apollo and Dionysos, where Dionysos weighs with greater weight than Apollo, yet without abolishing him.

S: The story ends with the acquittal of Orestes in *Les Euménides*. Thus with a sort of end to the tragic, a movement beyond it, an appeasement. Have *Les Euménides* presented a particular problem for you? [. . .] The play seems to be a sort of religious mystery, with something mystical about it.

M: Let's say that I don't really believe that. It is the establishment of a new order. Aeschylus tells us that the gods partially abdicate, that Athena foregoes her power of justice in favour of human justice. I don't see where the mysticism lies.

S: A lot of modern directors resort to a form of Brechtian distanciation, through derision and parody.

M: I reject derision. I take the play seriously. It is by taking things seriously that some possible derision can be unmasked. Derision is always an evasion. But I will tell you this: there is humour in the Furies. They are cunning and naive at the same time. They allow themselves to be taken in. But it's humorous rather than derisory.

S: The gods give up some of their power. The Greeks invent democracy – based not on a secular notion of humanity, but on a humanist notion of the gods; the gods become more human.

M: Yes, but Athenian democracy had taken shape a long time before Aeschylus wrote the *Oresteia*. Aeschylus wrote a parable about its birth, in sum. It's a commemoration through myth. This is no less astonishing.

From Alfred Simon, '*Les Atrides*: rencontre avec Ariane Mnouchkine',
Acteurs 84–5, November–December, 1990.

5.3 THE COMMUNION OF SUFFERING

Hélène Cixous

In the preface to Michèle Laurent's book of photographs of Les Atrides, *Cixous endeavoured to articulate the paradoxes of the Chorus and its ecstatic sufferings. Throughout this piece, Cixous plays on the French homophone* chœur/cœur *(chorus/heart). In this way, she suggests the Chorus's centrality as the affective 'pulse' in this cycle of plays, as well as the psychosomatic status of its presence: in other words, the choral dance as symptomatic embodiment and hystericised 'performance' of the psychic pain engendered by the actions of others – repressed affect written somatically, on and in their bodies* (écriture corporelle).[22] *Cixous implicates us in the Chorus's plight as spectators torn between the daemons of fear and hope, both here at the Théâtre du Soleil and in wider contexts where the 'nameless' suffer 'economies of death': Cambodia, Ethiopia, the Gulf, Algeria, Bosnia.*

They fear, they suffer, they strike, they are struck, they fall under the blows of those closest to them, Iphigenia, Agamemnon, Clytemnestra, each of them suffers in his place in the family scene, each man and each woman in their name and in the name of the parent, Iphigenia as the daughter on one hand of Agamemnon, on the other of Clytemnestra, she suffers at least three times, for her for him for her, each one suffers, kills, is killed, each man each woman is in the atrocious net woven by the ties of the Atreus family – it's not only Agamemnon who is in the net, the whole family is in the net, the family weaves the net, the family is the net, each one shoots and kills another by the name, by the ties that bad fate poisons.

The net spreads, next Cassandra, then Orestes, each of them takes from it, each of them is taken in it.

And not only all these heroes brought together by the ties of blood, of love, of hate, and the names that hold them,

But we too, we whom the poet named the Chorus, we are in the net, and we suffer, and many times, we suffer otherwise and in a way that is terrible and otherwise tragic, we who are the innumerable and Nameless Character of these tales.

I will speak of the Chorus. Of our role, of our action, of our destiny.

I will speak of the Nameless Hero, who occupies such an important place in the plays which tell us the cruel story of the Atridae, of his mystery and necessity: nothing is without him (without them, without her), nothing is with him. This Character who doesn't kill and who isn't killed, what is his function, what is he doing here?

Later on – after the Greeks – this Nameless one will disappear, did you notice?

We no longer find him in Shakespeare, nor in Racine, neither to the North nor to the West, unless in the form of slender people, reduced to a near 'uselessness', a nurse, an attendant, a few dead people. That is all that is left of this powerful partner.

Look closely, look at these young women who tremble from their feet to their heads, traversed as they are by fateful messages.

Look at these old men who struggle furiously to stand up in the storm, and that time has led to the end of the path of life to the wavering state of the last childhood, look at these beings whose febrile flesh is rocked with presciences and apprehensions.

Look closely at them, for they are going to disappear, these mediums. This is the last time, perhaps, that, with the Chorus and as chorus, we are to be admitted once more into this terrestrial theatre in convulsion.

– What use is it, since it doesn't kill, it doesn't avenge, it doesn't cause, and it doesn't prevent anything?

– Well, the necessity of the Chorus is precisely there: it is there to *suffer otherwise*, to bear the pain of those who, caught in the Net, don't do anything, can't do anything, it is there to live the pain of powerlessness, the dreadful pain without consolation, without compensation, of those who watch people suffer, our pain.

The Chorus has its own tragedy, that of the Powerless Witness, the tragedy, always begun anew, of exile, of interdiction, of exclusion, which is the lot of all those who are deprived of that most precious possession: the possibility of *acting*.[23]

The Chorus embodies the passion of passions, that of mothers who do not save their children. The Chorus is pinned in place by invisible nails, and it writhes in anguish. Riveted to our places as spectators, we are bound by invisible ties, and we recognise, by the anguish that squeezes our hearts, that we are of the same familial flesh as the Atridae, the same as that of the Chorus.

But to the Chorus has devolved the time to fear and the time to complain, which the characters who bear the names in the family do not have.

The Chorus is always there. Without respite. The body of the Chorus is over-run, trampled, criss-crossed by the racing assassins and victims.

The Chorus always 'knows' too much, too far in advance, and for nothing. It is not a seer, it is human: it does not affirm what it senses will come, it is not prophetic, it is not the spokesperson of a deity, it is the trembling and furious spokesperson of memory. [. . .]

The Chorus is the Hero of Presentiment. It is in the state of Tragic Rage. 'I sense it will end badly, it will end badly, it will end badly' – finally, the worst is that it ends badly.

The Chorus suffers from Job's illness: all its fears are fulfilled.

Now, within fear the feeble hope that the fear won't be fulfilled is always beating. I'm afraid she will be condemned, she will die, we think, and yet, saying this, we do not believe ourselves, we run away our head lowered under the storm of the thought, we do not think all that we think, we lie to ourselves, we are mistaken, we are not mistaken. It is because we are living, we inhabit the country of life, and what is beyond, the outside, death, we don't have eyes to see it, only a heart to fear it. Death: we cannot believe in it in advance – that would mean being its instrument – the living do not *believe* in it, even if they know it will come.

This is our immortality: 'not-to-believe-in-death'. This does not prevent us from trembling. To die is to lose the immortality we have for the duration of our life. It is this paradox, this madness, which animates the Chorus. The Chorus resists, to the very end.

Ah! The horror we experience when what we dread is realised. 'That's what I was afraid of!' we exclaim to ourselves, humans-insistent-on-hoping that we are. Up to the last second we have feared while hoping, have hoped while fearing. On one hand we expect the worst, on the other we do not want to expect it. The anger of the Chorus is immense when evil triumphs.

We rebel. Century after century. Massacre after massacre. We do not want to believe that we are mortal. And yet there is the proof.

The Chorus has an infinite aptitude for hoping against all hope. The Chorus is made for deception.

But this is not all. The Chorus is not only the audience that we are, ready for mourning, in mourning. It is also identified with each of the members of the condemned family, separately, it is the one against the other; and it is also the family, this whole that splits and tears itself apart.

– In Agamemnon's place, I wouldn't kill Iphigenia – I say to myself.

– Is this true? – I say to myself.

I no longer know. I am such a mixture. I no longer know who I am. I vacillate. Sometimes I am angry with Agamemnon. Sometimes I am angry with Clytemnestra. I take sides diversely, the pain of one convinces me, the pain of the other persuades me.

It's because I am of the family. Under the net, on the stage, around the bed, the table, the altar, the Chorus is in the place of the children who are summoned by destiny to choose, in the quarrel, between father and mother. It is impossible. Every choice entails a counter-choice.

As soon as there is Family, the dance of identifications begins. (N.B. I, personally, H.C., am for Clytemnestra, N.B. N.B.: and I do not agree with Iphigenia. But I only speak for H.C. in this parenthesis.) Poor chorus, poor old children, orphans even while their parents live, without a say, and Nameless.

We, human creatures, when misfortune strikes (us) brutally, all of a sudden we feel alone in the world, persecuted, there we are running away before us, with neither father nor mother. In us awakens the ancient memory of the most distant exiles, those that struck humans thirty thousand generations ago.

There we are swirling around like straw in the tragic wind, we are not in control of the events. So we experience the unpleasant sensation of the Nameless, well known by those that find themselves thrown into situations of illegitimacy. We are no one, even if we're the whole town and the whole world. But we endure personally, in our nameless body, the passion of the country, the tribe, the family, the race. The Chorus is there to express the immemorial anguish which arises on the occasion of a precise threat.

An obscure fear warns us: what we have never yet lived our ancestors in us have lived. Of course, events which take place on stage, or are going to take place, will only occur once. They are extraordinary. And yet, the Chorus senses, we (when we were not born) have already lived it, before our birth.

This is what makes the Chorus shudder:[24] terrors that have come from former lives. And we too, sitting in the theatre, we sense that the story taking place here and which is not our own, was our own or will be, one day or another.

The Chorus is hurting. The Chorus has the 'honours' (attributions) of feeling all the hurts of all the protagonists in its flesh, in horrible translation. And also all the words that are so penetrating. It has the time, and it is the place, of torments. Those of others and its own. It has a double portion of passion.

Under the blows of the words pronounced by Agamemnon, or Clytemnestra, or Iphigenia, or Cassandra,

I am wounded by a purple bite

A saffron colour flood has flowed back towards my heart

The mouth of my heart is filled with a bitter taste

My own blood sickens me [*m'écœure*], it seems to me that I am going to die, spiteful words act on my organs like daggers and poisons, yes, I could die of hate, of anger, of fear.

The Chorus takes us into the regions where the physical sorrows of the soul rage, they leave the heart and spread from the chest to the feet in intolerable convulsions, they make us stagger, the vertigos that turn the world upside down and stretch the earth above our heads.

Look at them, these old enraged dancers.

What the Chorus expresses, for once, is the seismic vocation of our soul–body. In the soul's affliction, the heart, contracted like a uterus, tries to expel the pain, and in vain: for it is the heart itself that the heart tries to vomit out. The entire earth is convulsed in the crazed effort to rip the source of the torture from its own chest.

Bent double, arched, contracted, a grimace on its face, the Chorus, prey to the attack, sobs the names of the visceral sufferings:

– Ah, I have aching memory, I have aching tenderness, I have aching justice, I ache in my mother, I ache in courage, I ache in all the subtle, spiritual parts of my being.

I dance the strange savageries of the family tied heart

I who cannot break the bonds that bind me to the other.

– Your pain hurts me, you hurt me, as I hurt you – we are atoms of a single body.

We are a part. Useless to deny it. What happens in Argos happens to us in Paris. We do everything to forget it, but we do not escape. We are in the circle – it concerns us. In its round the Chorus traces the human circle. Marking the rhythm that reminds us: You too, you too.

From Hélène Cixous, 'La Communion des Douleurs', in Le Théâtre du Soleil, *Les Atrides 1: Iphigénie à Aulis, Agamemnon*, Paris: Théâtre du Soleil, 1992.

5.4 THE ART OF THE SYMPTOM
From an interview with Ariane Mnouchkine
by Odette Aslan

*In this short interview recorded in 1991, Mnouchkine describes the genesis of the physical work
for* Les Atrides. *She refers to the influence of Kathakali in a production which foregrounded
choric odes as* choros *(dance), and to the need for tragic actors to find gestural forms to short-
circuit the gap between inner impulse and external action. Her psychosomatic discourse
recuperates Artaudian 'affective athleticism' and Aristotelian catharsis as performative embodiment (corpo-reality dis-played).*

ODETTE ASLAN: Did Kathakali help you in the search for a form?

ARIANE MNOUCHKINE: In *La Nuit des Rois* [*Twelfth Night*], we found our
inspiration in Bharata Natyam, but in *Les Atrides*, apart from Catherine Schaub
(Plate 5.2) who studied it in India, Kathakali is an entirely imaginary source of
inspiration.[25] It isn't the techniques that are important to us, but a demand for
clarity, for form, for great precision in detail. In the course of certain rehearsals, I
sensed bodies being shaken, attacked by the feelings that were being unleashed;
like shivers or rub-downs, the dances were liberating. We experienced them like
a vital, necessary element. Which Nietzsche had perceived very well intuitively.

    The characters in *Les Atrides* are rather like entities, gods or demi-gods (in
L'Indiade, we had only theatricalised a gestural vocabulary stemming from everyday life in India). They are larger than life. Heads of hair and beards have
importance because they are man's symbols of strength, of his virility, of his
aggressiveness, of his power. The actors are also helped by make-up/masks: I
insisted on them being masked, but I did not want opaque masks that would
have concealed their faces. From the first day of rehearsals, they practised
Kathakali make-up, which both amplifies their expressions and supports their
performance.[26] It's well known that all Théâtre du Soleil actors have learnt to
work with masks.

A: Does performing tragedy imply particular body work?

M: In *Les Atrides*, the actors have allowed thoughts, terrible feelings to pass
through them, and the work has been more trying than for the Shakespeares.
Perhaps at that time we were at a level of acting that was less permeable than
now. When an actor progresses, he becomes more athletic in his corporeal

Figure 5.2 Les Atrides: Iphigénie à Aulis. The chorus in rehearsal; on the right, chorus leader
  Catherine Schaub. Photo: Martine Franck/Magnum

performance and at the same time more fragile. He doesn't only strengthen his
body, he ends up flaying it.

A nervous influx passes visibly into the bodies of the actors. Theatre is the art
of the 'symptom'. The actor is someone who knows how to show the symptoms
of all the illnesses of the soul. His task is to suffer them in his body and to show
them. The spectators recognise their own passions there. In order to find the
symptoms, the actor accepts having the fever. Tragic characters have anxiety
right to their guts; the chorus in *Les Choéphores* [*The Libation Bearers*] is full of
hatred and cries for vengeance. One must seize works bodily and hang on to the
end. Push internal feeling and external form to the limit. Then emotion is born
and catharsis is produced.

The chorus is very important, as is the vital energy it represents. Dance
imposed itself on us right away. Besides, tragedy is essentially tied to music, to

rhythms. Undoubtedly I would not have staged *Les Atrides* had there not been the collaboration with Jean-Jacques Lemêtre, a musician who has an extraordinary intuition for theatre.

First published as 'Ecorchement et catharsis', in Odette Aslan (ed.), *Le Corps en jeu*, Paris: CNRS Editions (collection 'Arts du Spectacle'), 1993.

5.5 LEAVING ROOM FOR THE OTHERS
From an interview with members of the Théâtre du Soleil
by Béatrice Picon-Vallin

In a wide-ranging interview recorded in March 1993, various members of the company discuss the ideals and practices of cross-art form collaboration during the creation and performance of Les Atrides. *Béatrice Picon-Vallin invites the company director, designer, composer-musician and two of the performers to describe their roles in the collective elaboration of a multi-textual, multi-vocal performance form akin to a Wagnerian* Gesamtkunstwerk. *The conversation touches on the nature of improvisation, the impact of Asian performance forms and the physical and emotional demands of theatre-making as research. Underpinning the discussion as a whole is a call to an ethics of interrelatedness and of exchange, and a conviction that by definition creativity always – and only – occurs in relation to others. Béatrice Picon-Vallin is Director of Research in the Laboratoire de Recherches sur les Arts du Spectacle, CNRS, Paris.*

BEATRICE PICON-VALLIN: In his reflections on the 'total work of art' (*Gesamtkunstwerk*), Richard Wagner privileged Greek tragedy, a grand synthesis of the arts in which music, poetry and dance are implicated. [. . .] Is this concept [. . .] of help to you in articulating the processes of creation of the *Atrides* cycle at the Théâtre du Soleil? Today, in a period when there are fewer and fewer 'pure' genres, the borders between the performing arts are becoming more and more porous, but your approach is different. Have you been guided by a utopia of totality in production, as Bernard Dort reported at the time of the Shakespeares?[27] Or by that of a work which is communal in its modes of creation?

ARIANE MNOUCHKINE: The question of the presence and alliance of related art forms in theatre is no longer posed at the Théâtre du Soleil: we have responded 'yes' for a long time [. . .] Even if it has nothing to do with *Les Atrides*, our next show will be built from what we take to be the essentials: music, text, space and light, bodies. Of course, the actors are always at the centre of theatre, of any theatre. But without music, without light, it wouldn't be the theatre I like, even if the actors are very good and it is nonetheless theatre. The necessity of this alliance became apparent to us very quickly, and the question that was posed is 'how can one realise it?' A mystery.

P: In the history of the Soleil, there is an evolution leading up to these *Atrides*, which convoke the different arts nearly equally, since music and dance intervene more than in the preceding productions?

M: If the music and the dance interpenetrate to such an extent, it's because Aeschylus and Euripides required it of us. So long as we had not admitted defeat, they did not budge. And so long as our bodies did not understand it, we simply suffered.

P: How did the collaboration between the different artists function?

JEAN-JACQUES LEMÊTRE: [. . .] The theatre that I love is a collective theatrical art. When he began composing, Wagner knew that he would have to use a symphony orchestra and choruses. In my own case, starting with a 'musical stage' that is empty, naked, which is filled progressively during the work, if I told myself that I absolutely had to use such and such an instrument – a Cretan *lyra*, for example – I would spend all my time in rehearsals wondering where to put it. I would not be attentive and receptive to make musical propositions, listen to the responses and be able to formulate other propositions. People sometimes say to us, 'You're very close to opera' . . . But it's quite different. Besides, we don't sing, although there is a form of singing-speaking in the productions.

M: There could be singing without it being opera. If we had the same affinity with singing as with dance, there would have been song. But we were not ready. For me, a real theatre – and I mean both the building and the works – is first of all made of encounters. I often say that I would not have done *Les Atrides* if Jean-Jacques hadn't been with us. Working with someone doesn't mean imposing things on each other; it is an exchange which is very mysterious, very profound, very internal, which creates a sort of circulation of blood, and where the fact that someone is not 'in on things' is a source of terrible suffering for everyone. It doesn't come easily, there's a lot of sweat, a lot of work. First you need to cross a few rivers, a few deserts and a few mountains together.

CATHERINE SCHAUB: As Ariane said, the actors are at the centre, they're in the spotlight. But what's so rich about this way of working is that all the arts – all the artists – are together. We know that we all have a share of responsibility for the development of things on stage. The direction in which we're 'pushed' will determine the acting. And the décor will be realised because a certain movement appeared in the acting. It is not an imposed décor within which we have to act. It really is like that: we move forward together.

M: The presence of a particular voice entails the use of a particular instrument . . . Sometimes it's very clear, Jean-Jacques follows a voice, he grabs a tonality. But then, did he already have this theme running around inside him a few days beforehand? Or did it really come to him during the work? Or on the contrary, did Jean-Jacques think to himself, 'We're not getting anywhere here, I'll try something else'? I don't know, but an actor reacted, seized his proposition – and I'm not talking about dance yet, I'm talking about a particular impulse, a particular rhythm, a particular emotion, a particular violence. One day a woman in the audience said, 'In this production, the music is the second lung.' She spoke of the text as being the first.

L: I think that both the music and the scenography fight for the theatre here. Some are not obliged to submit to the others, whereas perhaps Wagner first looked for an idea in a text to defend his music. I don't need to defend my music because it's theatre music, which is to say that it stems from theatre, from the body of the actor performing a text. One cannot talk here of 'musical theatre', because that would imply that the music would command at some point. It's much more interesting if it defends theatre, instead of fighting for itself alone. Composing a score for the Soleil first means finding the turning-points in the text that I hear, which will correspond to changes of timbre and theme, and therefore of instruments. Then it involves indicating in the margin of the text a codification that can be memorised, in other words, the melodic and rhythmic modes.

P: There's no hierarchy of the arts at the Théâtre du Soleil, in the process of creation?

M: Theatre is what leads. Evidently the problem is knowing what is theatre and what isn't. Music, light, actors, *mise en scène*, fine: but is it theatre? Is there both form and content here, or is there only form? Or only content, in which case it won't be perceived? In order to live, we need air, we need blood.

P: Theatre as an organism?

M: I wouldn't use the word 'organism'. No, it's rather a quest. When we are 'good', when something circulates and is, as a result, both magnificent and totally humble, it is natural, artistically natural, which is to say that there is nothing aprioristic, there are neither theories nor whims in the music or the staging. There is something that is indispensable, vital, at every instant. This is what makes 'primitives' of us. Yes, we are often called primitives, I admit.

GUY-CLAUDE FRANÇOIS: The Théâtre du Soleil has given itself the means to go as far as possible in theatre; it's the only theatre that allows itself to gather everyone and say: 'We are going to do theatre' – quite simply. To take an architectural image that is closer to me: if there's a wall over there that bothers us, we move it. This image is true for each one of the actors in the company. I believe it's at the Théâtre du Soleil that this idea of a collective art has been taken to the very limit.

P: Ariane speaks of a sort of alchemy, of mystery. How can one nonetheless penetrate a part of that shadow? And first, is it possible that everything really comes from the group? Isn't there first a director's vision, a scenographer's vision?

F: I have the feeling it's like a game of ping-pong involving fifteen or more people. For example, the idea of the arena space came from an actor who was hiding one day behind a flat in the rehearsal room, because Ariane didn't know what to do with the chorus at a particular moment. This then generates repercussions in such a way that everything follows, and even the text is included in this process. We say that the text comes first, but in reality it is shaped alongside, it can be reworked as a function of what happens on stage. Perhaps this isn't the case with the Greek tragedies, but it is for the texts of Hélène Cixous, who is present during the elaboration of the productions.

M: You spoke of vision. When I read a play, I have many 'visions'. But on the day of the first rehearsal, I have more of an emptiness inside me, as if I were on the roof of the world; I try to see a domed stage, this is an expression we used for the Shakespeares. What could appear there? . . . It's more than emptiness – in fact it isn't an emptiness.

P: It's a space of apparition?[28]

M: Yes, a space of apparition. One needs singularly courageous actors to bear this idea. There are people who gain strength from the demand for apparition. Others only want to say their text, and don't have the courage to wait. A company comprises actors of varying degrees of training, some more advanced than others, some not trained at all. So their training takes place during rehearsal times. The possibilities for discovery are different for each one. With some, one must try to teach them to appear: that too is part of the 'communal work of art'. So there are different levels to reconcile, just as there are different art forms that must figure out how to get along.

Musicians have notes. They have a precise, quasi-scientific language: these notes. All the rest comes afterwards. An actor does not have any. If I say to an actor: 'No, that's realistic', and he replies: 'I don't understand', that is where the pain begins. Jean-Jacques could say: 'No, you're off, you did a C sharp, it's a C in the score.' When I say: 'You're saying that you're crying, but you're not crying', and the actor replies: 'But yes, I am crying', I have no scientific proof to confront someone who is lying to me and lying to himself. No need for proof with Jean-Jacques, we no longer even need to discuss things. We work in total complicity. With Guy-Claude too, we know how to wait for each other, it's undefinable.

L: The Théâtre du Soleil offers the privilege of being able to start from zero. The music really does begin at zero: in other words, with hands, with feet, with the heart. The heart. The heart? Sensing what's on stage, sensing the actors, the way they move, breathe, speak. It all starts with the drums, because in so far as none of the roles is cast at the outset, as everything remains open and I have no preconceived idea, I don't play a melodic or harmonic theme, but the beat, the pulse, the 'fundamental of the actor', man or woman. Next comes the notion of the 'drone', which is an extremely simple melody that begins to follow the pitch of the voices.

I learn along with everyone else. There is an evolution in the music, firstly through the simple task of creating a rhythm, in such a way that the tempo of the actor on stage doesn't become humdrum or realistic, supported by too much slowness. A certain speed is necessary to be able to start working, and for a scene not to collapse. And little by little it all takes shape, the characters awake and the music awakes with them, because the casting is concretised progressively. What I love about the work here is that in fact we don't need to theorise first. The score is created as we go along, 'live'.

P: When you began to work on *Les Atrides*, this 'space of apparition' was really all that existed? Anything was possible?

M: Anything, anything. It is difficult to believe, but it's true, we go that far. Clearly, my great problem was with the chorus. I didn't know what a chorus was.[29] All I knew was that I didn't want a chorus dressed in bed-sheets . . . With the first entrances of the chorus members, although we knew well that they were homogeneous groups of women or old men, since the text says so, there was a Japanese princess, an Indian, two Eskimos . . . The whole world became part of the chorus, and of course nothing worked, but we had to go through such a phase. And I'm convinced that the fact that, at a particular moment, we had a Japanese princess, an Indian, two Eskimos, prevented us from becoming like clones; and we were able to find a chorus of old men who were all the same, but at the same time not at all the same, all together, but each one different from the others. For us, the 'zero degree' is not a figure of style. We even imagined: Aeschylus just sent us his play, and sometimes during an exercise, I tore up the pages of the text and gave out the sentences as they came, to break up the whole accumulation of clichés on Greek theatre.

P: How did the actors react?

SIMON ABKARIAN: The great playwrights, and in particular Aeschylus, seem to us to be surprised by what they wrote. So we were doubly surprised. And whenever something happens at the level of music, the space, the direction of the actors, there are always surprises, either agreeable or painful. For example, when the palisades arrived, for four or five months, we performed behind these rather unstable palisades which were only about five centimetres thick. But we managed to sit on them. The day the little walls were built, we could dance on them, because we had succeeded in performing on the five centimetres of the palisades . . .

P: What part does improvisation play?

M: A major one in our work. We don't improvise with the text when we work on plays, whether they're by Shakespeare, by Aeschylus or by Hélène Cixous. There is too great a difference between the paucity of our language and the force of theirs . . . But everything apart from the text is improvised.

A: From my first 'apparition', confronted with Aeschylus' text, it was as if I had to make myself smaller, become small again, then suddenly grow, awaken. Come out of the ground. We've often talked of exhumation, and we always crawled behind the palisades to get into position, but it was a poetic voyage that lasted ten metres. For the costumes, each one searched: I had to build a costume for a month, I made a head-dress seventy centimetres high. I came on-stage with the costume, it lasted thirty seconds – for us to realise. Achilles ended up with a simple stocking on his head. But it was necessary that I do all that, and that Ariane see it.

L: To me, it's really a matter of improvisation in the Asian sense. In other words, there is the 'mode', which is the text, and then there are rules, laws, spoken and unspoken, those that we know, and the others that we discover little by little in the course of improvisation. There is always a moment at which you go back to technical bases, because you get lost; from there you can start out again towards something much more poetic, more mysterious, more grand. When an opera composer speaks using the words of the musical vocabulary, I don't think theatre practitioners understand him, and he doesn't listen or hear through the screen of his music. Between the composer and librettist of a contemporary opera there is a dialogue of the deaf. I believe that music for theatre shares exactly the same vocabulary, the same way of thinking, of speaking with the actor, of listening to the exchange between actor and director. There's no transposition to be made; I provide something to be heard, and someone responds, and vice versa . . .

P: You're criticising an overly technical language?

M: He uses that language when he's with musicians, but not with the actors, nor with me. I think Jean-Jacques means that, in order for the arts or the artists of each art to be able to commune, they must not look to impose hegemony or even superiority; the arrogance of the arts and of artists has to disappear, one must yield. In fact, at a certain moment, everything yields to this strange small single suffering in the middle of the stage, including fear, because fear must yield also. It is the character who never yields, but the actor must yield to the interest of the group.

P: Yield to help each other?

M: Yes, to help each other, one must yield. If not, one is in a power struggle.

P: Jean-Jacques says: 'I make music for theatre.' Can one listen to his music without the theatre? Why has the Théâtre du Soleil released four compact discs of music for *Les Atrides*? Edison Denissov [. . .] does not want his theatre music played outside of the production for which it was written. It is made to be seen, heard in a context outside of which it has no meaning.

L: There is real pressure from the audience who buy the disc, partly to be able to remember the performance. But I think the disc lacks something fundamental, it lacks the soloist. It lacks the actor. It's as if one listened to Beethoven's Fifth without the upper section of violins.

M: It lacks the text, of course. But as a 'spectator' I've had a lot of pleasure listening to the music, because the images return – and the text also, by the way. And at moments, since Jean-Jacques's music is tuned to the actors' voices, when I hear the music, it evokes for me the tonality of the voices of Simon, Catherine, Niru, Juliana, of each one . . . And also, it is popular music, popular theatre music, there are themes, melodies that are pleasurable to 'see'. Even if of course one regrets not being able to hear a particular cry, a particular sound of footsteps, sometimes a particular breath – in short, the entire production . . .

L: It's not film music in the sense that the words ambience, sound illustration, atmosphere have been banished.

M: Ah, no . . . and it is not opera music. In film music, what is surprising is that they often manage to do realism with the abstract . . .

F: Film-makers justify their realism by referring to how 'it happens in life', and yet the cinema uses entirely conceptual means like music or time compression . . .

M: The other day, at the Vidéothèque de Paris, where I am watching films on the poor, I saw *La Zone* by Georges Lacombe, who filmed the ragmen of Paris in 1928. What beauty! Nothing realistic about it and yet they are real characters, it's a documentary: you see the ragmen going on their rounds, you would think it was Chaplin, Eisenstein. So one wonders: why persist obstinately in doing realism when such documentaries exist?

P: Doesn't Jean-Jacques's notion of the 'actor-soloist' recall the image of the orchestra? [. . .] Could this metaphor help us to account for the ways in which the relations between the different arts on stage function?

M: The word orchestra is not quite right. If I remember correctly, the *orkestra* is the performance space itself, the place in which the chorus moves. But I think what happens is closer to the relationship between musicians and actors in Kathakali, or even in Noh. When you evoke the orchestra, I see a conductor. In our case, once everything is set up, certain rules are established, we do not do just anything each night, and if the production lasted four or five minutes longer, I would bring it to people's attention. But if the actors give an extra breath, the musicians will accompany them, and similarly, if one day Jean-Jacques is more brutal with particular themes, they accompany him in turn. They accompany him in the sense that they go with him, which does not mean that they add something on top of him. Unlike the current sense of 'to accompany', which is often understood as 'to add', 'to accompany' means 'to go with', 'to be a companion'. That is why I don't really see the image of the orchestra, which is first of all an ensemble led by a baton, even if there is an element of that in putting together a production. At the moment of the performance, if it is a beautiful production, it's the theatre, it's the ear that conducts.

P: It's the audience?

M: No, I do not know if you can go that far. I think that something unites the actors, the audience, the music, which is really of the order of the spirit, which stems from the possibility of forgetting oneself at a particular moment, and no longer being anything other than listening, when the musicians, the actors, the audience are all ears. This is dependent upon total discipline, an absolute rigour and a magical freedom.

P: An orchestra is composed of artists who practise a single art, it's very different from theatre.

M: Yes, but a very good conductor must feel magic moments too, in a very good concert where he senses that with the slightest thing it would 'take off'.

L: Measure bars were invented so that the orchestra musicians could talk between themselves through the conductor. But they create a certain rigidity. At the Soleil, with the absence of these measure bars, we avoid the notions of breadth, of the return of the strong beat, and of the cycle. Which allows the actors greater flexibility. In every performance, the beginning of a theme remains the same, so an actor senses that I'm with him, but the ending is re-adapted every evening. Alongside the word *orkestra*, there's another Greek term, *orkestik*, which has been completely forgotten and which would be appropriate here since it signifies the alliance of acting, dance and music. According to the Greek definition, I believe that acting addresses the heart, dance addresses the body, and music the soul. The ensemble addresses the entire being.

A: With Jean-Jacques, for all of this there was an apprenticeship. He didn't want to speak to us with the coded language of musicians, so he provided us with very simple keys; he looked for an instinctive, poetic relationship with the music. He never said to us: 'At this point I'll put in a B flat.' Instead he would say, 'This instrument is tuned to the mode of so-and-so's voice', or 'to your voice'. At the beginning we didn't know how to listen to the music, we would even talk over what Jean-Jacques was doing. Or else at times an actor would start speaking before he had stopped moving, and Jean-Jacques continued playing because he was going by the body. This happened until we learnt a particular discipline, which is to say the discipline of the stop, so as to go to another stop.

M: There is no movement without stopping. If you watch a dancer closely, he goes from immobility to immobility, even in mid-air: he stops in mid-air! The music exposes the absence of stops, because if Jean-Jacques plays on a movement, and the actor speaks while still in movement, nothing works at all. I think this is the law of every gesture, of every movement which has meaning. At the theatre, one's perception is extremely deep, but very narrow. The audience cannot see more than one thing at a time, and even if they manage to see ten things in a second, it's always successively, one after the other. The music imposes a cleanness of the movement and of the text, which is essential. It prevents stammering – in the feet, in the mouth, in the eyes and above all in the heart.

A: Once you have entered into this apprenticeship, you don't yet feel at home, but you begin to understand something and another aspect of the music appears. At certain moments, when Jean-Jacques 'came in', he would begin to play the theatrical situation, the scene, the characters present, and the emotion would come. It takes time to learn how to listen to this kind of thing. One day I said to Ariane that even a rock could perform if Jean-Jacques played in that way for that scene. Except that if the rock can't hear it won't perform. For us, it's an apprenticeship in listening to the music and also in listening to each other; often we're so preoccupied with what we're about to say that we don't hear our partner, or we don't see what's in the process of being created.

M: We talk about the relationship between Jean-Jacques and the actors because it's – almost – a skin to skin contact, and we don't talk about the relationship between the actors and Guy-Claude because it's very bizarre. I don't think actors understand anything about décor. I can remember at the very beginning, when we didn't yet have the possibility of having an initial approximation of the décor (like the palisades for *Les Atrides* that Simon mentioned just now), we rehearsed in an empty space. This meant that, when the time came to rehearse with the décor in construction, there was always a terrible trauma when the actors discovered that they were going to perform in a space that seemed gigantic to them . . . While actors (when they are really actors) have a sense of the music and of their costume, the space is always disturbing for them, even if subsequently they settle into it very well. But now, as rehearsals progress we create a simulacrum of the décor, as soon as it has been determined.

P: [. . .] The designer is not always present during the lengthy work on the production. What is the designer's role at the Théâtre du Soleil?

F: The place that we use for performances, the Cartoucherie, plays a very important role. I have the sense that I'm building something that must serve as a tool more than be beautiful. A tool is only invented in response to needs, and these are indicated to me by Ariane, by the actors. The aesthetics are not added on later. Something which is perfectly functional, which corresponds perfectly to a need – firstly that of a poem, of a text, then that of the actors – becomes beautiful. At least I think that's how I would define beauty in theatre.

L: Guy-Claude's constraints are also different from ours. If I make a mistake, I put the instrument down and pick up another. If Ariane or the actors make a mistake at a particular moment, they stop and try something else. Whereas he can't knock down an entire wall and rebuild it in ten minutes.

M: That can happen, but it's better if it happens to him less often than to us. Guy-Claude came to the Cartoucherie at the same time as me; and as the technical director of the company, he shared our fourteen-hour working day for a long time. Subsequently, and though this was difficult for me, it became clear that there wasn't enough work for him, with one design to create every year or every two years; so, without leaving us, he has taken his own path. But he knows every layer of the Cartoucherie, from the bottom of the sewers to the tip of the roof. I prefer to call him constructor or architect, rather than designer. When we discuss a décor, first we use the language of building, then that of the feel, of the colour – that is, I think we look subsequently for a kind of sensuality.

P: How did you decide on the relations between the timbres of different instruments, the sonorities of voices, and the play of colours and materials?

F: Nothing was predetermined.

M: It's the result of the work, of the time devoted to working! And then, the fact that at some point someone can say: 'No, that doesn't go together.' I remember a costume in *Les Euménides* – for the Dogs – which we had a lot of trouble finding, and indeed it was a question of materials. That's where the time factor is important. Thinking of certain other ways of working, or of the obligations some directors endure, it's as if money hasn't been used where it should have been. It is used on quantity, eighteen shows are done instead of doing one. As for us, we need time, because we learn to walk with each new production. I feel as though I've learnt a great deal with *Les Atrides*, as I did with *L'Indiade*. Nevertheless, for the next production, once again, I will know nothing, and what's more I don't want to know. Because the day I tell myself 'I know', I'll do the same thing over.

L: It's very difficult to take the 'timbre' of one character and reuse it for another who is as important. Take the harp, for example: its timbre was so deeply associated with the Congress in *L'Indiade* that it was impossible for me to reuse it, and for the actor to re-hear it, in the following production. [. . .]

M: He told me the other day he's up to 1,400 instruments now.

L: And yet gradually in the course of the work we've eliminated the majority of modern and contemporary Western instruments, because of the overly realist or cinematographic images they engender. I would also like to say that from time to time the music is a décor – that is, not in the sense of an iron collar.

M: Yes, at times Jean-Jacques is the sky, the sea, the clouds . . . destiny.

L: And there are also moments when an actor manages to be the décor, which is strange.

M: What we're calling décor is precisely that space of apparition you spoke of earlier, which must be my inner state, and which is not always easy to hold on to. It is clear that this space of apparition concerns Guy-Claude. He moves towards a concrete space of apparition, which is solid (even if it's in cloth), 'real'. But if Guy-Claude makes too much sky, then neither Jean-Jacques nor the actors will be able to perform the sky, and thus the audience will only see a single sky, that is, Guy-Claude's sky. Yet the absence of sky, or earth, or sea, or boat, or onions, or sides of ham hanging on the wall of the tavern, allows everything. What I am saying is utterly banal. But what is curious is that this rule, which is banal and true in theatre which has neither décor nor music, remains true when there is décor, music, dance.

F: It's at the Théâtre du Soleil that I've learnt what emptiness in architecture can mean; it makes it possible to bring out all that man, in this case an actor, offers in himself.

M: The other day I saw the beautiful production by Pina Bausch, *Orpheus and Eurydice* with the music of Gluck. And I asked her: 'Have you done any other operas?' 'Yes, *Iphigenia in Tauris*'. 'Do you want to produce any others?' She replied, 'I listen and I listen, but I can't find any operas in which there's room for me.' She's quite right; what do you want her to do with Verdi, for example? Verdi suffices for Verdi. One must get used to the idea of yielding [*céder*], one must yield. Hélène Cixous says, 'If the writing of theatre doesn't stop before the end, if one does not remember in writing that in any case the work is completed in the incarnation of the text on stage, then one will write a text that is too much.' The author too must . . . be suspended.

P: Knowing how to yield to others, not to take up too much space: how can one direct actors according to this principle?

M: I think it's above all in this way that one can direct actors. But 'yielding' doesn't mean 'allowing anything at all to happen'.

S: Leaving space, letting things come. If you are ahead, wanting to move forward too quickly, you tear the piece of paper, the text, and you collide with Jean-Jacques, you crash, you crash into the décor. Listening is what is most important. One has to be concave.

M: Which doesn't mean being limp, being devoid of energy. To be as rich and as free as possible, the actor must have as few obstacles as possible in front of him; but the actor, even the actor, must yield to the theatre, to the text, to the meanings. He must yield because although he may be king – the actor is king, the actress is queen – there is a moment when a poor little character worth nothing at all is more king than he is.

P: In the single scenic space of *Les Atrides*, there seems to be a search for a totality without monumentality: a cycle of plays (the practice of 'complete works'), the involvement of all the arts – poetry, music, dance, circus, acting, fine arts, mask and make-up arts. The orchestra involves dozens of instruments. The casting brings together men, women, different nationalities, contrasting physiques – the range of sizes, for example. It even involves animals – the chorus of Dogs in *Les Euménides*. Was this totality pursued from the outset, or did it impose itself progressively?

M: We weren't looking for totality, we were looking for Aeschylus and Euripides. Although there was barking at the end of each play, the idea of the chorus of animals, of masks, only came during rehearsals for *Les Euménides*. As far as the actors are concerned, I never cast anything in advance, and when Juliana [Carneiro da Cunho] arrived she worked on the role of Clytemnestra that Simon [Abkarian] had rehearsed previously. Both of them are quite tall. Sizes should not have any importance: they are realistic facts. But the relationship between the mother and her child, Clytemnestra and Iphigenia, was apposite: it's good that she is really treated as a very small creature.[30]

We only became aware of our struggle as we went along, the project was beyond anything we could have imagined, and it's no surprise that productions of Greek tragedies have failed so often. People scoffed: '*Les Euménides* is unstage-able.' But all of the difficulties that are encountered stem from not taking the text literally. Worse: people do not believe the text and focus on the complexity of the task; they get blocked in the face of a sort of enormous tangle of idiocies that have accumulated over the centuries. Everything in our production was found in the text, at a particular moment.

S: References in the texts are very sensual, not at all intellectual. There are things like, 'Bile wells up near my heart.' It's very physical.

P: *Einstein on the Beach* by Robert Wilson [. . .] is a work where all the arts are involved, but it is above all a visual artist's production.

M: There is a big difference between making a beautiful image on the stage by placing someone, not necessarily an actor, in lighting, and making theatre by finding the lighting that is necessary for an actor, or rather for a character. Personally, I like lighting up characters and I like it when one can really see them. I cannot hear someone I cannot see, and I think that an actor who is not lit cannot perform. If you leave an actor a bit too long in darkness, he can't perform, and this is not because of his exacerbated narcissism: he can't perform because he can't see, if he isn't seen.

F: At the school of design where I teach, the students of scenography have a good command of plastic elements. But they must learn to imagine with and for others (author, actors, technicians) so as to avoid isolated and sometimes introverted plastic work. Theatre cannot be made alone. Each thing in theatre only has value in so far as one needs others in order to express oneself.

M: To return to the theatre of images: it is narcissistic, it says: 'Look at me, look at my world.' But I want to know in what ways you share my world, in what ways do we live in the same world and what can I do in this world. There should be a stimulation in the production. I believe that the theatrical text is made to call people to understand, to react at times, to learn, to receive. In *Les Atrides*, the chorus enters and speaks to us: 'Try to understand, you are so stupid, you do not understand. I, an old man, a servant, am telling you something useful, that you have forgotten, I am telling you what you are, hurry up and understand, because if not you are going to kill your mother, you are going to kill your daughter.'

P: In the collaboration between the different arts, the cinema has very little place at the Soleil. [. . .]

M: I adore the cinema. One day, perhaps, in one of our productions, there will be some cinema, a character who will go to the cinema or will watch cine-matographic images. But it is not a question of competing with the cinema. It's something else. Indeed I think that no art can compete with another. They can only accompany each other for a time. For example, Chaplin owes every-thing to the theatre and at the same time he is the greatest cinema actor that ever walked the earth. I do theatre, I love the theatre. If the cinema is on-stage one day, if one day characters watch a screen, it will remain on the stage only if it becomes theatrical and if the cinema performs like a theatre actor. I will try it, and after a week, if it remains cinema, we will say good-bye: 'Glad to have met you, but it will have to be another time.'

F: I've been designing for film for some time, and I've heard many directors say that they like working with theatre designers because they possess particular qualities, like, for example, the mastery of metaphor, and that of emptiness.

M: It is true that this can give depth to cinema. Nevertheless, I realise that we're talking here about our work and the convictions that we share. But all of this should not seem too triumphalist. Though we're convinced we're right to proceed in this way, one must not forget the months and sometimes years of doubt, the days and the weeks in which this space of apparition, this magnificent emptiness, remains a mortal void which can take actors to the brink of nervous breakdown. At such times I think I'm wrong, that we shouldn't work like this, that perhaps I want too much, and that I would do better to say to the chorus: 'Line up single-file, enter slowly, stop there, say your text and then sit down.' Actors and aspiring musicians must know that this art, this 'communal work of art' – I like that expression – gains resolution through very intense work, through renunciation which at times is cruel. There is 'yielding', which is one thing, and then 'renouncing', which is worse.

The human cost does not appear in *Les Atrides*, and that's how it should be: for the audience, it should not appear, I find it immodest, indecent and histrionic to show to the audience what it cost. On the other hand, I believe one must say that it takes real actors, who accept doubt, darkness, the black hole, who accept that the director says: 'I don't know what a chorus is like, I want to know, but I don't. All I know is what it isn't.' If not, people imagine that some kind of recipe exists, and they fail to understand that to make it work, one must burn one's arms right up to the elbows. Here we are, after the work has been accomplished, with two of the actors who were the 'dynamos' of the production, thus who suffered, but not all that much since they were creating. But there are also all those who were less creative, or not at all. We should write on all our pediments: 'If you don't want to suffer, do not enter.' If you're afraid of pain, don't do theatre.

A: To continue in Ariane's direction, I spoke with one of Pina Bausch's dancers about physical injuries. I am wary of people who are intact, who are untouched by any pain. Even if you emerge unharmed from a battlefield, you at least have the blood of others on you. If you emerge limpid, immaculate, it's that somewhere you have a problem with engagement. The dancer had bruises all over, they all have bruises all over. And inevitably one loves to complain about them, to talk about them. I am proud of my war wounds, and yet God knows I would rather have avoided them. But to get there one must stumble, one must fall; you can't learn to ride a bike without falling, you can't remain intact.

S: It's the price to pay, which is worth the pain, but you must know that you will have to pay it. It's not enough to have the address of a Kathakali school and to intend to make a three-month trip to the Kalamandalam in India.

M: There's a misunderstanding. Nowadays lots of young actors, even here, want to have *the* recipe that will make everything easy and quick. Catherine means that the Kalamandalam – and first of all, she didn't spend three months there but two years – is not a recipe, but only the beginning of a difficult trail: from the moment you decide to take this path, everything becomes very difficult. As soon as one begins to know something, the grave danger is the illusion of facility; and it's the same in music or drawing, you both said it. Theatre is difficult, and although it doesn't really concern them, audiences often recognise this, and come tell us: 'What work, what a lot of work.' Moreover, they too have to work during these productions, as in all our productions. Future professionals are very surprised by the intensity of what's required in workshops at the Théâtre du Soleil. But nobody forces them . . . So total work of art or not, but it's total and communal even more . . . [. . .]

P: Could we go back to the dance in *Les Atrides* – the choral dances led by the chorus leader, as well as the dances of certain characters; I'm thinking in particular of the dance of Orestes in *Les Choéphores*, or Clytemnestra's, when she moves forward on her knees. At such moments, the intense emotion is no longer conveyed through words, but exclusively through the moving body. Is it still in this case collective work? It seems that it's more a matter of an actor implicated in his totality. [. . .]

S: I remember that in rehearsal, when the old men in the *Agamemnon* chorus began to dance, these were spontaneous interventions, which were neither imposed nor premeditated. They clearly came from the music and the text, but it was always moments in which the emotion was at such a point that it could only express itself through the body, through . . .

M: . . . we called them little 'therapeutic frictions' . . .

S: . . . yes, through these 'therapeutic frictions'. I don't think this kind of phenomenon can happen in regular theatre, because it doesn't have the space. But during the work on *Les Atrides*, there were always violent impulses one could express, and whether it followed us or pushed us forward, the music was always like a flying carpet; it enabled us to develop this emotion with our body, the sound, perhaps in a primitive way. All of the choral dances were born in this way.

M: Orestes' dance is indeed one of the most flamboyant, dazzling and trying moments, for both actor and audience.[31] But it is a collective moment – which doesn't take anything away from Simon, for it's also a great acting moment. It's totally collective because this dance brings everything together: music, grand music, percussion, very particular lighting, the entire chorus behind, and then Aeschylus, even if there is no text, because one feels all the weight of the preceding scene. At that moment, clearly you only look at Simon, and Simon merits your looking only at him, but this moment is the point at which the three preceding plays come together. The scene between Clytemnestra and Orestes in *Les Choéphores*, Clytemnestra's murder, that dance, is the tragic summit of Aeschylus' trilogy. Afterwards he will try to put a little balm on the wounds, he will write *Les Euménides*. But I think Orestes' dance really is a 'collective work of art'. Otherwise it's a bit like if you said that the one who arrives at Olympia with the flame brought it by himself. I say this all the more willingly since Simon had a creative role in these productions that clearly went way beyond the roles he ended up playing on-stage. If one accepts that there are 'collective works of art', then it exists at every instant, whether a single actor is on-stage or they all are. Ultimately, when there's no longer anyone on-stage and the lights go down, the stage is still charged with all the phantoms, with all the sweat of the characters, with the blood of Iphigenia, of Clytemnestra. For an actor to be total at a given moment, all the others must yield.

A: One cannot speak after having killed someone on stage. Something theatrical must happen – which was translated by the dance, by cries, by a bloodied sword, [. . .] I know I had this problem of 'yielding'. It's true, because after wanting so much to perform . . . Until the day Ariane said to me: 'It's the story of Cassandra, at this moment it's Cassandra that people want to watch. Not you!' It takes time to stop, to 'yield', so as then to give oneself, transmit oneself. Sometimes you think, 'That's mine.' But no, it's hers, it's his, it's ours, it's the audience's. And Orestes' dance is also Clytemnestra's dance, the chorus leader's, the chorus's, it's Jean-Jacques's dance, and it's also Ariane's dance.

P: What is the Asia that inspired you to realise this conflation of arts on stage?

M: For *Les Atrides* we were more involved with Kathakali than with Kabuki. But it's common knowledge that there are basic elements which unite Kathakali, Kabuki, Noh, Topeng and Greece . . . Now that I'm reading the documentation, I realise that in fact we've returned to Greece, but we came back intuitively: our documentation, which began in Turkey, and moved through the Caucasus, did not concern the Greeks. I didn't want to consult documents on ancient Greece because I was afraid of sliding into the old clichés of the Greek vases, of the togas, the draping. I continue to believe that in the West there is dramaturgy, but that in the East there is the art of the actor, which I cannot do without, and I will continue to draw from it without scruples.

I come back to *La Zone*, to this little film of 1928 where one sees dump trucks on the outskirts of Paris literally pouring the refuse on the ragmen. They take it all in the face.

So why go to India for a performance that has nothing to do with India?

Because all that's bad is worse there, and all that's beautiful is even more beautiful. We need these extremes – extreme cruelty, imbecility, whatever – because at the moment everything here seems tepid and grey. I have only got one life, and I need extremes to feed me. Beauty from everywhere helps me to recognise beauty here. There is an underground river connecting cultures. Meyerhold undertook the same research, and to my mind, without sounding arrogant, for the same reasons.

P: How do you locate the creation of the music in relation to these multiple sources? Where do all these different instruments come from? Do you invent some of them?

L: It's not a matter of invention. In India, one of the wide range of musical theories is exactly the same as that of ancient Greece. I use modes that I deem to be Greek, but that doesn't stop them being Indian at the same time. I began with the idea that Greece, at a particular time, must have thought it was the centre of the world, and Greek culture spread very widely. The advantage of Greece is that it contained elements of both East and West, at least in terms of music. A Brazilian or a Turk will recognise certain passages in my music; as would someone from China, Cambodia or Greece.[32] It's astonishing, there's certainly something there that is universal.

P: What is the role of an audience in this collective art form? On one hand you have suggested that it is the audience that brings the performance to completion. And on the other, that you're looking for particular qualities through this cross-art form collaboration: intelligibility, maximum clarity and 'ecstasy' – in other words, a state that takes spectators out of themselves.

M: The performance must be intelligible, but there's something else. When you watch, you're no longer just who you are, you are also Iphigenia or Orestes; you bear the characters and their terrible feelings, you understand and recognise them. A connection with their humanity is woven, a compassion in the etymological sense of the word. I'm not talking about catharsis. Being taken out of oneself can include forgetting oneself [. . .] I think people are big enough to experience moments of ecstasy, to try to reflect on them afterwards, to understand what happened. One needs moments of intense emotion and intense pleasure. In the end, wasn't this what Brecht was looking for, although he said the opposite? Audiences are royalty, and they must be able to leave at the end thinking: 'You have fed me, you've given me strength; you've enabled me to return to the city a little better, a little more conscious, a little clearer, a little more generous, a little stronger.' And they renew our strength, they feed us, in all senses of the word. Through their witnessing and recognition, they justify us, they re-elect us; in other words, they agree to let us represent them again [. . .]

S: When we were on tour, in Bradford, it was so hot that all of the spectators had fans; in front of us it was like a human sea with fans. It was extraordinary to observe the effects at moments of tension or relief; the movement of the fans came in waves, and it was always orchestrated.

P: What's the role of the director?

M: I don't think I've ever managed to explain this well, and anyway it varies from production to production.

P: Are you a guide?

M: Sometimes yes, sometimes no. Sometimes I'm a wall; at other times, a boxer. The director is the only person in a group who doesn't produce anything in the physical sense of the word. And the relative freedom of their qualities of perception and discrimination may be more developed because they don't have the constraints of the 'instrumentalists' (actors with their bodies, scenographers and their structures and materials).

P: Does the director always have the last word?

M: Your phrase 'the last word' suggests incessant conflict. In fact, if anyone has to have the last word, it's a bit of a shame. Normally you shouldn't need to, things should be sufficiently self-evident to all that it won't be necessary. Having said all that, sometimes a 'last word' is needed, and at those times it's better that it comes from the director. Otherwise you lose huge amounts of time and personal factors intervene. But if your working practice is based on creation, rather than antagonism or narcissism, there's no need for any 'last word'. What we call 'the evidence' is characterised by the fact that it is collectively recognised [. . .]

It makes me think of the way in which work was shared during the construction of a cathedral. The building would have been conceived by someone, the plans may be drawn up by someone else; then there were those who sculpted a particular ornament or a particular gargoyle, while others were responsible for the stained-glass windows. These different arts must have been extraordinarily well co-ordinated, in order for a particular stone, for example, to be there at the right moment. What's curious in our work is the continuously shifting relationship between the detail and the overall picture. Some people focus on the details, some work on the bigger picture; and then quite suddenly those working on detail have to move on to the wider frame, and vice versa. We shift constantly from close-up to wide shot.

From Béatrice Picon-Vallin, 'Une œuvre d'art commune: rencontre avec le Théâtre du Soleil', in *Théâtre/Public* 124–5, July–October 1995.

NOTES

1 'Extreme fidelity', in Susan Sellars (ed.), *Writing Difference: Readings from the Seminar of Hélène Cixous*, Milton Keynes: Oxford University Press, 1988, p. 35.
2 'Thought of the heart', in Thomas Moore (ed.), *A Blue Fire: the Essential James Hillman*, London: Routledge, 1989, p. 304.
3 Judith Butler, *Gender Trouble: Feminism and the Subversion of Identity*, London and New York: Routledge, 1990; and 'Performative acts and gender constitution: an essay in phenomenology and feminist theory', *Theatre Journal* 20, Winter 1988. [SBB].
4 Teresa de Lauretis, *Technologies of Gender*, Bloomington: Indiana University Press, 1987; and *Alice Doesn't*, Bloomington: Indiana University Press, 1985. [SBB]
5 Hélène Cixous, who actively collaborated on *Les Atrides*, critiques the *Oresteia* as a narrative of the formation of patriarchal imperialism, in the influential book she co-wrote with Catherine Clément in the mid 1970s, *La Jeune Née* (Paris: Union Générale d'Editions, 10/18, 1975). As Morag Schiach points out, however, 'Cixous's interest in *The Oresteia* [. . .] does not lie simply in the ways in which it dramatises the origins of patriarchy; her aim is not to reprimand Aeschylus. Instead, she wants to read what is repressed in this myth of origins, to recapture the violence, the excess and the death that are an inescapable part of this putting-in-place of patriarchy; her project in reading *The Oresteia* is to challenge the seamless teleology of the narrative, and its apparent equation with progress'; *Hélène Cixous, a Politics of Writing*, London: Routledge, 1991, p. 12.
6 One line represented Agamemnon's fleet's journey, another the route of the signal of fire beacons sent from Troy at the beginning of *Agamemnon*. For *Sihanouk*, the entrance hall contained an enormous map of South-East Asia, with a red Cambodia at the epicentre of coloured shock-waves rippling out over the wider region. For *L'Indiade*, a gold, red and blue mural represented a map of India, Pakistan, Bangladesh and their immediate South-East Asian neighbours. Like the map for *Les Atrides*, which continues the westward itinerary of the Soleil while sustaining the displacement of Eurocentrism, these iconic and symbolic figurations of history-as-epic trace some of the human movements and differences (and their repercussions) to be further explored and animated in the shifting cartographies of performance.
7 Bryant-Bertail is referring to the army of figures buried to accompany the Chin dynasty emperor Chin-Shi-Huang-Ti after his death. Performatively this transitional space, a concretised metaphor of excavation and exhumation between the worlds of the everyday and of theatre, seems to infer a return to/of the repressed through some ritual act of sympathetic magic, rather than any archaeological reconstitution. In addition, however, as Sarah Bryant-Bertail has reiterated in correspondence with David Williams, 'the statues in *Les Atrides* expose our own historical discourse of digging objects out of (other people's) ground.' The recuperation of Emperor's (and Empire's) claim to eternal life forms part of the Soleil's 'critique of using myths to write our history – "myth" in Barthes' sense: not at all a "magical" entity or creation, but rather a historical construct that is made and used (and reused) by real people to legitimise concrete power arrangements'. These mythical figures of the past are to be disinterred, re-membered and reincarnated in the present on-stage, but by real bodies writing real histories.
8 Cf.: 'The high solid walls, the brusquely rectangular shape, the handholds and footholds

set into the walls at strategic points, the partition walls that divide each entrance from the open central plaza, clearly place the space in the category of the corral, the *corrida*, the hockey rink, the wrestling ring, the jai-alai [a Basque ball game] court and the gladiatorial arena: a place where encounters happen, where blood might be spilled'; Robert Bethune, 'Le Théâtre du Soleil's *Les Atrides*', *Asian Theatre Journal* 10: 2, Fall 1993, p. 183. Cf. also Michael Ratcliffe: 'It is a kind of corral in which some sort of violence has already taken place: stock-car racing, perhaps, or the breaking-in of wild horses or young bulls; but more likely, to judge from the stains on the walls, mass-execution of enemies without trial'; 'The Greeks, with an accent on the French', *New York Times*, 28 July 1991.

9 The *ekkyklêma*, or 'roll-out machine', was a mechanical device used in Greek theatre to show interior scenes externally, like a dramaturgical jump-cut from a public place to the tableau exposure of a private space (although notions of 'inside' and 'outside', 'public' and 'private' are transitive and blurred in Greek dramaturgy); these tableaux were usually formal representations of the aftermath of violence. *Les Atrides* also employed mobile platforms to 'fly' performers into the playing space from the central 'vomitorium' in the audience seating area; again, these platforms were operated invisibly from off-stage. There are parallels here with Meyerhold's use of mobile 'truck-stages' in his celebrated production of *The Government Inspector* in 1926; see Edward Braun (ed.), *Meyerhold on Theatre*, London: Methuen, 1969, pp. 215–16.

10 For a discussion of visual and gestural parallels with *Iphigenia at Aulis* in this sequence which create an 'alliance' between the two women and give a 'feminist, Euripidean' reading of Aeschylus, see Marianne McDonald, 'The atrocities of *Les Atrides*: Mnouch-kine's tragic vision', *TheatreForum* 1, Spring 1992, pp. 16–17.

11 See Linda Winter, 'The splendid pageantry of Greek tragedy', *New York Newsday*, 6 October 1991, and Frank Rich, 'Taking the stage to some of its extremes', *New York Times*, 6 October 1992. [SBB]

12 Jack Kroll, 'Blood and bones of tragedy', *Newsweek*, 5 October 1992. [SBB]

13 Cf. Denis Salter on Carneiro da Cunha's performance of both Clytemnestra and Athena: 'This not only enhances the structure of moral continuity and moral account-ability throughout the tetralogy, but, in a brilliant stroke, forces Clytemnestra and Athena to judge each other in a reciprocal action which makes absolute judgement impossible'. 'Hand Eye Mind Soul: Théâtre du Soleil's *Les Atrides*', *Theater* 24: 1, April 1994, p. 60.

14 Cf.: 'The peace Athena finds at the end is more like an armistice than a heartfelt rapprochement. Mnouchkine noted [in a public forum in New York, October 1992], "We have to forget the victims to have peace. The people we forgive are not the people who have been murdered".' In the light of our witnessing of the act of ritual murder in *Iphigenia*, 'Athena's solution appears as an accommodation, not as a resolution [. . .] It is a way for the living to go on living, not a way for the dead to be put to rest.' Robert Bethune, 'Le Théâtre du Soleil's *Les Atrides*', op. cit., pp. 188–9.

15 *Iphigenia at Aulis* was first produced in Athens *c.* 406 BC, the *Oresteia* in 458 BC.

16 For an informative discussion of the differences between Aeschylean and Euripidean choruses, and of the dramaturgical and political implications of their gendering, see Victor Castellani, 'The value of a kindly chorus: female choruses in Attic tragedy', in *Themes in Drama 11: 'Women in Theatre'*, Cambridge: Cambridge University Press, 1988, pp. 1–18.

17 For a detailed discussion of *Iphigenia at Aulis*, see Helene P. Foley, *Ritual irony: poetry and sacrifice in Euripides*, Ithaca: Cornell University Press, 1985, pp. 65–105.

18 As Sarah Bryant-Bertail points out, the addition of *Iphigenia at Aulis* 'brings new historical evidence to an old crime case' ('Gender, empire and body politic as mise en scène', *Theatre Journal* 46: 1, March 1994, p. 14). In *Iphigenia*, Agamemnon's decision to have his daughter sacrificed unlocks Clytemnestra's memories of her past, and 'she reveals the violent pre-history of their marriage: Agamemnon killed her first husband,

raped her, and crushed her baby to death for fear he would grow up to avenge the father's murder. Clytemnestra's father then married her to Agamemnon against her will' (p. 16).

19 Friedrich Nietzsche, *The Birth of Tragedy* (trans. Francis Golffing), New York: Doubleday, 1956, pp. 77–81.

20 The Messenger suggests that Iphigenia has been spared, blessed and carried off by the gods to serve them; it is a day of 'imperishable glory'. In performance, the Messenger (Georges Bigot) knelt on the floor beside Clytemnestra, who lay prostrate and unmoving as if asleep or stunned. Bigot's white head-dress and robe were spattered in blood.

21 'C'est par la souffrance que vient la connaissance'; *Agamemnon* (trans. Ariane Mnouchkine), Paris: Théâtre du Soleil, 1990, p. 17.

22 Cf. Hélène Cixous's and Catherine Clément's recuperation of hysteria as critical and subversive excess in Cixous and Clément, *La Jeune Née*, op. cit.

23 Cf.: 'The chorus [. . .] remains forever an *attending* chorus; it sees how [Dionysos] suffers and transforms himself, and it has, for that reason, no need to act.' Nietzsche, op. cit., p. 57.

24 Cf. Elin Diamond, 'The shudder of catharsis', in Andrew Parker and Eve Kosofwsky Sedgwick (eds), *Performativity and Performance*, London: Routledge 1995, pp. 152–72. Diamond's re-corporealising of catharsis is very pertinent to Cixous's text – particularly her discussion of Helene Weigel's gestic silent scream in *Mother Courage*; here she locates the 'shudder' as sentient embodied knowledge of 'the otherness of the other' (161), and quotes Adorno: 'The subject is lifeless except when it is able to shudder in response to the total spell. Without shudder, consciousness is trapped in reification. *Shudder is a kind of premonition of subjectivity, a sense of being touched by the other*' (161–2, my italics).

25 For *La Nuit des Rois*, the Soleil collaborated with Maïtreyi, a choreographer trained in Bharata Natyam. For *Les Atrides*, Nadejda Loujine supervised the choric dances, led by Catherine Schaub (trained in Kerala in Kathakali), Simon Abkarian (an Armenian actor with experience in the folk dances of the Caucasus) and Nirupama Nityanandan (extensively trained in Bharata Natyam in India). The cultural hybridity of the choric dances stemmed primarily from these three forms, montaged into an unfamiliar 'imaginary' form.

26 According to performer Catherine Schaub, the make-up was adapted primarily from Kutiyattam, the form from which Kathakali probably evolved. See Schaub in Denis Salter, 'Hand Eye Mind Soul', op. cit., p. 71.

27 Bernard Dort, *La représentation émancipée*, Arles: Actes Sud/Le temps du théâtre, 1988, p. 63. [BPV]

28 Mnouchkine has used this phrase on a number of occasions in recent years. It carries traces of Hannah Arendt's 'space of appearance', a notion of civic responsibility, collaboration and ethical action with and in political communities, drawn from Arendt's reading of the Greek *polis*, which she describes as 'the space of appearance in the widest sense of the word, namely, the space where I appear to others as others appear to me, where men exist not merely like other living or inanimate things but make their appearance explicitly'; *The Human Condition*, Chicago: University of Chicago Press, 1958, pp. 198–9. In addition, there are echoes of Herbert Blau's articulation of the double-binds of representation – the 'play of appearances' in performance, and the struggle for 'the liberation of the performer as an *actor* who, laminated with appearance, struggles to *appear*'; 'Universals of performance; or amortizing play', in Richard Schechner and Willa Appel (eds), *By Means of Performance: Intercultural Studies of Theatre and Ritual*, Cambridge: Cambridge University Press, 1990, p. 257 (italics in original). Finally, the term suggests theatre as a site for critical re-memberings, for the restorative embodiment of mythical revenants (*apparitions*) in the actual body of the 'actor-medium'; cf. Sarah Bryant-Bertail in note 7 above, and Abkarian's notion of 'exhumation' below.

29 Mnouchkine is being somewhat ingenuous here. Her training with Jacques Lecoq

would have included extensive choral work, and the ensembles in her own productions from the late 1960s onwards are massively informed by choral notions. Cf. for example Jacques Lecoq, 'Comment bouge un chœur?', in *Le Théâtre du geste*, Paris: Bordas, 1987, p. 112.

30 For a discussion of the different physicalities of Abkarian (as Agamemnon), Nityanandan (as Iphigenia) and Carneiro da Cunho (as Clytemnestra), see Odette Aslan, 'Au Théâtre du Soleil les acteurs écrivent avec leur corps', in *Le Corps en jeu*, Paris: CNRS Editions, pp. 294–5.

31 Cf.: 'At the end of *Les Choéphores*, Orestes dances a frenzied dance in which he dares Aegisthus and Clytemnestra to return to life, so he can kill them again. His madness proceeds naturally from the hysterical ecstasy he exhibits after the brutal murder. The ecstatic dances of each central figure in these plays express a strange mixture of triumph linked with tragedy. They are apt renditions in the private area of the public slaughter of every war. Iraq, with its screams of mothers and children, is not far from our imagination.' Marianne McDonald, 'The atrocities of *Les Atrides*', op. cit., p. 18.

32 Cf. John Chioles's description of Lemêtre's 'virtual symphony' in *Les Atrides*: 'Greek and Asia Minor mountain music from a variety of reed instruments, Balinese dance music, Indian Kathakali (the stutter step) music, Kabuki *aragoto*, and for good measure he uses as a motif the small fragment of music that we have extant from the ancient period (slow and pensive mounting to momentary exaltation)'; '*The Oresteia* and the avant-garde', *Performing Arts Journal* 45, September 1993, p. 5. Chioles's essay offers a useful account of productions of the *Oresteia* by Martha Graham, Tyrone Guthrie, Peter Hall, Karlos Koun and Peter Stein, as well as of *Les Atrides*.

APPENDIX

1959 Aged 20, Mnouchkine returns to Paris after a year studying at Oxford University, and enrols to read Psychology at the Sorbonne. With Martine Franck, she establishes l'Association Théâtrale des Etudiants de Paris (ATEP). President – Ariane Mnouchkine; Honorary President – Roger Planchon. At the invitation of ATEP, Jean-Paul Sartre gives a lecture ('Théâtre épique et théâtre dramatique').

1960 *Noces de Sang* (*Blood Wedding*), by Federico Garcia Lorca (ATEP); directed by Dominique Sérina, costumes designed by Ariane Mnouchkine.

1961 *Gengis Khan*, by Henri Bauchau (ATEP); directed by Ariane Mnouchkine, costumes by Françoise Tournafond, technical direction by Jean-Claude Penchenat. Performed in the Arènes de Lutèce, Paris, in June.

1962 Mnouchkine abandons her studies at the Sorbonne, works as scriptwriter and assistant producer on a film in Italy (*L'Homme de Rio*); then travels widely in the Middle East, Cambodia, Korea, China, Japan, India and Indonesia.

1964 May: creation of Le Théâtre du Soleil, Société Coopérative Ouvrière de Production ('The Theatre of the Sun, workers' production cooperative'). Ten initial members: Georges Donzenac (physical training), Myrrha Donzenac (actor), Martine Franck (photographer), Gérard Hardy (actor), Philippe Léotard (actor), Ariane Mnouchkine (director), Roberto Moscoso (designer), Jean-Claude Penchenat (actor/administrator), Jean-Pierre Tailhade (actor) and Françoise Tournafond (costume designer).

1964–5 *Les Petits Bourgeois*, by Maxine Gorki, translation and adaptation by Arthur Adamov; directed by Ariane Mnouchkine, décor by Roberto Moscoso, technical direction by Gérard Hardy, music by Roger Tessier. Premiered at the MJC de la Porte de Montreuil, in November 1964, followed by a short tour in the environs of Paris, then at the Théâtre Mouffetard, Paris, in October 1965. Audiences: *c.* 2,900.

1965–6 *Le Capitaine Fracasse*, by Théophile Gautier; adaptation by Philippe Léotard, directed by Ariane Mnouchkine, décor by Roberto Moscoso, costumes by Françoise Tournafond, lighting design by Serge Wolf. Premiered in Gennevilliers (June 1965), short tour in the environs of Paris (September–October), then to the Théâtre Récamier, Paris (January–February, 1966). Audiences: *c.* 4,000.

1966–7 Mnouchkine attends the Ecole Jacques Lecoq in Paris. In the evenings, she passes each day's lessons on to the other members of the company.

1967–70 *La Cuisine* (*The Kitchen*), by Arnold Wesker; translation by Philippe Léotard, directed by Ariane Mnouchkine, décor by Roberto Moscoso. Première season at the Cirque Médrano in Montmartre, Paris (April–July and September–November 1967). Subsequently toured in France, Belgium, Switzerland, Italy, before a season at L'Elysée-Montmartre, Paris (April–July 1970). Also a number of free performances given in striking/occupied French factories (May–June 1968). Awarded Prix de la Critique, Prix du Brigadier, etc. Audiences: *c.* 63,400.

1968 *Le Songe d'une Nuit d'Eté* (*A Midsummer Night's Dream*), by William Shakespeare; translation by Philippe Léotard, directed by Ariane Mnouchkine, décor by Roberto Moscoso, music by Jacques Lasry, costumes by Françoise Tournafond, lighting design by Roger Leuvron, technical direction by Guy-Claude François. Performed at the Cirque Médrano in Montmartre, Paris (February–April and June–July 1968).

L'Arbre Sorcier, Jérome et la Tortue, by Catherine Dasté; a children's play directed by Catherine Dasté, designed by Jean-Baptiste Manessier, music by Jacques Lasry, costumes by Marie-Hélène Dasté. Performed at the Cirque Médrano in Montmartre, Paris (from 24 March 1968), then on tour.

1969–70 *Les Clowns* (a collective creation); directed by Ariane Mnouchkine, décor by Roberto Moscoso, music by Teddy Lasry, costumes by Christiane Candries, technical direction by Guy-Claude François. Premiered at the Théâtre de la Commune d'Aubervilliers (April–June 1969), then 25 performances at the Festival d'Avignon (July–August), before returning to l'Elysée-Montmartre, Paris (January–March 1970), in rep with *La Cuisine*. Audiences: *c.* 40,000.

1970 24 August – arrival of Théâtre du Soleil at the Cartoucherie de Vincennes, Paris. Peppercorn rent of 500 francs per month. First opened to the public on 26 December for *1789*.

1970–1 *1789: la révolution doit s'arrêter à la perfection du bonheur* (a collective creation); directed by Ariane Mnouchkine, décor by Roberto Moscoso, technical direction by Guy-Claude François, sound by Jean-René Cluny, costumes by Françoise Tournafond and Christiane Candries, marionettes and props by Nicole Princet; director's assistant – Sophie Lemasson; historical adviser – Elisabeth Brisson; musical direction by Michel Derouin, with music by Lully, Rameau, Handel, Bach, Mahler, Julius Fucik. First performed at the Palazzo Lido, Milan (11–15 November 1970), at the invitation of the Piccolo Teatro di Milano; transferred to the Cartoucherie de Vincennes (26 December 1970–July 1971). Toured in France, then to Martinique, Lausanne (Switzerland), Berlin, London (The Roundhouse, 12–30 October 1971), Belgrade. Audiences: *c.* 281,370.

1972–3 *1793: la cité radieuse est de ce monde* (a collective creation); directed by Ariane Mnouchkine, décor by Roberto Moscoso, costumes by Françoise Tournafond, musical direction by Michel Derouin, technical direction by Guy-Claude François, lighting design by Jean-Noël Cordier; historical documentation by Jean-François Labouverie; director's assistant – Sophie Lemasson. Performed at the Cartoucherie de Vincennes (May–July 1972). Then from September 1972 to June 1973, revival of **1789**, performed in repertory with **1793**. Audiences: *c.* 102,100.

1974 Release of film version of **1789**, directed by Ariane Mnouchkine – filmed at the Cartoucherie in June 1973, during the final thirteen live performances.

1975–6 *L'Age d'Or: première ébauche* (a collective creation); directed by Ariane Mnouchkine, scenic design by Guy-Claude François, lighting design by Jean-Noël Cordier, costumes by Françoise Tournafond, Jean-Claude Barriera and Nathalie Ferreira, masks by Erhard Stiefel; director's assistant – Sophie Lemasson, dramaturgical assistant – Catherine Mounier, production manager – Emmanuel de Bary. Premiered at the Cartoucherie de Vincennes, Paris (4 March–May 1975). Toured in France, to Warsaw and Venice (1975), Louvain-la-Neuve (in Belgium), Milan and Venice (1976). Audiences: *c.* 136,000.

1976–7 *Molière, ou la vie d'un honnête homme* (a film); written and directed by Ariane Mnouchkine with le Théâtre du Soleil; designed by Guy-Claude François, costumes by Daniel Ogier, photography by Bernard Zitzermann, original music by René Clemencic. Audiences: *c.* 2,000,000.

1977–8 *Dom Juan*, by Molière: directed by Philippe Caubère, design and technical direction by Guy-Claude François, costumes by Françoise Tournafond, props by Erhard Stiefel, lighting design by Jean-Noël Cordier. Performed at the Cartoucherie de Vincennes (from 16 December 1977). Audiences: *c.* 30,500.

1979–80 *Méphisto: le roman d'une carrière*, adapted from Klaus Mann's novel and directed by Ariane Mnouchkine, designed by Guy-Claude François, costumes by Nani Noël and Daniel Ogier, music by Jean-Jacques Lemêtre (with Luciano Moro Marangone), masks by Erhard Stiefel, lighting design by Jean-Noël Cordier; director's assistant – Sophie Moscoso. Premiered at the

Cartoucherie de Vincennes (May–July 1979), then toured to the Festival d'Avignon and Louvain-la-Neuve (1979), Lyons, Rome, Berlin, Munich, Lons-le-Saunier (1980); return season at the Cartoucherie (June–July 1980). Audiences: *c.* 160,000.

1980 Video version of ***Méphisto***, by Bernard Sobel.

1981 ***Richard II***, by William Shakespeare; translated and directed by Ariane Mnouchkine, designed by Guy-Claude François, costumes by Jean-Claude Barriera and Nathalie Thomas, masks by Erhard Stiefel, music composed and performed by Jean-Jacques Lemêtre (with Claude Ninat), lighting design by Jean-Noël Cordier and Laurence Aucouturier, backdrops designed by Mehmet Ates; director's assistant – Sophie Moscoso. Premiered at the Cartoucherie de Vincennes (from 10 December 1981).

1982 ***La Nuit des Rois*** (*Twelfth Night*), by William Shakespeare; translated and directed by Ariane Mnouchkine, designed by Guy-Claude François, costumes by Jean-Claude Barriera and Nathalie Thomas, backdrops designed by Gérard Hardy, lighting design by Jean-Noël Cordier, music by Jean-Jacques Lemêtre (with Claude Ninat), choreography by Maïtreyi; director's assistant – Sophie Moscoso. Premiered in the Cour d'Honneur du Palais des Papes, as part of the Festival d'Avignon (from 10 July 1982); first performed at the Cartoucherie de Vincennes on 6 October.

1982–3 ***Richard II*** and ***La Nuit des Rois*** performed in repertory at the Cartoucherie de Vincennes, the Festival d'Avignon (July–August 1982) and the Festival of Munich (May 1983).

1984 ***Henry IV, première partie***, by William Shakespeare; translated and directed by Ariane Mnouchkine, designed by Guy-Claude François, costumes by Jean-Claude Barriera and Nathalie Thomas, lighting design by Jean-Noël Cordier, masks and props by Erhard Stiefel, music by Jean-Jacques Lemêtre; director's assistant – Sophie Moscoso. Premiered at the Cartoucherie de Vincennes (from 18 January 1984).

'*Les Shakespeares*': all three Shakespeare plays, performed as a cycle, toured to the Olympic Arts Festival of Los Angeles (June 1984), the Festival d'Avignon (July 1984), the Berliner Festspiele (September 1984). Audiences for the Shakespeare cycle: *c.* 253,000.

1985–6 ***L'Histoire terrible mais inachevée de Norodom Sihanouk, roi du Cambodge*** ('The terrible but unfinished story of Norodom Sihanouk, King of Cambodia'), by Hélène Cixous; directed by Ariane Mnouchkine, designed by Guy-Claude François, costumes by Jean-Claude Barriera and Nathalie Thomas, figurines and masks by Erhard Stiefel, lighting design by Jean-Noël

Cordier, music by Jean-Jacques Lemêtre (with Pierre Launay); director's assistant – Sophie Moscoso. Premiered at the Cartoucherie de Vincennes (from 11 September 1985). Subsequently toured to Amsterdam, Brussels, Madrid and Barcelona (June–October 1986). Audiences: *c.* 108,500.

1987 Mnouchkine and the Théâtre du Soleil awarded the first Premio Europa per il Teatro in Taormina, Sicily (August).

1987–8 *L'Indiade, ou l'Inde de leurs rêves* ('The Indiad, or the India of their dreams') by Hélène Cixous; directed by Ariane Mnouchkine, designed by Guy-Claude François, costumes by Jean-Claude Barriera and Nathalie Thomas, masks by Erhard Stiefel, music by Jean-Jacques Lemêtre, lighting design by Jean-Noël Cordier; Bharata natyam coach – Maïtreyi; director's assistant – Sophie Moscoso. Premiered at the Cartoucherie de Vincennes (from September 1987). Toured to the Jerusalem Festival, Israel (May 1988), before returning to the Cartoucherie (June 1988). Audiences: *c.* 89,000.

Confronted with deficits and funding difficulties, and resisting corporate sponsorship, the Théâtre du Soleil introduces '*le billet-mécène*' for the season of *L'Indiade*: a form of voluntary patronage whereby audience members can pay more for their tickets (250, 500 or 1000 Francs instead of 120).

1988 Film version of *L'Indiade*, by Bernard Sobel, shot July–September.

1989 *La Nuit miraculeuse* (film), written by Hélène Cixous and Ariane Mnouchkine, directed by Mnouchkine; photography by Bernard Zitzerman, music by Jean-Jacques Lemêtre, design by Guy-Claude François, costumes by Nathalie Thomas and Marie-Hélène Bouvet, figurines by Erhard Stiefel. Commissioned by the Assemblée Nationale on the bicentenary of the Declaration of Human Rights. Shot 1–4 September at the Cartoucherie and the Assemblée Nationale, Paris. Broadcast nationally in France on La Sept and FR3, 20 December, and in Germany.

1990 *Iphigénie à Aulis*, by Euripides; translated by Jean and Mayotte Bollack, directed by Ariane Mnouchkine, designed by Guy-Claude François, costumes by Nathalie Thomas and Marie-Hélène Bouvet, sculptures by Erhard Stiefel, music by Jean-Jacques Lemêtre (with Sergio Perera), lighting design by Laurence Aucouturier; make-up designs conceived by Catherine Schaub; choreography by Catherine Schaub, Simon Abkarian and Nirupama Nityanandan; director's assistant – Sophie Moscoso. Premiered at the Cartoucherie de Vincennes (from 16 November 1990).

Agamemnon, by Aeschylus; translated and directed by Ariane Mnouchkine, designed by Guy-Claude François, costumes by Nathalie Thomas, sculptures by Erhard Stiefel, music by Jean-Jacques Lemêtre (with Sergio Perera), lighting design by Laurence Aucouturier; choreography by Catherine Schaub, Simon

Abkarian and Nirupama Nityanandan; make-up design conceived by Catherine Schaub; translation adviser – Claudine Bensaïd; director's assistant – Sophie Moscoso. Premiered at the Cartoucherie de Vincennes (from 24 November 1990).

1991 *Les Choéphores* (*The Libation Bearers*), by Aeschylus; translated and directed by Ariane Mnouchkine, décor by Guy-Claude François, costumes by Nathalie Thomas, sculptures by Erhard Stiefel, music by Jean-Jacques Lemêtre (with Maria Serrão), lighting design by Jean-Michel Bauer; make-up design conceived by Catherine Schaub; choreography by Catherine Schaub, Simon Abkarian and Nirupama Nityanandan; translation adviser – Claudine Bensaïd; director's assistant – Sophie Moscoso. Premiered at the Cartoucherie de Vincennes (from 23 February 1991).

1991–2 *Iphigénie à Aulis*, *Agamemnon* and *Les Choéphores* toured together to Amsterdam (June 1991), Essen, Sicily, Berlin (August 1991), returning to the Cartoucherie (October–December 1991), then to Lyon (January 1992).

1992 *Les Euménides* (*The Eumenides*), by Aeschylus; translated by Hélène Cixous, directed by Ariane Mnouchkine, designed by Guy-Claude François, costumes by Nathalie Thomas, sculptures by Erhard Stiefel, music by Jean-Jacques Lemêtre, lighting design by Jean-Michel Bauer; director's assistant – Sophie Moscoso. Premiered at the Cartoucherie de Vincennes (from 16 May 1992).

All four Greek plays performed as a cycle ('*Les Atrides*'); toured briefly in France (June–July), then to Bradford, England (European Arts Festival, July), the Festival des Amériques, Montreal (September) and New York (BAM, October) and Vienna, before returning to the Cartoucherie (October–December). Audiences: *c.* 286,700.

1993 *L'Inde, de père en fils, de mère en fille*, directed by Rajeev Sethi, from an idea by Ariane Mnouchkine; a performance by thirty-two Indian artists (storytellers, musicians, dancers, acrobats, musicians). At the Cartoucherie de Vincennes, 15 May–6 June. Audiences: *c.* 8500.

1994–5 *La Ville parjure, ou le réveil des Erinyes* ('The Perjured City, or the Awakening of the Furies') by Hélène Cixous; directed by Ariane Mnouchkine, décor by Guy-Claude François, costumes by Nathalie Thomas and Marie-Hélène Bouvet, music by Jean-Jacques Lemêtre (with Morgane), puppets by Erhard Stiefel, lighting design by Jean-Michel Bauer; director's assistant – Sophie Moscoso. Premiered at the Cartoucherie de Vincennes in 1994 (season from 18 May; revived 18 September–30 October); in 1995, tour to Liège, Festival of Ruhr, the Wiener Festwochen, and Festival d'Avignon (July).

1995–6 *Le Tartuffe*, by Molière; directed by Ariane Mnouchkine, design by Guy-Claude François, costumes by Nathalie Thomas and Marie-Hélène Bouvet, lighting by Jean-Michel Bauer, songs by Cheb Hasni, musical score by Jean-Jacques Lemêtre, with François Leymarie and Yann Lemêtre. Premiered at the Wiener Festwochen (10 June 1995), then at the Festival d'Avignon (9–29 July) and the Cartoucherie de Vincennes (from 11 October). Audiences: *c.* 123,000 for 213 performances.

1995 'The Avignon Declaration' (August): Mnouchkine and others go on a hunger strike in protest at the inaction of Europe and the USA in relation to Bosnia; other signatories/strikers include Olivier Py, François Tanguy, Emmanuel de Véricourt, Maguy Marin and George Guérin.

1997 French television premiere of *Au Soleil, même la nuit*, a documentary on reherasals for *Le Tartuffe* at the Cartoucherie. Directed by Eric Darmon and Catherine Vilpoux; co-production by Agat Films, le Théâtre du Soleil and La Sept/ARTE.

BIBLIOGRAPHY

LE THÉÂTRE DU SOLEIL
PUBLISHED PRODUCTION TEXTS

Aeschylus (1990) *Agamemnon* (translated by Ariane Mnouchkine, with notes by Pierre Judet de la Combe), Paris: Théâtre du Soleil
—— (1992) *Les Choéphores* (*The Libation Bearers*, translated by Ariane Mnouchkine), Paris: Théâtre du Soleil
—— (1992) *Les Euménides* (translated by Hélène Cixous), Paris: Théâtre du Soleil
Cixous, Hélène (1985) *L'Histoire terrible mais inachevée de Norodom Sihanouk, roi du Cambodge*, Paris: Théâtre du Soleil
—— (1987) *L'Indiade, ou l'Inde de leurs rêves*, Paris: Théâtre du Soleil. Includes Cixous's 'Si vous le permettez, je vais vous parler d'amour', and 'Quelques écrits sur le théâtre' (pp. 11–7, 247–78)
—— (1994) *La Ville parjure, ou le réveil des Erinyes*, Paris: Théâtre du Soleil. Includes Cixous's 'Nos mauvais sangs' (pp. 5–7).
—— (1994) *The Terrible but Unfinished Story of Norodom Sihanouk, King of Cambodia* (translated by Juliet Flower MacCannell, Judith Pike and Lollie Groth), Lincoln and London: University of Nebraska Press
Euripides (1990) *Iphigénie à Aulis* (translated by Jean and Mayotte Bollack), Paris: Les Editions de Minuit
Léotard, Philippe (1966) *Le Capitaine Fracasse* (adapted from Théophile Gauthier by Philippe Léotard), Paris: Théâtre du Soleil
Mnouchkine, Ariane (1979) *Méphisto: le roman d'une carrière* (adapted from Klaus Mann's novel by Ariane Mnouchkine), Paris: Solin/Théâtre du Soleil
—— (1990) *Mephisto* (English translation of Mnouchkine's adaptation by Timberlake Wertenbaker), in *Theater and Politics: an International Anthology*, USA: Ubu Repertory Theater Publications, pp. 361–469
Shakespeare, William (1982) *La Nuit des Rois* (*Twelfth Night*, translated by Ariane Mnouchkine), Paris: Solin/Théâtre du Soleil
—— (1984) *Richard II* (translated by Ariane Mnouchkine), Paris: Théâtre du Soleil
—— (1984) *Henry IV: première partie* (translated by Ariane Mnouchkine), Paris: Théâtre du Soleil
Théâtre du Soleil (1971) *1789: la révolution doit s'arrêter à la perfection du bonheur*, Paris: Stock
—— (1971) *1789* (English translation by Alexander Trocchi, with an introduction by Michael Kustow), in *Gambit* 5: 20, pp. 5–52
—— (1972) *1793: la cité révolutionnaire est de ce monde*, Paris: Stock
—— (1973) *1789* and *1793*, in *L'Avant-Scène Théâtre* 526–7, 1–15 October
—— (1975) *L'Age d'Or: première ébauche ('Texte-Programme')*, Paris: Stock
—— (1989) *1789* and *1793*, Paris: Théâtre du Soleil
Wesker, Arnold (1967) *La Cuisine* (*The Kitchen*, translated by Philippe Léotard), *L'Avant-Scène Théâtre* no. 385, August

MATERIAL RELATING TO PARTICULAR PRODUCTIONS

La Cuisine

Copfermann, Emile (1967) Review in *Les Lettres Françaises*, 13 March
Godard, Colette (1967) 'Entretien avec Ariane Mnouchkine', *Les Nouvelles Littéraires*, 30 March
Poirot-Delpech, Bertrand (1967) '*La Cuisine*', *Le Monde*, 9–10 April
Saurel, Renée (1967) Review in *Les Temps Modernes*, May, pp. 2095–7
Wesker, Arnold (1961) *The Kitchen*, London: Jonathan Cape
Zand, Nicole (1967) Review in *Le Monde*, 8 April
—— (1968) '*La Cuisine* à l'usine', *Le Monde*, 17 June

Le Songe d'une Nuit d'Eté

Attoun, Lucien (1968) Review in *Europe* 468–9, pp. 492–3
Copfermann, Emile (1968) Interview with Mnouchkine, and review, *Les Lettres Françaises*, 7 February
Dumur, Guy (1968) 'Songes des nuits d'hiver', *Le Nouvel Observateur*, 28 February–5 March
Godard, Colette (1968) 'Songe cruel' (interview with Mnouchkine), *Les Nouvelles Littéraires*, 15 February
Nichet, Jacques (1968) Review in *Etudes* 4, April, pp. 540–5
Norès, Dominique (1968) Review in *Les Lettres Nouvelles*, May–June, pp. 181–3
Saurel, Renée (1968) 'Peaux de chèvres et peaux de lapins', *Les Temps Modernes*, March–April, pp. 1701–5
Zand, Nicole (1968) '*Le Songe d'une Nuit d'Eté*: une pièce sur nos fantasmes' (interview with Mnouchkine), *Le Monde*, 13 February

Les Clowns

Attoun, Lucien (1969) 'Avant-première pour *Les Clowns*' (interviews with Mnouchkine and Jean-Claude Penchenat), *Les Nouvelles Littéraires*, 17 April
Copfermann, Emile (1969) '*Les Clowns* à l'Elysée-Montmartre', *Les Lettres Françaises*, 28 January
Galey, Matthieu (1969) 'Parade foraine', *Les Nouvelles Littéraires*, 6 May
Lauroy, Nicole (1969) 'L'utopie vécue, ou l'éclat chaleureux du Théâtre du Soleil', *Femmes d'Aujourd'hui* no. 1271, 10 November, pp. 95–9
Madral, Philippe (1969) 'Héritiers ou bâtisseurs?' (interview with Mnouchkine), *L'Humanité*, 6 May
Rémy, Tristan (1945) *Les Clowns*, Paris: Grasset
Saurel, Renée (1969) 'Théâtre avec et sans auteur', *Les Temps Modernes*, May, pp. 2085–6
Simon, Alfred (1969) 'Des clowns et des hommes', *Esprit*, June, pp. 1091–4
Zand, Nicole (1969) 'Les clowns ne doivent pas mourir', *Le Monde*, 23 November

1789

Abirached, Robert (1971) '*1789* et la perfection du bonheur', *La Nouvelle Revue Française* no. 219, March, pp. 109–11

Bablet, Denis (1971) 'Une scénographie pour *1789*', *Interscaena* 4: 1 (Prague), Autumn, pp. 29–43.

Campos, Christophe (1972) 'Experiments for the people of Paris', *Theatre Quarterly* 2: 8, October–December, pp. 56–67

Casanova, Antoine *et al.* (1971) '1789 au théâtre et dans l'histoire' (interview with Mnouchkine), *La Nouvelle Critique* no. 45, June, pp. 74–82

Copfermann, Emile (1970a) 'Milan Ouvert: Théâtre du Soleil', *Les Lettres Françaises*, 25 November

—— (1970b) 'Le Soleil à la Cartoucherie', *Les Lettres Françaises*, 23 December

—— (1971) 'Entretien avec Ariane Mnouchkine', and 'Où est la différence?', *Travail Théâtral* no. 2, pp. 3–14, 15–20. (English translation in *Gambit* 5: 20, 1971, pp. 63–74)

Dort, Bernard (1973) 'L'histoire jouée', *L'Avant-Scène Théâtre* 526–7, 1–15 October, pp. 9–16

Faivre, Bernard (1987) 'Décentrements: *1789* et la Cartoucherie de Vincennes (Decembre 1970)', in *Le Théâtre dans la Ville*, Paris: Editions du CNRS, pp. 194–208

Godard, Colette (1970) '*1789*', *Le Monde*, 17 November

Kirby, Victoria Nes (1971) '*1789*', *The Drama Review* 15: 4, pp. 73–91

Lemasson, Sophie and Jean-Claude Penchenat (1971) 'From production to collective creation', *Gambit* 5: 20, pp. 53–62

Lusebrink, Hans-Jurgen and Axel Polleti (1989) 'Der vierzehnte Juli 1789: inszeniert vom Théâtre du Soleil', *Französisch Heute* 20: 2, June, pp. 117–29

Manceaux, Michèle (1970) 'La militante du théâtre: Ariane Mnouchkine', *Le Nouvel Observateur*, 28 December

Marcel, Gabriel (1971) 'Mise en place de la subversion', *Les Nouvelles Littéraires*, 4 February

Moscoso, Roberto (1971) 'Un théâtre pour chaque spectacle', *Travail Théâtral* no. 2, January/March, pp. 22–8

Poirot-Delpech, Bertrand (1971) '*1789*', *Le Monde*, 14 January

Ruyter-Tognotti, Danièle de (1991) 'Théâtre et Histoire: position critique dans *1789* du Théâtre du soleil', *Néophilologus* 75: 3, July, pp. 367–78

Schwartz, Helmut (1992) 'La révolution française dans le théâtre français contemporain, 1950–80', in Gérard Beauprêtre (ed.), *Révolution et littérature: la révolution française dans les littératures allemandes, françaises et polonaises*, Warsaw: University of Warsaw, pp. 209–17

Wardle, Irving (1971) 'Revolution in a military ghost-town', *The Times*, 8 March

—— (1971) 'Re-creation of revolution' (*1789* at the Roundhouse, London), *The Times*, 13 October

—— (ed.) (1972) 'Le Théâtre du Soleil: *1789*' (interview and public discussion with Mnouchkine), *Performance* 1: 2, April, pp. 132–6, 136–41

1793

Château, Gilbert (1972) '*1793* et le théâtre politique', *La Nouvelle Revue Française* no. 236, August, pp. 108–10

Copfermann, Emile (1972) '*1793*: une histoire mise à tour', *Travail Théâtral* no. 8, July/September

Decock, J. (1973) '*1793*: la cité révolutionnaire est de ce *monde*', *The French Review* 47: 1, October pp. 240–1

Dumur, Guy (1972) 'Spectacle glacial', *Le Nouvel Observateur*, 22 May

Godard, Colette (1972) '*1793*: un collectif artisanal', *Le Monde*, 4 May

Mounier, Catherine (1973) 'L'histoire de *1793*: de l'analyse historique à la création artistique', *Revue d'Esthétique* no. 1, pp. 85–92

—— (1977) 'Deux créations collectives du Théâtre du Soleil: *1793* et *L'Age d'Or*', in *Les Voies de la création théâtrale* vol. 5, Paris: Editions du CNRS, pp. 121–278

Poirot-Delpech, Bertrand (1972) '*1793* par le Théâtre du Soleil', *Le Monde*, 20 May

Rebérioux, Madeleine (1972) 'L'austerité spectacle révolutionnaire', *Politique Aujourd'hui*, December, pp. 97–9

Ristat, Jean (1972) 'Le théâtre de la différence', *Les Lettres Françaises*, 14 June

Sandier, Gilles (1972) 'La dynamique révolutionnaire', *La Quinzaine Littéraire*, 16 June

Saurel, Renée (1972) 'Le pain noir de l'égalité: *1793*', *Les Temps Modernes*, August, pp. 313–22

Simon, Alfred (1972) 'Théâtre et révolution: *1793*', *Esprit*, January, pp. 113–16

Théâtre du Soleil (1972) '*1793* à la Cartoucherie' (texts by company members), *Les Lettres Françaises*, 17–23 May

L'Age d'Or

Balazard, Simone (1978) 'La réference au théâtre dans *L'Age d'Or*', in Bernard Dort and Anne Ubersfeld (eds), *Le Texte et la scène: études sur l'espace et l'acteur*, Paris: Université de la Sorbonne Nouvelle III, pp. 111–24

Banu, Georges (1978) '*L'Age d'Or* et le conte', in Bernard Dort and Anne Ubersfeld (eds), *Le Texte et la scène: études sur l'espace et l'acteur*, Paris: Université de la Sorbonne Nouvelle III, pp. 137–56

Copeau, Jacques (1990) *Copeau: Texts on Theatre* (edited and translated by John Rudlin and Norman H. Paul), London: Routledge

Davis, Yvon, Michèle Raoul-Davis and Bernard Sobel (1975) 'Première ébauche: entretien avec Ariane Mnouchkine', *Théâtre/Public* 5–6, June–August, pp. 4–6

Dort, Bernard (1975) 'Entre le passé et le futur: *L'Age d'Or* au Théâtre du Soleil', *Travail Théâtral* no. 20, July–October

Dumur, Guy (1975) 'Les fables du monde', *Le Nouvel Observateur*, 17 March

Ezine, Jean-Louis (1975) 'Sur la sellette: entretien avec Ariane Mnouchkine', *Les Nouvelles Littéraires*, 3–9 March, pp. 19–20

Godard, Colette (1975) '*L'Age d'Or*, demain', *Le Monde*, 20 February

Hervic, Elizabeth (1976) '*L'Age d'Or*: une rencontre Mnouchkine–Copeau', *Revue d'histoire du théâtre* 28: 3, July–September, pp. 274–85

Kirkland, Christopher (1975) 'Théâtre du Soleil – *The Golden Age: first draft*', *The Drama Review* 19: 2, pp. 53–60

Kustow, Michael (1975) '*L'Age d'Or*', *The Guardian*, 31 March

Mnouchkine, Ariane (1975) '*L'Age d'Or*: the long journey from 1793 to 1975' (forum discussion), *Theatre Quarterly* 5: 18, pp. 4–13

Morand, Claude (1974) 'Le Théâtre du Soleil: mutation et nouveaux mythes' (interviews), *ATAC Informations* 62, 13–24 November, pp. 33–6

Mounier, Catherine (1977) 'Deux créations collectives du Théâtre de Soleil: *1793* et *L'Age d'Or*', in *Les voies de la création théâtrale* vol. 5, Paris: Editions du CNRS, pp. 121–278

Netto, Teixeira Coelho (1978) 'Le masque d'or de l'espace', in Bernard Dort and Anne Ubersfeld (eds), *Le Texte et la scène: études sur l'espace et l'acteur*, Paris: Université de la Sorbonne Nouvelle III, pp. 97–104

Rudlin, John (1986) *Jacques Copeau*, Cambridge: Cambridge University Press

—— (1994) *Commedia dell'arte: an Actor's Handbook*, London: Routledge, pp. 203–10

Sandier, Gilles (1975) 'La fable d'aujourd'hui: *L'Age d'Or*', *La Quinzaine Littéraire* no. 207, 1 April, pp. 3–5

Saurel, Renée (1975) '*L'Age d'Or* au Théâtre du Soleil', *Les Temps Modernes* 30: 2, pp. 1637–44

Sedel, Catherine (1978) 'Un espace en construction', in Bernard Dort and Anne Ubersfeld (eds), *Le Texte et la scène: études sur l'espace et l'acteur*, Paris: Université de la Sorbonne Nouvelle III, pp. 105–10

Seguin, Jean-Claude (1976) 'Rappresentare il mondo d'oggi', *Scena* 1, January–February, pp. 41–50

Simon, Alfred (1975) 'La création collective et la fonction sociale du théâtre', 'Un rêve vécu du théâtre populaire', and 'Ariane, c'est une grande chose qui commence: table ronde sur le Théâtre du Soleil' (interviews), *Esprit* no. 447, June, pp. 929–32, 933–44, 945–64

Thomadaki, Katerina (1978) 'Une comparaison entre le jeu des acteurs dans *L'Age d'Or* et les conduites des personnages de la bande dessinée comique: deux langages convergents', in Bernard Dort and Anne Ubersfeld (eds), *Le Texte et la scène: études sur l'espace et l'acteur*, Paris: Université de la Sorbonne Nouvelle III, pp. 125–36

Dom Juan

Andrade, Béatrix (1978) 'Molière, pile et face', *Les Nouvelles Littéraires*, 5–12 January

Attoun, Lucien (1978) Review in *Les Nouvelles Littéraires*, 5–12 January

Cournot, Michel (1977) 'Le *Dom Juan* de Philippe Caubère', *Le Monde*, 30 December

Sandier, Gilles (1978) Review in *La Quinzaine Littéraire*, 7 February

Molière (film)

Audibert, Louis *et al.* (1978) Review and interview with Mnouchkine, *Cinématographe*, June, pp. 14–19

Breton, Emile (1978) 'Longueurs du temps de l'histoire', *La Nouvelle Critique*, October

Comuzio, E. (1979) Review in *Cinéforum* 19: 11, pp. 700–13

Douin, Jean-Luc (1978) 'Molière, ou la vie d'un honnête homme' (interview with Mnouchkine), *Télérama*, 15 April, pp. 78–80

Gevaudan, Frantz (1978) 'Un grand absent' (review and interviews with Philippe Caubère and Daniel Ogier), *Cinéma* 77/78, August–September, pp. 132–42, 160–3

Godard, Colette (1981) 'La folie d'un honnête homme', *Le Monde*, 1 March

Grunfeld, Monique and Arnaud Spire (1978) 'De qui parle Molière? De Mnouchkine, Vitez et quelques autres', *La Nouvelle Critique*, no. 119, December, pp. 34–40

Hydak, Michael G. (1979) Review in *The French Review* 52: 6, May, pp. 957–8

Mançeron, Claude (1981) 'La résurrection de Molière', *Les Nouvelles Littéraires*, 19 March

Marcorelles, Louis (1978) 'A propos du Molière d'Ariane Mnouchkine: un récit contre l'histoire', *Le Monde*, 14 September

Mesnil, M. (1978) Review in *Esprit* 11, pp. 305–7

Sandrel, Carole (1981) 'Le *Molière* d'Ariane Mnouchkine', *Les Nouvelles Littéraires*, 5 March

Sarraute, Claude (1981) 'Un somptueux *Molière*', *Le Monde*, 10 March

Schepelern, P. (1980) Review in *Kosmorama* 26: 145, pp. 33–5

Torok, J.P. (1978) Review in *Positif* no. 211, pp. 58–9

Young, Vernon (1980) Review in *The Hudson Review* 33: 2, pp. 251–6

Méphisto

Denès, Max and Nicole Collet (1979) 'Théâtre du Soleil: sur la scénographie de *Méphisto*' (interview with Guy-Claude François), *Théâtre/Public* 27, June, pp. 22-4

Dort, Bernard (1980) 'Le Théâtre du Soleil à l'age d'acier', *Théâtre/Public* no. 31, January–February, pp. 52–7

Dumur, Guy (1979) 'Un bruit de bottes infernal', *Le Nouvel Observateur*, 28 May

Galey, Matthieu (1979) 'Mnouchkine: le cri de *Méphisto*', *L'Express*, 26 May–1 June, pp. 36–9

Godard, Colette (1979) '*Méphisto*: l'histoire ne se répète pas, elle se ressemble' (interview with Mnouchkine), *Le Monde*, 22 March

—— (1979a) '*Méphisto*: la farce des mortelles erreurs', *Le Monde*, 18 May

—— (1979b) '*Méphisto* et les communistes', *Le Monde*, 27 July

—— (1980) 'Re-écrire le théâtre pour l'écran' (re. Bernard Sobel's TV film of *Méphisto*), *Le Monde*, 16 November

Guibert, Hervé (1980) 'A qui appartient l'histoire?', *Le Monde*, 19 June

Guidi, Claudio (1980) 'Die Karriere des Hendryk Höfgen', and review of *Méphisto*, *Theater der Zeit* 35: 7, pp. 57–9

Léonardini, Jean-Pierre and Jacques Poulet (1979) 'A l'initiative des communistes, débat autour de *Méphisto*' (public discussion with Mnouchkine), *L'Humanité*, 28 June

Lion, Helen (1981) 'The storm over Mann's *Méphisto*', *International Herald Tribune*, 9 May

Lundstrom, Rinda (1985) 'Two *Mephistos*: a study in dialectics', *Modern Drama* 28: 1, pp. 162–70

Mann, Klaus (1977) *Mephisto* (trans. Robin Smyth), New York: Random House

Marcabru, Pierre (1979) 'La fin d'un monde', *Le Figaro*, 17 May

Mnouchkine, Ariane (1979) '*Méphisto*', *Les Nouvelles Littéraires*, 22 February

Morand, Claude (1979a) 'Ariane Mnouchkine: de nouveau le théâtre', *Les Nouvelles Littéraires*, 22 February

—— (1979b) 'Un nouvel auteur: Ariane Mnouchkine', *ATAC Informations* no. 101, April, pp. 16–18

Mounier, Catherine (1980) '*Méphisto*', in *Le Deux: Revue d'Esthétique* 1–2, Paris: Union General d'Editions, '10/18', pp. 409–20

Powell, Nicholas (1980) 'Tyranny down the ages', *The Financial Times*, 7 February

Richard, Lionel (1979) 'Klaus Mann, l'émigré', *Le Monde*, 22 March

Sandier, Gilles (1979a) 'Nazisme et théâtre', *La Quinzaine Littéraire*, 16 June

—— (1979b) 'Tumulte autour de *Méphisto*', *Le Matin*, 28 July

Schechter, Joel (1985) 'Théâtre du Soleil's *Méphisto*: Hitler in the Cabaret', in *Durov's Pig: Clowns, Politics and Theatre*, New York: Theatre Communications Group, pp. 108–19

Simon, Alfred (1979) 'Clowns, tragédiens et croix gammées', *Esprit*, July–August, pp. 166–70

Skasa, Michael (1981) Review in *Theater Heute* 22: 3, March, p. 4 ff.

Smyth, Robin (1986) 'Memories of Mephisto' (interview with Mnouchkine), *The Observer*, 30 March

Sohlich, Wolfgang (1986) 'The Théâtre du Soleil's *Méphisto* and the problematics of political theatre', *Theatre Journal* 38: 2, May, pp. 137–53

Suck, Titus Thomas (1988) 'Representing power/power of representing: aestheticization v. production in the Théâtre du Soleil's *Méphisto*', *Journal of Dramatic Theory and Criticism* 2: 2, Spring, pp. 105–33

Wardle, Irving (1986) 'An artist's response to guilt and complicity' (interview with Mnouchkine), *The Times*, 2 April

Zipes, Jack (1980) 'Theatre and commitment: Théâtre du Soleil's *Méphisto*', *Theater*, Spring, pp. 55–62

Les Shakespeares

Alter, Jean (1988) 'Decoding Mnouchkine's Shakespeare: a grammar of stage signs', in Michael Issacharoff and Robin F. Jones (eds), *Performing Texts*, Philadelphia: University of Pennsylvania Press, pp. 75–85

Aslan, Odette (1993) 'Entraînements des comédiens du Théâtre du Soleil' (interview with

Maïtreyi re. *La Nuit des Rois*), in Odette Aslan (ed.), *Le Corps en jeu*, Paris: CNRS Editions (collection 'Arts du spectacle'), pp. 297–8

Becker, Peter von (1984) 'So schön, um war zu sein' (*Henry IV*), *Theater Heute*, April, pp. 15–17

—— (1984) 'Die Theaterreise zu Shakespeare' (interview with Mnouchkine), *Theater (Theater Heute Yearbook)*, pp. 13–19

Billard, Pierre and Anne Pons (1982) 'Mnouchkine et compagnie', *Le Point* no. 515, 2 August, pp. 52–7

Boquet, Guy (1982) 'De Shakespeare à Artaud' (*Richard II*), *Historiens et Géographes*, February, pp. 589–90

Clément, Catherine (1981) 'Shakespeare ne supporte pas qu'on apporte en plus son manger' (interview with Mnouchkine re. *Richard II*), *Le Matin de Paris*, 10 December

Costaz, Gilles, (1984) 'Mnouchkine, la reine soleil' (interview re. *Henry IV*), *Le Matin*, 17 January

Dasgupta, Gautam (1982) '*Richard II, Twelfth Night*', *Performing Arts Journal* 18, 6: 3, pp. 81–6

Debroux, Bernard (1983) 'Entretien avec Ariane Mnouchkine' (*Les Shakespeares*), *Alternatives Théâtrales* no. 15, July, pp. 46–51

Déprats, Jean-Michel (1982) 'Voyage en Shakespeare', 'Le besoin d'une forme' (interview with Mnouchkine), and 'Un texte masqué' (interviews with Georges Bigot and Philippe Hottier, re. *Richard II*), *Théâtre/Public* 46–7, July–October, pp. 5–7, 8–11, 12–14

—— (1983) 'Le mot et le geste', in Marie-Thérèse Jones-Davies (ed.), *Du Texte à la scène: langages du théâtre*, Paris: Touzot, pp. 205–24

Dort, Bernard (1984) 'Aux deux bouts de Shakespeare' (*Les Shakespeares*), *Le Monde*, 8 April

Double Page (1982) *Le Théâtre du Soleil: Shakespeare* (with an introduction – 'Ariane Soleil' – by Claude Roy, and photographs by Martine Franck), *Double Page 21*, Paris: Editions SNEP

—— (1984) *Le Théâtre du Soleil: Shakespeare 2e partie* (with essays by Sophie Moscoso and Raymonde Temkine, and photographs by Martine Franck), *Double Page 32*, Paris: Editions SNEP

Dragovitch, Valida (1983) 'Deux mises-en-scène de *Richard II*', in Marie-Thérèse Jones-Davies (ed.), *Du Texte à la scène: langages du théâtre*, Paris: Touzot, pp. 69–89

Dumur, Guy (1981) 'Les oiseaux noirs du Soleil levant' (*Richard II*), *Le Nouvel Observateur*, 19 December

—— (1982) 'Plein Soleil sur Avignon' (*Les Shakespeares* in Avignon), *Le Nouvel Observateur*, 24 July

—— (1984) 'Stratford-sur-Seine: le triomphe d'Ariane' (*Henry IV*), *Le Nouvel Observateur*, 3 February, pp. 52–3

Frendenrich, Frank (1981) 'Nous avons voulu montrer l'histoire grâce au Théâtre (interview with Mnouchkine), *Tribune de Genève*, 19–20 December

Giesbert, Franz-Olivier (1984) 'Le triomphe d'Ariane' (*Les Shakespeares* in Los Angeles), *Le Nouvel Observateur*, 6 July

Gleiss, J. (1985) 'Shakespeare cycle at the Théâtre du Soleil', *Theater der Zeit* 40: 1, pp. 19–22

Godard, Colette (1981a), '"L'histoire pas seulement": le théâtre du Soleil joue Shakespeare' (interview with Mnouchkine re. *Les Shakespeares*), *Le Monde*, 24 November

—— (1981b) 'Les samouraïs de Shakespeare' (*Richard II*), *Le Monde*, 15 December

—— (1981c) 'Shakespeare at Vincennes: passion and fear' (interview with Mnouchkine re. *Les Shakespeares*), *The Guardian Weekly*, 27 December

—— (1982) 'Tudor Kabuki: Mnouchkine's *Richard II*', *The Guardian Weekly*, 7 March

—— (1982) 'Voyage en Illyrie' (*La Nuit des Rois*), *Le Monde*, 13 October

—— (1984) '*Henry IV*: les derniers jours de l'enfance', *Le Monde*, 25 January

Haye, Bethany (1984) 'Ariane Mnouchkine's Théâtre du Soleil: astonishing audiences with grand spectacle' (*Les Shakespeares*), *Theater Crafts* 18: 9, November–December, pp. 24–7, 80–1

Héliot, Armelle (1982a) 'Du Shakespeare dans le droit fil d'Ariane', *Le Quotidien de Paris*, 17 July

—— (1982b) 'Ariane en Illyrie' (*La Nuit des Rois*), *Acteurs* no. 9, November, pp. 39–40

—— (1982c) 'La vie au soleil' (interviews), *Acteurs* no. 10, December, pp. 30–4

—— (1984a) '*Henry IV* par le Théâtre du Soleil' (inerview with Mnouchkine), *Acteurs* no. 18, March–April, pp. 32–4

—— (1984b) 'Le règne du Soleil' (*Les Shakespeares* in Los Angeles), *Acteurs* no. 20, July–September, pp. 41–2

Hugo, Joan (1984) 'Théâtre du Soleil' (*Les Shakespeares* in Los Angeles), *High Performance* no. 27, pp. 18–19

Jongh, Nicholas de (1984) 'Why the bard's all shook up' (*Les Shakespeares*), *The Guardian*, 22 June

Kennedy, Dennis (1993) *Looking at Shakespeare: a Visual History of Twentieth-Century Performance*, Cambridge: Cambridge University Press, pp. 285–8

Laroque, F. (1982) Review of *La Nuit des Rois*, *Cahiers Elizabéthains* 22, October, pp. 102–4

Liégeois, Jean-Paul (1982) 'Ariane Mnouchkine: "Je mets Shakespeare devant tous les autres, même Molière"', *Le Nouveau Figaro Magazine*, 1 February, pp. 81–6

Marat, Pierre (1982) 'Ariane Mnouchkine – Shakespeare: l'atelier d'un maître', *La Charente Libre*, 8 January

Miller, Judith G. (1983) Review of *Richard II* and *La Nuit des Rois* in Avignon, *Theatre Journal* 35: 1, March, pp. 114–16

Neuschäfer, Anne and Frédéric Serror (1984) *Le Théâtre du Soleil: Shakespeare – Richard II, Heinrich IV, Was Ihr Wollt*, Cologne: Prometh Verlag

Pascaud, Fabienne (1982) 'Les soleils d'Ariane Mnouchkine' (interview), *Télérama*, 7 July, pp. 11–13

Ratcliffe, Michael (1984) Review of *La Nuit des Rois* and *Henry IV, The Observer*, 1 April

Schulman, Barbara S. (1982) Review of *Richard II, Plays and Players*, March, pp. 36–7

Simon, Alfred (1982) '*Richard II*: retour à Shakespeare, retour au texte?' and 'Les dieux qu'il nous faut: entretien avec Ariane Mnouchkine', *Acteurs* no. 2, February, pp. 16–24

—— (1983) 'Le grand jeu Shakespearien de la cour d'honneur' (*Richard II, La Nuit des Rois*), *Esprit* no. 73, January–June, pp. 236–47

Tremblay, Anne (1984) 'A French director gives Shakespeare a new look', *New York Times*, 10 June

Norodom Sihanouk

Alexandrescu, Liliana (1991) '*Norodom Sihanouk*: l'inachevé comme lecture shakespearienne de l'histoire contemporaine', in Françoise van Rossum-Guyon and Myriam Diaz-Diocaretz (eds), *Hélène Cixous: chemins d'une écriture*, Paris: Presses Universitaires de Vincennes, pp. 187–204

Birkett, Jennifer (1992) 'The limits of language: the theatre of Hélène Cixous', in John Dunkley and Bill Kirton (eds), *Voices in the Air: French Dramatists and the Resources of Language*, Glasgow: Glasgow French and German Publications, pp. 171–86

Blumenthal, Eileen (1986) 'The unfinished histories of Ariane Mnouchkine', *American Theatre*, April, pp. 4–11

Boquet, Guy (1985) 'Chronique théâtrale', *Historiens-Géographes* no. 307, December, pp. 805–6

Catalyse (1986) 'A l'école de Shakespeare: l'histoire en scène' (interview with Mnouchkine), *Catalyse* no. 4, June–August, pp. 6–23

Cixous, Hélène (1989) 'From the scene of the unconscious to the scene of history' (translated by Deborah W. Carpenter), in R. Cohen (ed.), *The Future of Literary Theory*, London: Routledge, pp. 1–18

Costaz, Gilles (1985a) 'La déchirure d'Ariane Mnouchkine' (interview), *Le Matin*, 12 September, pp. 23–4

—— (1985b) 'La chronique Shakespearienne du Cambodge' (interviews with Mnouchkine, Cixous and Odile Cointepas), *Acteurs* no. 29, October, pp. 12–16

Delorme, Olivier (1986) Review in *Espoir*, June, pp. 48–50

El Publico (1986) *El Théâtre du Soleil: amanecer en otoño*, special supplement to *El Publico* no. 36, September, Madrid: Centro de Documentación Teatral (83 pp.)

Ertel, Evelyne (1986) 'Entre l'imitation et la transposition', *Théâtre/Public* no. 68, March/April, pp. 25–9

Godard, Colette (1985) 'Ariane Mnouchkine, Hélène Cixous et le Petit Prince', *Le Monde*, 28 September

Graver, David (1986) 'The Théâtre du Soleil, Part 3: the production of *Sihanouk*', *New Theatre Quarterly* 2: 7, August, pp. 212–15

Guerin, Thierry and Thierry Mack (1986) 'L'histoire et les acteurs' (interview with Mnouchkine), *Drama: revue sur le théâtre*, January–February, pp. 4–7

Hotte, Véronique (1986) 'Une temerité tremblante: entretien avec Hélène Cixous', *Théâtre/Public* no. 68, March–April, pp. 22–5

Kiernander, Adrian (1985a) 'Confronting history: Shakespeare for our times', *Times Higher Educational Supplement*, 1 November

—— (1985b) 'The King of Cambodia', *Plays and Players* 386, November. p. 17–18

—— (1986) 'The Théâtre du Soleil, Part 1: a brief history of the company', and 'The Théâtre du Soleil, Part 2: the road to Cambodia', *New Theatre Quarterly* 2: 7, August, pp. 195–212

Lagorio, Michele (1986) 'Sculpting the silent majority', *Theater Crafts*, March, pp. 29–31, 65

Lamar, Celita (1987) 'Norodom Sihanouk, a hero of our times: character development in Hélène Cixous's Cambodian epic', in Karelisa V. Hartigan (ed.), *From the Bard to Broadway*, Lanham, MD: University Presses of America, pp. 157–66

Léonardini, Jean-Pierre (1985) 'L'art de passer entre les gouttes', *L'Humanité*, 28 October

Lerrant, Jean-Jacques (1985) 'Norodom Sihanouk, héros shakespearien par le Théâtre du Soleil', *L'Espoir*, 23 November

Marrero, Mara Negron (1991) 'Comment faire pour écrire l'histoire poétiquement, ou comment faire pour ne pas oublier?', in Françoise van Rossum-Guyon and Myriam Diaz-Diocaretz (eds), *Hélène Cixous: chemins d'une écriture*, Paris: Presses Universitaires de Vincennes, pp. 205–12

Pidoux, Jean-Yves (1987) 'Le soleil de la tragédie', *Théâtre/Public* no. 75, May–June, pp. 4–12

Presko, Jean-Jacques (1985) 'Le Cambodge ressuscité', *Phosphore*, November, pp. 61–4

Sabatier, Patrick (1986) 'Portrait du prince en héros shakespearien' (interview with Sihanouk), *La Libération*, 7 September

Sabouraud, Frédéric (1985) 'Coup de Soleil pour Sihanouk', *Le Nouvel Observateur*, 6–12 September, pp. 56–8

Shawcross, William (1986) *Sideshow: Kissinger, Nixon and the Destruction of Cambodia*, London: The Hogarth Press

Simon, Alfred (1985) 'Sihanouk, héros shakespearien', *L'Express*, 27 September, pp. 124–5

Sullivan, Scott (1985) 'Cambodia as history play', *Newsweek*, 11 November

L'Indiade

Boquet, Guy (1987) 'L'Inde déchirée', *Historiens et Géographes*, October, pp. 307–8

Carlson, Marvin (1990) 'Peter Brook's *The Mahabharata* and Ariane Mnouchkine's *L'Indiade* as examples of contemporary cross-cultural theatre', in Erika Fischer-Lichte, Josephine

Riley and Michael Gissenwehrer (eds), *The Dramatic Touch of Difference: Theatre, Own and Foreign*, Tübingen: Gunter Narr Verlag Tübingen, pp. 49–56

—— (1996) 'Brook and Mnouchkine: Passages to India?', in Patrice Pavis (ed.), *The Intercultural Performance Reader*, London: Routledge, pp. 79–92

Cixous, Hélène (1987) 'Si vous me permettez, je vais vous parler d'amour', *Acteurs* no. 53, October, pp. 8–9

—— (1988) 'De la colonisation à l'indépendence et de l'indépendence à la partition', *Itinéraire Sartrouville*, March/April

—— (1989a) 'Writings on the theatre' (trans. Catherine Anne Franke), in *Qui Parle* 3: 1, Berkeley: University of California, Spring, pp. 133–52

—— (1989b) 'A realm of characters', in Susan Sellers (ed.), *Delighting the Heart: a Notebook by Women Writers*, London: The Women's Press, pp. 126–8

Coen, Lorette (1987) 'Soleil sur l'Inde', *Mensuel Européen/Emois*, 5 October, pp. 37–42

Costaz, Gilles (1987) '*L'Indiade*: un troupeau d'animaux furieux' (interview with Mnouchkine and Cixous), *Le Matin*, 28 September

Double Page (1987) *Le Théâtre du Soleil: L'Indiade* (with an introductory essay by Hélène Cixous, 'Invisible visible, visible invisible', and photographs by Martine Franck), *Double Page 49*, Paris: Editions SNEP

Dumur, Guy (1987) 'De l'ombre de Brecht au soleil de Gandhi', *Le Nouvel Observateur*, 16 October

Gastellier, Fabian (1987) 'L'India Song d'Ariane Mnouchkine' (interview with Cixous), *Le Quotidien de Paris*, 28 September

Godard, Colette (1987) 'Images cruelles d'un rêve de paix', *Le Monde*, 10 October

Golfier, Bernard (1988) 'Le tragique de la partition' (interview wtih Cixous), *Théâtre/Public* 82–3, June.

Goy-Blanquet, Dominique (1987) 'An Indian dream', *Times Literary Supplement*, October 16–22, p. 1140

Grewal, Mojanheet and Anees Jung (1987) 'Scenes from an Indian pageant', *The Times of India*, 22 November

Hassoun, Pascal, Chantal Maillet and Claude Rabant (1988) 'Entretien avec Hélène Cixous', *Patio* no. 10, pp. 61–76

Hill, Diane (1987) 'By the nose to India', *The Times*, 24 November

Karl, Patrick (1987) '*L'Indiade* de Mnouchkine: une danse d'amour', *Pour la Danse* no. 143, December, pp. 44–5

Lagorio, Michele (1988) 'Mnouchkine company visits the India of its dreams', *Theater Crafts* 22: 7, pp. 36–7

Lecoq, Dominique (1988) 'Les motions contre l'émotion de l'Histoire' (interview with Cixous), *Politis*, 7 July, pp. 77–88

Le Roux, Monique (1987) 'Gandhi et l'ourse', *Quinzaine Littéraire*, 16 November

Libération (1987) 'Eclipse de Soleil sur les Indes', *Libération*, 19 October (review by 'M.S.')

Méreuze, Didier (1987) 'Le théâtre avec les dieux' (interview with Mnouchkine), *La Croix*, 25 September

Miller, Judith G. (1988) 'La Fin de Siècle (again)', *Theater*, Spring, pp. 86–8

—— (1989) 'Medusa and the Mother/Bear: the performance text of Hélène Cixous's *L'Indiade ou l'Inde de leurs rêves*', *Journal of Dramatic Theory and Criticism* 4: 1, Fall, pp. 135–42

Neuschäfer, Anne (1987) 'Männermacht aus Frauenperspektive: *L'Indiade* im Théâtre du Soleil', *Lendemains* 48, pp. 135–7

Pavis, Patrice (1990) 'Interculturalism in contemporary mise en scène: the image of India in *The Mahabharata* and *L'Indiade*', in Erika Fischer-Lichte, Josephine Riley and Michael Gissenwehrer (eds), *The Dramatic Touch of Difference: Theatre, Own and Foreign*, Tübingen: Gunter Narr Verlag Tübingen, pp. 57–71

Picard, Anne-Marie (1989) '*L'Indiade*: Ariane's and Hélène's conjugate dreams', *Modern Drama* 32: 1, March, pp. 24–38

—— (1989) '*L'Indiade, ou l'Inde de leurs rêves*', *Dalhousie French Studies* 17, Fall/Winter, pp. 17–26

Rathbone, Christopher (1987) 'A sparkling Paris jewel', *Times Higher Education Supplement*, 27 November

Scheie, Timothy (1993) 'Body trouble: corporeal "presence" and performative identity in Cixous's and Mnouchkine's *L'Indiade ou L'Inde de leurs rêves*', *Theatre Journal* 46: 1, March, pp. 31–44

Temkine, Raymonde (1987) 'L'épopée indienne' (interview with Mnouchkine), *Acteurs* no. 53, October, pp. 10-11

—— (1988) 'Grandes maisons et petits lieux', *Europe*, January–February, pp. 189–91

Théâtre du Soleil (1988) 'Lettre aux Israéliens' (*L'Indiade* in Israel), *Le Nouvel Observateur*, 22 April

La Nuit Miraculeuse (film)

Dumur, Guy (1989) 'La nativité laïque d'Ariane Mnouchkine' (interview with Mnouchkine), *Le Nouvel Observateur*, 14 December

Giudicelli, Anne (1989) 'Mnouchkine revisite la révolution', *La Libération*, 28 August

Héliot, Armelle (1989) 'Le film d'Ariane', *Le Quotidien de Paris*, 19 December

Mingalon, Jean-Louis (1989) 'Un soir à l'Assemblée Nationale', *Le Monde*, 20 December

Pascaud, Fabienne (1989) 'Naissance d'une passion' (interview with Mnouchkine), *Télérama*, 13 December

Sotinel, Thomas (1989) 'Miracle à l'Assemblée', *Le Monde*, 28 August

Les Atrides

Banks, Daniel (1990) 'Family at war' (interview with Mnouchkine), *Paris Passion*, October, pp. 22-3

Becker, Peter von and Eberhard Spreng (1991) 'Die Inszenierung: *Les Atrides*' (review and interview with Mnouchkine), *Theater Heute*, June, pp. 1–10

Bethune, Robert (1993) 'Le Théâtre du Soleil's *Les Atrides*', *Asian Theatre Journal* 10: 2, Fall, pp. 179–90

Billington, Michael (1991) 'Frank and fearless on the Parisian stage', *The Guardian*, December 31

Bost, Bernadette (1992) 'Chroniques des temps de barbarie', *Le Monde*, 2 January

Bryant-Bertail, Sarah (1993) 'Gender, empire and body politic as *mise en scène*: Mnouchkine's *Les Atrides*', *Theatre Journal* 46: 1, March, pp. 1–30

Chioles, John (1993) '*The Oresteia* and the avant-garde: three decades of discourse', *Performing Arts Journal* no. 45, XV: 3, September, pp. 1–28

Coveney, Michael (1991) Review of *Les Choéphores*, *The Observer*, 15 December

Dumur, Guy (1990a) 'Le fil d'Ariane' (*Iphigénie à Aulis*), *Le Nouvel Observateur*, 6 December

—— (1990b) 'La bonne étoile d'Ariane: *Les Atrides* revisités', *Le Nouvel Observateur*, 20 December

Godard, Colette (1990) 'Les enfants d'Atrée' (*Iphigénie à Aulis*), *Le Monde*, 8 December

—— (1991) 'La fureur d'Atrée' (*Les Choéphores*), *Le Monde*, 27 March

Goetsch, Sally (1994) 'Playing against the text: *Les Atrides* and the history of reading Aeschylus', *The Drama Review* 38: 3, Fall, pp. 75–95

Goy-Blanquet, Dominique (1991) 'Exposing the fathers of tragedy: *Les Atrides*', *Times Literary Supplement*, 18 January, p. 14

Héliot, Armelle (1990) '*Iphigénie à Aulis*: le grand retour du Soleil', *Le Quotidien de Paris*, 5 December
—— (1991) 'Le sang de la vengeance, la nuit du délire' (*Les Choéphores*), *Le Quotidien de Paris*, 25 March
Hewison, Robert (1992) 'La grande illusion', *Sunday Times*, 26 July
Lallias, Jean-Claude, with Jean-Jacques Arnault (eds) (1992) *Théâtre aujourd'hui no. 1: 1a tragédie grecque – Les Atrides au Théâtre du Soleil*, Paris: CNDP (56 page booklet with 32 slides)
Liégeois, Jean-Paul (1990) 'Nos ancêtres, les Grecs: Ariane Mnouchkine, en prise avec la liberté', *Le Nouveau Politis*, 22–28 November
Louchet, Jean-Claude (1991) 'Ariane Mnouchkine: retour à la source des sources' (interview), *Textes et documents pour la classe*, 23 January
Mathieu, Bénédicte (1990) 'Soleil grec' (interview with Mnouchkine re. *Iphigénie à Aulis*), *Le Monde*, 1 September
McDonald, Marianne (1992) 'The atrocities of *Les Atrides*: Mnouchkine's tragic vision', *TheatreForum* 1, Spring, pp. 13–19
Mnouchkine, Ariane (1993) 'Ecorchement et catharsis', in Odette Aslan (ed.), *Le Corps en jeu*, Paris: CNRS Editions, p. 296
Nightingale, Benedict (1992) 'Epic rewoven in human terms', *Life and Times* (London), 20 July
Picon-Vallin, Béatrice (1995) 'Une œuvre d'art commune' (interview with Mnouchkine and members of le Théâtre du Soleil), *Théâtre/Public* 124–5, July–October, pp. 74–83
Pons, Anne (1991) 'Ariane, déesse de l'antique' (*Les Choéphores*), *L'Express*, 25 April
Ratcliffe, Michael (1991) 'The Greeks, with an accent on the French', *New York Times*, 28 July
—— (1992) 'Mnouchkine's dance of life and death', in the programme for *Les Atrides*, European Arts Festival, Bradford
Rockwell, John (1991) 'An Oresteia' (*Iphigénie à Aulis, Agamemnon*), *New York Times*, 27 March
—— (1992) 'Behind the masks of a moralist', *New York Times*, 27 September
Rogoff, Greg (1992) 'Carnal knowledge', *The Village Voice*, 29 September, pp. 41–3
Salter, Denis (1994) 'Hand, eye, mind, soul: Théâtre du Soleil's *Les Atrides*', *Theater Magazine* (Yale), 24: 1, April, pp. 59–74; includes an interview with Simon Abkarian, Nirupama Nityanandan, Juliana Carneiro da Cunha, Brontis Jodorowsky and Catherine Schaub
Schlocker, Georges (1991) 'The myth dances: *Iphigenia in Aulis* and *Agamemnon*', *Euromaske* 3, Spring, pp. 55–6
Simon, Alfred (1990) '*Les Atrides*: rencontre avec Ariane Mnouchkine', *Acteurs* 84–5 November–December, pp. 24–31
—— (1991) '*Les Atrides* – suite: *Les Choéphores*', *Acteurs* 88–9, March–April, pp. 18–24
Solis, René (1991) 'Mnouchkine à la grecque' (interview), *La Libération*, 3 January
Théâtre du Soleil (1992a) *Les Atrides 1: Iphigénie à Aulis, Agamemnon*, Paris: Théâtre du Soleil. Photographs by Michèle Laurent, preface by Hélène Cixous ('La communion des douleurs')
—— (1992b) *Les Atrides 2: Les Choéphores, Les Euménides*, Paris: Théâtre du Soleil. Photographs by Michèle Laurent, preface by Hélène Cixous ('Pas de réponse, ou l'appel du mort')
Thornber, Robin (1992) Review of *Les Atrides* in Bradford, *The Guardian*, 21 July
Toffin, Janine (1991) 'Viser la perfection pour atteindre la beauté' (interview with Mnouchkine), *Messages des Postes et Télécommunications*, February
Weitzmann, Marc (1990) 'Allons nous faire voir chez les Grecs!' (interview with Mnouchkine), *7 à Paris*, 14–20 November, pp. 18–23

La Ville Parjure, ou le réveil des erinyes

Brock, Julie (1995) 'Un regard sur *La Ville Parjure*', *Théâtre/Public* no. 121, January–February, pp. 46–8

Casteret, Anne Marie (1992) *L'Affaire du sang*, Paris: La Découverte

Godard, Colette (1994) 'Notre tragédie nécessaire', *Le Monde*, 1 June

Grapin, Jean (1994) 'Ariane et Hélène: de la tragédie à la tragédie', *Impact Médecin Hebdo* no. 241, 17 June, pp. 104–5

Héliot, Armelle (1994) 'Le Théâtre du Soleil rouvre le dossier du sang contaminé', *Le Quotidien du Médecin*, 27 May

Léonardini, Jean-Pierre (1994) 'Ranimer la flamme d'un courroux collectif', *L'Humanité*, 13 June

Morelle, Aquilino (1993) 'L'institution médicale en question: retour sur l'affaire du sang contaminé', *Esprit* no. 195, October, pp. 5–51

Quirot, Odile (1994) 'Ce sang impur', *Le Nouvel Observateur*, 23–9 June, p. 64

Shevtsova, Maria (1994) 'Diving into a lake' (interview with Renata Ramos Maza), *Western European Stages* 6: 3, Fall, pp. 13–18

—— (1995a) 'Le mal social' (interviews with Renata Ramos Maza and Juliana Carneiro da Cunha), *Théâtre/Public* no. 121, January–February, pp. 36–45

—— (1995b) 'Sur *La Ville Parjure*: un théâtre qui parle aux citoyens' (interview with Mnouchkine), *Alternatives Théâtrales* no. 48, May, pp. 69–73. Published as 'A theatre that speaks to citizens', in *Western European Stages* 7: 1, Spring 1996

Le Tartuffe

Schmitt, Olivier (1995) '"*Le Tartuffe*", théâtre de guerre contre tous les fondamentalismes', *Le Monde*, 7 November

Théâtre du Soleil (1995) *Molière: Le Tartuffe*, programme in the form of a newspaper

OTHER MATERIAL ABOUT THE THÉÂTRE DU SOLEIL

Acteurs (1982) 'De la vie collective au one-man show: sept ans au Soleil' (interview with Philippe Caubère), *Acteurs* no. 4, April, pp. 48–51

Althaus, Jean-Pierre (1984) *Voyage dans le théâtre*, Lausanne: Editions Pierre-Marcel Favre

Aslan, Odette (1985) 'Le créature de masques et sa participation au spectacle' (interview with Erhard Stiefel), in Odette Aslan and Denis Bablet (eds), *Le masque: du rite au théâtre*, Paris: Editions du CNRS, pp. 241–4

—— (1993) 'Au Théâtre du Soleil les acteurs écrivent avec leur corps', in Odette Aslan (ed.), *Le Corps en jeu*, Paris: Editions du CNRS, pp. 291–5

Attoun, Lucien (1969) 'La création collective', *Les Nouvelles Littéraires*, 13 November

—— (1972) 'La Cartoucherie: un piège', *Les Nouvelles Littéraires*, 12 June

Bablet, Denis (1975) 'Rencontres avec le Théâtre du Soleil', *Travail Théâtral* 18–19, January–June

Bablet, Denis and Marie-Louise (1979) *Le Théâtre du Soleil, ou la quête de la bonheur (Diapolivre 1)*, Ivry, Paris: CNRS. With 84 slides, 1 sound disc, 2 booklets

Balazard, Simone (1989) 'Du Soleil à nous, ou de *1789* à 1989', in *Le Guide du théâtre*, Paris: Syros, pp. 124–39

Barbaroux, Monique (1979) 'Entretien avec Ariane Mnouchkine', *ENA Promotions*, September–October, pp. 13–14

Becker, Peter von (1984) 'Dossier: 20 Jahre – Théâtre du Soleil', *Theater (Theater Heute Yearbook)*, p. 10–23

Berger, Anne *et al.* (eds) (1984) 'Voir 1: En plein soleil', *Fruits* 2–3, Paris: Presses Universitaires de Vincennes, June (223 pp.)

Bigot, Georges (1984) 'Im spiel finde ich das Abenteuer meines Lebens', *Theater (Theater Heute Yearbook), pp. 21–2*

Bonnaud, Georges (1976) 'Des moutons, pas de dragon', *Travail Théâtral* 22, Winter

—— (1983) 'Chronique de l'illusion efficace, 1968–80', in Claudine Amiard-Chevrel (ed.), *Le Théâtre d'intervention depuis 1968, Tome 1*, Lausanne: L'Age d'Homme

Bradby, David (1991) *Modern French Drama, 1940–1990*, Cambridge: Cambridge University Press, pp. 191–213, 266–7

Bradby, David and David Williams (1988) *Directors' Theatre*, Basingstoke: Macmillan, pp. 84–111

Caubère, Philippe and Jean-Claude Penchenat (1985) 'Les rescapés du Soleil', *Autrement* no. 70 ('Série Mutations: acteurs – des héros fragiles'), May

Champagne, Lenora (1984) 'The Golden Age of Collective Creation', in *French Theatre Experiment since 1968*, Ann Arbor: UMI Research Press, pp. 23–49

Champagne, Lenora and Françoise Kourilsky (1975) 'Political theatre in France since 1968', *The Drama Review* 19: 2, June, pp. 43–52

Cixous, Hélène (1988) 'Comment arriver au théâtre?', *Lettre International*, Summer

—— (1990) 'The two countries of writing: theater and poetical fiction', in Juliet Flower MacCannell (ed.), *The Other Perspective in Gender and Culture*, New York: Columbia University Press, pp. 191–208

Cofman, Saril Sorana (1991) *Mnouchkine, Kantor, Brook: the Discourse on Total Theatre*, Ph.D. Thesis, University of Minnesota

Cohn, Ruby (1985) 'Ariane Mnouchkine: twenty-one years of Théâtre du Soleil', *Theater* 17: 1, Winter, pp. 78–84

—— (1989) 'Ariane Mnouchkine: playwright of a collective', in Enoch Brater (ed.), *Feminine Focus: the New Women Playwrights*, Oxford: Oxford University Press, pp. 53–63

Cointepas, Odile (1984) 'Actors on acting: an international perspective', *Olympia Arts Festival Conversations*, 21 June

Conley, Verena Andermatt (1992) *Hélène Cixous*, Toronto: University of Toronto Press

Costaz, Gilles (1987) 'Mnouchkine invente le billet-mécène', *Le Matin*, 8–9 August

Dégan, Catherine (1984) 'L'acteur est un scaphandrier de l'âme' (interview with Mnouchkine), *Le Soir*, 20–22 July

Donahue, Thomas J (1991) 'Mnouchkine, Copeau and Vilar: popular theatre and paradox', *Modern Language Studies* 21: 4, Fall, pp. 31–42

Dort, Bernard (1979) *Théâtre en jeu: essais de critique 1970–1978*, Paris: Editions du Seuil

—— (1986) 'A l'heure du Soleil', in *Théâtres*, Paris: Editions du Seuil, pp. 212–29

—— (1988) *La Représentation émancipée*, Arles: Actes Sud/Le temps du théâtre

Féral, Josette (1990) 'Mnouchkine's workshop at the Soleil: a lesson in theatre', 'Building up the muscle: an interview with Ariane Mnouchkine', and 'Théâtre du Soleil – a second glance: an interview with Sophie Moscoso', in *The Drama Review* 33: 4, Winter, pp. 77–87, 88–97, 98–106

—— (1995) *Rencontres avec Ariane Mnouchkine: dresser un monument à l'éphémère*, Montreal: XYZ Editeur, and Paris: Editions Théâtrales

François, Guy-Claude (1976) 'Un lieu à chaque fois renouvelé', in *Technique et architecture* no. 310, August–September, pp. 52–3

Franke, Catherine Anne and Chazal, Roger (1989) 'Interview with Hélène Cixous', in *Qui Parle* 3: 1, Berkeley: University of California, Spring, pp. 152–79

Frost, Anthony and Ralph Yarrow (1989) *Improvisation in Drama*, New York: St Martin's Press

Gauvin, Lise (1979) 'L'itinéraire d'une troupe' (interview with Mnouchkine), *Etudes Françaises* 15: 1–2, April, pp. 174–85

Godard, Colette (1980) *Le Théâtre depuis 1968*, Paris: Lattes

Godard, Colette (1994) 'Ariane Mnouchkine: le théâtre en révolutions', *Le Monde*, 26 May

Gourdon, Anne-Marie (1973) 'Le Théâtre du Soleil: un théâtre populaire?', *Revue d'Esthétique* 2–4, January/March, pp. 93–6

Guerrin, Michel (1994) 'Regards sur le mouvement' (interview with Martine Franck), *Le Monde*, 26 May

Héliot, Armelle (1985) 'Rêve oriental: entretien avec Ariane Mnouchkine', *Autrement* no. 70 ('Série Mutations: acteurs – des héros fragiles'), May, pp. 141–5

Hill, Victoria W. (1978) *Bertolt Brecht and Post-War French Drama*, Stuttgart: Akademischer Verlag Hans-Dieter Heinz, pp. 249–60

Hottier, Philippe (1982) 'Un texte masqué', *Théâtre/Public* 46–7, July–October

—— (1984a) 'Un entretien avec Philippe Hottier', *La Libération*, 12 July, pp. 28–9

—— (1984b) 'Ariane ist mein Meister', *Theater (Theater Heute Yearbook)*, pp. 20–2

—— (1985) 'La structure du masque agit sur le corps et le mental du comédien', in Odette Aslan and Denis Bablet (eds), *Le Masque: du rite au théâtre*, Paris: Editions du CNRS, pp. 235–9

Hyslop, Gabrielle (1985) 'Has Ariane Mnouchkine sold out?', *Australasian Drama Studies* no. 7, October, pp. 31–42

Innes, Christopher (1993) *Avant-Garde Theatre*, London: Routledge, pp. 209–13

Jazdzewski, Catherine (1984) 'La parole à Ariane Mnouchkine' (interview), *Agence Femmes Information* 118, 30 July, pp. 10–12

Jeffery, David (1992) 'France: towards *création collective*', in Ralph Yarrow (ed.), *European Theatre, 1960–1990: Cross-cultural Perspectives*, London: Routledge, 1992, pp. 27–31

Jouve, Nicole Ward (1990) 'Hélène Cixous: from inner theatre to world theatre', in *White Woman Speaks with Forked Tongue: Criticism as Autobiography*, London: Routledge, pp. 91–100

—— (1991) 'The faces of power: Hélène Cixous', in *Our Voices, Ourselves: Women Writing for the French Theatre*, New York: Peter Lang

Kiernander, Adrian (1990) 'The role of Ariane Mnouchkine at the Théâtre du Soleil', *Modern Drama* 33: 3, September, pp. 322–32

—— (1992a) 'The Orient, the Feminine: the use of interculturalism by the Théâtre du Soleil', in Laurence Senelick (ed.), *Gender in Performance: the Presentation of Difference in the Performing Arts*, Hanover, New Hampshire: University Press of New England, pp. 183–92

—— (1992b) 'Reading(,) Theatre(,) Techniques: responding to the influence of Asian theatre in the work of Ariane Mnouchkine', *Modern Drama* 35, pp. 149–58

—— (1993) *Ariane Mnouchkine*, Cambridge: Cambridge University Press

—— (1996) '"The theatre is oriental"; Ariane Mnouchkine', in Patrice Pavis (ed.), *The Intercultural Performance Reader*, London: Routledge, pp. 93–8

Kourilsky, Françoise (1971) 'L'Exemple' (interview with Mnouchkine re. Jean Vilar), *Travail Théâtral* no. 4, July–September, pp. 117–8

Lamar, Celita (1995) 'Dialogues of the heart: Norodom Sihanouk and Mahatma Gandhi as portrayed by Hélène Cixous', *Contemporary Theatre Review* 2: 3, pp. 31–7

Lauroy, Nicole (1969) 'L'utopie vécue, ou l'éclat chaleureux du Théâtre du Soleil', *Femmes d'Aujourd'hui*, 10 October, pp. 94–6, 99

Manceaux, Michèle (1986) 'Mnouchkine, la prêtresse du dieu théâtre', *Marie-Claire*, April 1986, pp. 99–101, 122

Merschmeier, Michael (1983) 'Paris: ein neues Theaterwunder?', *Theater (Theater Heute Yearbook)*, pp. 67–9

Mignon, Paul Louis (1973) 'Le théâtre de A à Z: Ariane Mnouchkine', *L'Avant-Scène Théâtre* 526–7, October, pp. 17–18

Miller, Judith G. (1977) 'Le Théâtre du Soleil: theatre as revolution, revolution as theatre', in *Theatre and Revolution in France since 1968*, Lexington, Kentucky: French Forum Monographs 4, pp. 52–75

—— (1989) 'Contemporary women's voices in French theatre', *Modern Drama* 32, March, pp. 24–38

Mnouchkine, Ariane (1968) 'Une prise de conscience', in *Le Théâtre 1968–1: cahiers dirigés par Arrabal*, Paris: Christian Bourgeois, pp. 119–26

—— (1973) 'L'œuvre de tous' (re. Brecht), *L'Arc* 55: 4, pp. 41–4

—— (1985) 'Le masque: une discipline de base au Théâtre du Soleil', in Odette Aslan and Denis Bablet (eds), *Le Masque: du rite au Théâtre*, Paris: CNRS, pp. 231–4

—— (1995) '"Cette Bosnie-là!"': le message d'Ariane Mnouchkine' (text read to Bosnian President Alija Izetbegovic at the Cartoucherie), *Le Nouvel Observateur*, 7–13 September, p. 41

Mnouchkine, Ariane and Jean-Claude Penchenat (1971) 'L'aventure du Théâtre du Soleil', *Preuves* no. 7, Autumn, pp. 119–27

Monod, Richard, Sophie Moscoso and Jean-Claude Penchenat (1989) 'La vie d'une troupe', in Daniel Couty and Alain Rey (eds), *Le Théâtre*, Paris: Bordas, pp. 210–29

Mounier, Catherine (1977) 'Le plaisir de raconter nos histoires, l'histoire, notre histoire: l'évolution du récit dans quatre créations collectives du Théâtre du Soleil', *L'envers du théâtre (Revue d'Esthétique 1–2)*, Paris: 10/18, pp. 153–68

Neuschäfer, Anne (1983) *Das Théâtre du Soleil: commedia dell'arte und création collective*, Germany: Schauble Verlag Rheinfelden

Noetzel-Aubry, Chantal (1988) 'Halte au désert culturel!' (interview with Mnouchkine), *La Croix*, 16 April

Pavis, Patrice (1992) 'Interculturalism in contemporary mise en scène: the image of India in the *Mahabharata*, the *Indiade*, *Twelfth Night* and *Faust*', in *Theatre at the Crossroads of Culture*, London: Routledge, 1992, pp. 183–216

Perret, Jean (1987) 'Entretien avec Ariane Mnouchkine', in Jacques Lecoq *et al.* (ed.), *Le Théâtre du geste*, Paris: Bordas, pp. 127–30

Pouy, Jean-Bernard (1990) 'Ariane Mnouchkine: entretien serein', *Autrement* 1 ('Série France': ed. Jean Viard), June

Richardson, Helen Elizabeth (1991) *The Théâtre du Soleil and the Quest for Popular Theatre in the Twentieth Century*, Ph.D., University of California, Berkeley

Roubine, Jean-Jacques (1990) 'The Théâtre du Soleil: a French postmodernist itinerary', in Erika Fischer-Lichte, Josephine Riley and Michael Gissenwehrer (eds), *The Dramatic Touch of Difference: Theatre, Own and Foreign*, Tübingen: Gunter Narr Verlag Tübingen, pp. 73–82

Rossum-Guyon, Françoise von and Myriam Diaz-Diocaretz (eds) (1991) *Hélène Cixous: chemins d'une écriture*, Paris: Presses Universitaires de Vincennes

Salina, Brigitte (1981) 'Ariane Mnouchkine, demiurge et tyran', *Les Nouvelles Littéraires*, 10 December, pp. 52–3

Samary, Jean-Jacques and Jean-Pierre Thibaudat (1984) 'L'ombre d'Ariane dans le Soleil' (interviews with Philippe Hottier and Georges Bigot), *La Libération*, 12 July, pp. 28–9

Sandier, Gilles (1982) *Théâtre en crise: des années 70 à 82*, Grenoble: Editions la Pensée Sauvage

Saurel, Renée (1973) 'Deniers publics ou cassette royale?', *Les Temps Modernes* no. 321, April, pp. 1907–18

—— (1974) 'Opération survie pour le Théâtre du Soleil', *Les Temps Modernes* no. 336, July, pp. 2478–9

Schiach, Morag (1991) *Hélène Cixous: a Politics of Writing*, London: Routledge

Sellers, Susan (ed.) (1994) *The Hélène Cixous Reader*, London: Routledge

—— (1996) *Hélène Cixous: Authorship, Autobiography and Love*, Cambridge: Polity Press, Chapter 4, 'Cixous and the theatre', pp. 74–93

Simon, Alfred (1976) *Les Signes et les songes: essai sur le théâtre et la fête*, Paris: Editions du Seuil

—— (1979) *Le Théâtre à bout de souffle*, Paris: Editions du Seuil

—— (1984) 'Dossier: le Théâtre du Soleil – Naître et renaître au théâtre' (interviews with Mnouchkine and members of the Théâtre du Soleil), *Théâtre en Europe* no. 3, July, pp. 78–99

Singleton, Brian (1996) 'Body Politic(s): The Actor as Mask in the Théâtre du Soleil's *Les Atrides* and *La Ville Parjure*', *Modern Drama* 39: 4, Winter, pp. 618–25

Stiefel, Erhard (1985) 'Le créateur des masques et sa participation au spectacle' and 'Au retour du Japon', in Odette Aslan and Denis Bablet (eds), *Le Masque: du rite au théâtre*, Paris: Editions du CNRS, pp. 77–80, 81

Temkine, Raymonde (1972) 'La Cartoucherie de Vincennes, ou théâtre-sous-bois', *Europe* no. 522, October, pp. 205–13

—— (1977) *Mettre en scène au présent 1*, Lausanne: La Cité/L'Age d'Homme

—— (1983) 'Les acteurs sont des poètes' (interview with Mnouchkine), *Europe* no. 648, April, pp. 56–60

Textes et documents pour la classe (1981) 'Ariane Mnouchkine et le Théâtre du Soleil: une utopie humaniste', *Textes et documents pour la classe*, 5 November, pp. 8–11

Théâtre du Soleil (1972) 'La justice telle qu'on la rend', *Esprit* 40: 417, pp. 524–55

Thibaudat, Jean-Pierre (1984) 'Lumières, Monsieur Lux!' (interview with Jean-Noël Cordier), *La Libération*, 17 July

Thompson, Juli Ann (1986) *Ariane Mnouchkine and the Théâtre du Soleil*, Ph.D., University of Washington

Travail Théâtral (1971) 'Quelques comédiens du Théâtre du Soleil' (interviews re. a visit to Paris by the Berliner Ensemble), *Travail Théâtral*, Summer, pp. 105–6

—— (1976) *Différent: le Théâtre du Soleil*, Lausanne: La Cité (collection of articles, interviews and reviews from *Travail Théâtral* re. *1789, 1793* and *L'Age d'Or*)

Whitton, David (1987) *Stage Directors in Modern France*, Manchester: Manchester University Press, pp. 255–76

INDEX

AM = Ariane Mnouchkine; TdS = Théâtre du Soleil